MANIPUR MISCHIEF

The injured Lieutenant Grant being carried on a dooly.

MANIPUR MISCHIEF

Rebellion, Scandal and the Dark Side of the Raj, 1891

WILLIAM WRIGHT

AMBERLEY

First published 2018

Amberley Publishing
The Hill, Stroud
Gloucestershire, GL5 4EP

www.amberley-books.com

British Library Cataloguing in Publication Data.
A catalogue record for this book is available from the British Library.

ISBN 978 1 4456 7183 3 (hardback)
ISBN 978 1 4456 7184 0 (ebook)

Typesetting and Origination by Amberley Publishing.
Printed in the UK.

Contents

The truth is rarely pure, and never simple.

Oscar Wilde

Introduction

In 1891, without any warning, the peaceful and remote Indian hill state of Manipur exploded into violence. Not since the days of the Indian Mutiny had the British Raj been rocked in this way. It was to see the largest expedition mounted on the north-east frontier of India until the Second World War.

I first became fascinated by the Manipur Uprising more than 40 years ago. No Victorian small war – by which I mean the numerous expeditions on the Indian frontiers – can compare with it for displaying such a cast of colourful characters and dramatic events. For a century afterwards the only full-length account outside India was the memoir by Ethel Grimwood, the beautiful young wife of the murdered British Political Agent. Hers was a thrilling and vivid narrative that also left many unanswered questions. *My Three Years In Manipur* tells the story through Ethel's eyes, but her view of things was distorted by her own perceptions and prejudices and went unchallenged and unextended for far too long. A Calcutta barrister, Mano Mohun Ghose, also wrote an account of the princes' trials, which saw a limited publication in England (and has never been reprinted).

The tale is an astonishing one – a peaceful Indian hill state, nominally independent, suddenly broke into violence with an attack on British soldiers sent to arrest a popular local prince. Then, after a peaceful durbar aimed at finding a solution, the unarmed Chief Commissioner of Assam and his entourage, including Frank Grimwood, were taken prisoner without warning before being swiftly beheaded, their feet lopped off, and their bodies thrown into a common grave. Immediately a fierce attack was launched on the British Residency where inexperienced officers, confused and scared, led a humiliating retreat out of the country, losing more than half their force along the way. During the attack on the residency and the retreat Mrs Grimwood became a legendary heroine, assisting the wounded and displaying incredible reserves of courage. A subsequent invasion was launched by three columns, but meantime a lone officer, supported by just 80 troops, fought off an attacking force ten times in size and restored British honour.

These are the bare bones of the tale, but I wanted to know what made the peaceful and hitherto friendly Manipuris suddenly erupt into violence? Had they been provoked in some way? Why did the British not make a better defence of the residency? Why was a subsequent military tribunal hushed up? Why was the trial of the Manipuri princes also apparently unfair? Answering these questions, and many others, revealed a complex and intriguing story of British arrogance, mistakes and ineptitude going up as high as the Viceroy himself – Lord Lansdowne. Policies were pursued by the Indian Government contrary to all common sense. At a local level these errors were compounded by a civil official who tried to push through his agenda too quickly and in a heavy-handed way. There was a compendium of bad military planning right from the start, made worse when action became necessary. Plain bad luck also played its part.

Then a document, marked 'Secret', came to my attention. It revealed that the tale told in Mrs Grimwood's book deserved to be challenged. It cast a completely different light on her and her husband – and offered an alternative theory as to why the murders of the Political Agent and Chief Commissioner took place. It spoke bluntly of things not normally mentioned in the context of the Victorians and certainly not of their military campaigns – of orgies, sexual infidelities, miscegenation and implied paedophilia. I decided this document, bypassed in other accounts, deserved to be scrutinised and put under the historical microscope.

One hundred and one years after the Manipur Uprising two historians in India, John and Saroj Parratt, wrote the first full-length account of the debacle in detail. The book was not published outside India, concentrates on the trials of the princes, and suffers from a limited bibliography, though displaying good scholarship. Sixteen years later Lady Belinda Morse authored a most entertaining but all-too-brief biography of Ethel Grimwood, which is understandably partisan towards this fascinating woman. Finally, in 2015, a scholar who has written on the princely states, Caroline Keen, produced a well-researched account, though limited to an academic audience. She covers all aspects of the uprising though chose not to debate the Secret Report in any detail.

In *Manipur Mischief* I have simply attempted to put some flesh on the bare bones of the story by telling the tale, where possible, in narrative style and using first-hand accounts or reporting. The events are peopled by a fascinating cast of characters, both British and Manipuri. I also wanted to try to place the Manipur War in the context of its times, to say something of the Raj in 1891, and how India was governed. This was the heyday of the British Empire and also of imperial conceit. I have tried to take you back to another age with the hope that you understand a little better what the British Raj felt and looked like to people at the time. By the end, I hope you will agree with me that the British reaction to local events in Manipur was ill-conceived, without any properly executed plan and carried out in such an arbitrary manner that, as one officer said at the time, the mud stuck. The Manipuris, to their credit, defended their land bravely, literally the last gasp of traditional rule in India. Queen Victoria, who took her duties as Empress of India very seriously, also weighed in on the side of the Manipuris seeing, quite rightly from the start, that the reasons for the war as explained by her Viceroy simply did not make sense. Imperialist though she was, Her Majesty's letters at the time reveal the monarch to have been remarkably perceptive about the best way of ruling subject peoples.

My thanks go to Her Majesty the Queen for permission to quote from the letters of Queen Victoria as printed in Buckle's edition of her correspondence. Among librarians I owe a debt to are the splendid and patient staff of the British Library, Euston Road; the National Archives, Kew, London; and the National Archives of India, New Delhi. The illustrations were photographed from my collection by Krisztina Elias, who has assisted on all my previous five books. Finally, sincere thanks to Shaun Barrington, who has guided me through the pitfalls of publishing throughout all my attempts at writing history.

William Wright, Budapest

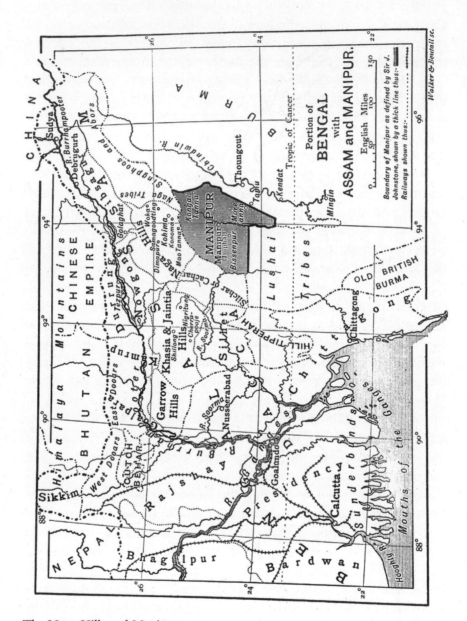

The Naga Hills and Manipur.

MANIPUR FORT

Scale : 1 inch = 640 feet.

a a a a ... Lieutenant Brackenbury's route.
b b b b ... Captain Butcher's route.
c ... Bastion where Captain Butcher was challenged and from which Manipuris first opened fire.
d ... Gateway captured by Lieutenant Chatterton.
e e ... Two 7-pounder guns which shelled Residency
f ... One 7-pounder gun commanding Cachar Road and approach to *d*.
g ... Residency Gateway in which were Treasury and Telegraph Office.
k ... Quarters of Resident's permanent guard.
x x x ... Spot where Lieutenant Brackenbury lay after being wounded.

N

From Tammu

Village

School

Hospital

Residency

Village

From Kohima

Bridge

Jungle

Jungle

River

Bridge

Palace

Durbar Hall

Dragons

Palo Ground

Bustee

Bustee

Inner wall

Bustee

Bridge

West Ditch

From Cachar

Camp

Palo Ground

Bustee

Women's
Bazar

Wet Ditch

Dry Ditch

Outer wall in ruins

Jubraj Temple

Outer wall broken

Ditch (dry)

Ditch (dry)

Bustee

N.B.—Buildings exaggerated Principal buildings ▨

Bustees shewn ▨ shaded

11

1

Ethel and Frank

They were, everyone agreed, a perfect couple. The bride looked beautiful, wasp-waisted and corseted in her tight-fitting white satin gown with some of her giggling sisters as bridesmaids. Her groom was, people remarked, considerably older than his 19-year-old fiancée – yet at 33, they murmured, almost at the perfect age for a gentleman to marry. He was handsome with neatly-parted brown hair, a neat military-style moustache and expressive eyes that could turn in a twinkle into a smile, which was something they did often.

The girl's maiden name was Ethel Brabazon Moore. Her middle name demonstrated a distant family connection to the Earls of Meath. She had been born in Muttra, West Bengal, on 4 October 1867, eldest of four daughters, to Charles Moore, a judge in the Bengal Presidency. Three years earlier, Ethel's parents had been the centre of a scandal when they had eloped together; mother Margaret was at that time married to a rising officer (and later major-general) named Boisragon. When she ran off with Charles Moore she took with her Boisragon's only son, a boy called Alan, who would grow up close to his step-sisters. Despite much gossip and the stigma attached to elopement, the act had little effect on Judge Moore's career since his employer, the Indian Civil Service, was a remarkably forgiving institution. (Charles was later to re-marry at the age of 53 to a girl barely seven years older than Ethel while at the same time he had fathered a son by a mistress he was keeping at a house in Beaufort Street, Chelsea).

The Moores had a long association with India and also with the British Army. One of Charles's brothers was a colonel and another was a major, so Ethel had various officer cousins (step-brother Alan had also entered the army). Like all the other children of the British elite in India, Ethel and three of her siblings – Lillian, Beatrice and Sydney (listed as a boy in the census but decidedly a girl), were all shipped back to England to be educated. This was frequently a miserable experience for thousands of children, separated for several years from their parents, natural surroundings and ever-doting *ayahs* (Indian nursemaids). Ethel at least had the good fortune to share what must have seemed a strange banishment to a windy seaside town and the vagaries of the English weather with her sisters. The education of girls at this time was not given the serious attention or the expense expended on sons. There was no Eton, Harrow or Winchester for Judge Moore's daughters. Instead the girls went to Hove, to a genteel school run by Mrs Moulson, a widow, assisted by her daughters, Ada and Emily. What the Moore girls were taught we can only guess at, but Mrs Moulson did employ a foreign governess, so that her charges at least had a smattering of French. It seems that Ethel was a bright girl, and showed great skill and promise as a pianist.

She returned to India with 'the fishing fleet' as girls looking for husbands were called. It appears that fairly quickly she made a great catch in reeling in Frank St Clair Grimwood. Frank was just a junior official of the Indian Civil Service (ICS) but it was well-known that civilians were better paid than their only social equals – army officers. 'Worth three hundred pounds dead or alive,' notes David Gilmour in his history of the ICS, 'was a saying that reflected in pounds sterling both the initial salary and the pension they would bequeath their widows.' It is hardly surprising that Frank was smitten; the few surviving photographs we have of Ethel, all dating from her return from Manipur in 1891, clearly show that she was a great beauty. She bore more than a passing resemblance to Alexandra, Princess of Wales, considered one of the loveliest women of the 1880s, her face seeming noble and innocent, her expression dignified, her grace winning and her smile enchanting. Ethel was tall and slender, long-necked, with a mass of dark auburn hair, sensuous bow lips and innocent, penetrating eyes. She comes across as so lively in her writing that it seems a shame we have no photographs of her looking less like the tragic heroine, yet clearly, like all young women, she had a natural zest for life and an abundant sense of humour, especially so in 1887, long before her life took a more serious turn.

Frank had been born in 1853, the third son of Jeffrey Grimwood, a magistrate belonging to the Essex landed squirearchy (the gabled hall of Woodham Mortimer still stands). His mother, Zoë, had been born on a plantation at Demerara, British Guiana. Frank had four brothers and sisters and seems to have had a happy childhood. Like most sons of the landed gentry, he learned at an early age to ride well and handle a gun. Most of Frank's schooling was done at Winchester College, then, as now, one of Britain's leading public schools. Classics had dominated the curriculum but during Grimwood's years a forward-thinking headmaster, George Ridding, had introduced the teaching of modern languages and history. From public school Frank moved on to Merton College, Oxford, where he achieved a third in finals in 1875. To be fair to him at this time less than half of Merton's students attempted an honours degree. A contemporary (at Magdalen) later complained 'one of the curses of the place was that there was no discipline, either self or outside at all.' Oxford did not encourage study, snobbery was rife, along with 'a great deal of gambling and card-playing...The other predominant evil was an unchecked tendency to drink, which at this time prevailed all over the University.'[1]

From Oxford Frank moved into a Lincoln's Inn law practice as a barrister, but in 1884 he went to Burlington House, Piccadilly, to sit the exams for entry into the Indian Civil Service. On average about 200 students competed each year for about 40 places. The I.C.S., on behalf of the Crown, administered British India and dictated the lives of its 287 million inhabitants, who spoke a bewildering 800 languages. Despite its British arrogance, the I.C.S. was remarkably free from corruption, acquiring a prestige, as Jan Morris has written, 'so towering that to many simple people it seemed infallible if not divine'. Successful I.C.S. applicants could be expected to be sent out to India and work phenomenally hard, first as lowly 'griffins' (newcomers), but with dedication and luck, their upward path might lead via years toiling in native villages listening to claims as a district officer, collector and magistrate, often administering areas larger than Belgium, to the all-powerful realms of a Chief Commissioner or Lieutenant-Governorship. Frank was accepted. Next came a medical examination followed by two years on probation in England. More exams followed periodically with a view to testing his progress in ancient Sanskrit, the vernacular languages of India, law, political economy and the history and geography of the country.

We cannot be sure how well Frank did in his exams but it seems certain that he was not top of his class; the most successful candidates always had a pick of the provinces they were being sent to and the most popular were the Punjab and the North-Western Provinces. Frank was sent to Bengal, not in itself the worst destination, which was Madras, yet apart from Calcutta this was a place 'of almost constant humidity, a land consisting mainly of rice fields and villages and so many enormous rivers that travel was usually difficult and invariably slow.' Chittagong, notes Gilmour, 'was regarded as a sort of penal institution for insubordinate Civilians, a place so damp that one's books rotted and one was lucky to escape from it without breaking down.' Even worse, Assam, on the Bengal frontier with Burma, was regarded as 'a perilous and undesirable exile, a place where Anglo-Indian society consisted of truculent tea-planters and where the dangers of being killed by hostile tribesmen was greater than anywhere else.'[2] It would soon be Grimwood's posting.

Since Frank reached India in 1886 and duly courted the daughter of Judge Moore, another civilian, we must assume the young pair met shortly after Grimwood's arrival. What is more surprising is that Frank was allowed to return home to England for the wedding since a first furlough normally required eight years' service. It seems he used his four weeks annual entitlement of holiday and may also have asked for special leave, which was usually granted in an emergency (such as the death of a parent). There was an old I.C.S. maxim – 'Don't marry till you have five years' service' since marriage often affected promotion; assistant commissionerships usually went to bachelors able to spend long hours away from home and in the saddle. Marriage, it was thought, made a man poorer and less mobile.

Yet Frank was at the right age to marry. In a society very different from our own, 'gentlemen' of the upper classes were expected to wait until they had attained sufficient income and advancement before looking for a wife. Thirty-one was considered the perfect year. Socially and sexually this enforced delay led to many virile young men in their twenties resorting to prostitutes or, if wealthy enough, to acquiring a mistress.

As a 19-year-old bride, we can assume that under the strict middle-class morality of the 1880s young Miss Ethel Moore stepped up to the altar *virgo intacta*. Without a mother alive to offer advice and not, it seems, very close to her father, one wonders if Ethel went to her marriage bed with more than the faintest idea of what was in store for her. We can also conjecture, probably accurately, that her groom, Frank, knew all about the delights of the marital bedchamber. He hardly had time in India to acquire a native mistress, a hobby contemporaries called 'getting an Indian dictionary', but it seems inconceivable that a sensualist such as Frank, a man who events were to prove enjoyed the company of young women, had not in his London days explored the fleshly delights of the metropolis with an estimated 5,000 brothels or houses where prostitutes congregated. It is worth remembering that it was only in 1885 that the Criminal Law Amendment Act raised the minimum age of consent to 16 years and made procuring a criminal offence (for centuries consent had been fixed at just 12 years). London was notorious for its child prostitutes and 'willing' young teens. One year after the Grimwoods got married, the 1,200 full-time prostitutes of the Whitechapel slums and their thousands of part-time sisters who sometimes sold their bodies to survive would face the bloody knife of a fiend called 'Jack the Ripper'. Frank, of course, being a gentleman, had no need to have gone to East London. Piccadilly and Holborn were the haunts of hundreds of street girls. Their nightly promenades, dressed in all their flashy finery, at the Alhambra and the Pavilion music halls, or the Argyle Rooms (later the famous Trocadero Restaurant) were a sight to behold.

Two years younger than Frank Grimwood was B. De Sales la Terriere, an officer in the smart 18th Hussars; he recalled in his memoirs how the girls waited for clients to buy them a port and lemonade at the bars in the music halls. Down Lower Regent Street the prostitutes gathered, like moths around the gas lamps, 'all ages, sizes and colours', booted and gloved, in feather boas and gauche hats. La Terriere remembered how in the early 1880s 'the fashions just then made them lace in their skirts behind from the waists down to the heels so tightly, that they could not move their legs at all, and if they fell down they could not get up again.' Dresses showed every curve of a woman's figure. 'They had to *fall* into a cab for they could not step in,' he wrote, 'and I actually remember having to actually cut one poor lady out of her dress, as the kicking-strap had got knotted and she could not move.'[3] Beneath every gown, was an equally tight-fitting and restrictive corset.

Ethel and Frank had a suitably stylish summer wedding on 19 July 1887 at the fashionable St Peter's Church, Cranley Gardens, Kensington. The church is still there (now the Armenian church of St Yeghiche), and so are the London addresses of the bride and groom as given in the register. The Moores were either staying at or renting 3 Cranley Gardens, a classic porticoed London townhouse of at least eight bedrooms. It is just down the road from the church, which perhaps explains why St Peter's was chosen. Frank's address is given as '22 Victoria Square SW'. Occupying a corner of this small but select early Victorian square that lies just behind Buckingham Palace, No. 22 had a morning room, library and five bedrooms. We must assume Grimwood was staying here with either friends or relatives (oddly enough, living next door at No. 20 was the retired and much disliked Zulu War general, Henry Hope Crealock, who died at this address while the Manipur War was taking place).

History does not record what kind of wedding breakfast the happy couple had or whether they enjoyed a honeymoon or not. Honeymoons only later became the conventions they are today and not everyone rushed off to a sunny resort. One suspects that this good-looking pair were in love and the journey to India they were about to embark on was in itself romantic enough. They might have taken a ship all the way from Southampton to Bombay, a journey of three weeks, but it was quicker and far more attractive to start the sea leg in the Mediterranean. One can imagine the newlyweds taking the mail train from Victoria to Dover, then on to Paris, where most people broke their journey for a few hours' sight-seeing. Possibly they went via Marseilles but travellers generally preferred the scenic route through Italy. The 8.40pm steam express from the Gare du Lyon gave the option of breakfasting at Culoz, followed by the Mount Cenis tunnel and the glorious vistas of the snow-capped Dora Valley before the locomotive chugged into Turin. There was a chance to sight-see there, and also in Florence and Rome, before boarding the steamship at Brindisi docks. Suez was reached in four days, the thermometer steadily rising as they crossed a sea as smooth as glass. The Grimwoods would have had a first-class compartment and if possible facing north, portside, to avoid the sun, hence the almost certainly erroneous derivation of 'portside out and starboard home' for 'P.O.S.H.'. By Aden many passengers would have been sleeping on deck to escape the stuffy heat below. Suez to Bombay took about 16 days, but one suspects that Ethel and Frank went via Ceylon (Sri Lanka) to Calcutta, the imperial capital and administrative centre of Bengal. At Ceylon it was a popular pastime for those new to the East to take the midnight mail train up to beautiful Kandy, 'through swarms of fireflies and wake up to their first views of tropical scenery, palm trees and paddy-fields, tea gardens and mountain torrents.'[4]

None of these oriental sensations were new to either Ethel or Frank. Yet it seems hard to believe that their hearts did not beat a little faster when Calcutta hove into view. Unlike Bombay or Madras, which the traveller could observe while still at sea, Calcutta was 100 miles up a gloomy estuary where newcomers were often shocked to see decaying corpses floating in the waters. Garden Reach gave an indication that something special lay around the corner. Behind a series of cypresses came the Botanical Gardens, followed by a long succession of villas whose lush, well-manicured lawns ran down to the river's edge. The high walls of old Fort William lay just past The Reach 'with a forest of masts in the river before it'. Flags of all nations, masts and sails fluttered in the breeze before the 'City of Palaces', its great mansions often blazingly white after their annual coating of *chunam* (lime).

Calcutta (Kolkata) was a city of huge contrasts (it still is). It was famous in Victorian times for its stenches. Hindus burned their dead but many partially-consumed bodies were left by the side of the *Hooghly* (Hughli) River to be borne away. If the wind blew from the land, newcomers were also greeted by the smell of the open drains which made the city one of the least healthy in India. Kipling wrote of 'the big Calcutta stink ... sickly ... indescribable.' Close to the resplendent open space known as the maidan, 'Clapham Common, Hyde Park and Sandown Park all in one,' as one late nineteenth-century visitor called it, was Spence's Hotel, opened in 1830 and considered the best in the city. Nearby stood its great rival, the Auckland, opened in 1840 (in 2017 it looks grander than ever, now called the Great Eastern). Dominating the maidan and river was the imposing Georgian portico and steps of Government House, 'the finest governor's palace in the world', with a ballroom so vast that it could accommodate 2,000 guests. The building was the official winter quarters of the Viceroy – the Queen-Empress's representative in India – a potentate who lived in such splendour that he had his own throne room and emblems of royalty.

The Viceroy combined the duties of a Prime Minister and President and ruled for a five-year term, assisted by a council of advisors. Usually the Viceroys were British aristocrats with no previous knowledge of India. In 1887 the position was held by Frederick Temple Hamilton-Temple-Blackwood, Marquess of Dufferin and Ava, a career diplomat who had previously been Governor-General of Canada. A recent biographer has called him 'imaginative, sympathetic, warm-hearted and gloriously versatile'. In truth Dufferin was brilliant, urbane and famously vain. One suspects that the Burmese used other names to describe him as he had two years previously annexed their country, thus adding another jewel to the Imperial Crown. Knowledgeable about the Islamic World, Lord Dufferin had pleased many educated, moderate Indians by extending to them a palm leaf of involvement in provincial legislative councils. In all his work he was aided by the vicereine, Lady Hariot, a strong-minded though rather plain woman, but a lady of great dignity. The King of Greece had once remarked 'that there was no lady in Europe who can enter a room like Lady Dufferin.'⁵

One can imagine Ethel's delight at returning to the heat, sights and smells of her childhood. Children of the Raj usually remembered India with great affection, especially those born there, for whom banishment to a cold and wet island in the North Sea, despite its historical associations, always seemed oddly alien. Frank, no doubt, had calls to make on his superiors before he and his wife set out for his post at Sylhet in Assam. Ethel's job was to make sure the couple had all they would need for a home with them. Calcutta had every kind of shop for Anglo-Indians including – then as now – many excellent tailors. The couple's list would have included Assam silk suits, evening dress and dinner-jacket (for 'informal occasions' advised the guide books) for Frank, besides Ethel's own dresses and personal items. Frank would have been advised to take plenty of flannel shirts and his own guns and saddlery. Guide books recommended that iron baths should be brought from England since the zinc baths sold in the bazaars were unreliable. Women were advised to take three pounds of Windsor soap with them and a case of Cologne-water.

Frank and Ethel were not overjoyed about his posting to Sylhet as deputy commissioner. The district had been acquired by the British in 1765 and the little town, a provincial backwater, lay in a broad valley near the Khasia and Jaintia Hills. A Frontier Police recruiting depot had been opened there in 1865 so there was a strong military presence. The soldiers were necessary to overawe the local tribes, especially hill men, who periodically swooped down on the indigo plantations and tea gardens that dotted the valley. However, the tribesmen were less troublesome than the local white owners and managers of the plantations, a breed notorious throughout India for their short tempers and violent manners. Frequently drunk, often living miles from civilization of any sort, these men seemed to live on 'brandy pawnee' (brandy and water) and were ready to shoot at visiting magistrates who were foolish enough as to ask why, for instance, a native woman had been whipped. Henry Cotton, a contemporary I.C.S. official of Frank Grimwood's, recalled how, when he was acting as a magistrate, a white planter on a charge of common assault actually entered his courtroom and came and sat next to him, even putting his feet on the bench. Cotton had great pleasure in having him restrained and administered a stiff sentence. On another occasion Cotton visited a lonely tea garden and found the Scottish owner had reverted entirely to native ways, growing his beard long and wearing only a *dhoti* to cover his loins. It seemed incongruous to the civilian to hear a Scottish accent emanating from this grimy apparition.

Luckily for them the Grimwoods did not have to endure Sylhet for long. Within a few months of their arrival, news came that the British Resident of the native state of Manipur, based at Imphal, had died. To their astonishment and delight Frank was now given the post. 'Visions of glories heard of, but not seen, floated in both our minds,' wrote Ethel. The couple must be forgiven their dreams of opulence and glamour. Who can blame them? Ethel fantasised:

I pictured to myself the dignity of being the mistress of a Residency, of possessing servants in scarlet and gold, with 'V.R.' on their buttons and a guard-of-honour to walk out with me whenever I chose.

I saw visions of a large house and extensive grounds, and I pictured the ensign of Old England dominating over all.[6]

Frank was equally excited; quite apart from the honour of his I.C.S. promotion, which was totally unexpected, were his memories of Manipur where he had once spent a couple of days in 1886. He recalled with delight a lake in the residency compound swarming with wild ducks and most especially had 'played a never-to-be-forgotten game of polo with three royal princes on a ground worthy of Hurlingham.'[7]

The Grimwoods hardly cared that Manipur had an unenviable reputation as a backwater where British Residents and their families seemed to die of fever or disease with unpleasant regularity. The I.C.S. clearly chose Frank Grimwood because he was the best man who happened to be on the spot. They viewed his appointment, as events were to prove, as only a temporary replacement until someone better could take up the post. He was not a first choice but simply a necessary one.

Ethel began packing in high spirits. She remained unfazed even when a gale blew down the kitchen and sent her new cooking pots to the winds. Seeing this event perhaps as a bad omen, the Grimwoods 'highly valued and talented cook' gave notice to quit immediately. The promise of extra pay and new cooking pots quickly solved the problem. The Grimwoods made a short trip to Shillong, the bracing hill station in the mountains where the Chief Commissioner of Assam had his residency, then returned to Sylhet to collect their belongings. Both Ethel and Frank were about to embark on a momentous adventure, the outcome of which they could not possibly have imagined. For a short time their names were destined to be front page news all over the world. First they had a journey to make. Not some short trek, but sixteen days of hard travelling via swift-flowing rivers and lush jungle, through thick forests and over spectacular hill ranges, by boat, on horseback and on foot, to one of the remotest corners of British India – the princely state of Manipur.

2

The Grave of Fame

They set off late one night after dinner by boat. Ethel pointed out in her memoirs that travelling 'on a broad smooth river, with the moon shining overhead as only an Indian moon can shine,' sounded very romantic, but the reality was an awkwardly small vessel 'of the Noah's ark type' with a roofed area of coarsely woven bamboo matting 'so low that it necessitated crawling in on all fours... Once in you had to lie down and shuffle off your clothes and tumble in your blankets, which were spread upon the floor.' The noisy crew, vibrations from the rudder, 'and, worst of all, the insects that swarmed in the woodwork,'[1] all made sleep impossible. To add drama to the occasion, one crewman knocked another into the water during an argument, and Ethel and Frank had to hastily organise a rescue.

Next morning, 'cold and very hungry', the Grimwoods arrived in a chilly dawn at the landing stage where their horses awaited them. After *chota hazri* (a light early breakfast), the couple's next task was to assemble a long line of grumbling porters who were to carry their luggage. A number of these men complained that each of the *memsahib's* 'enormous' boxes required at least three coolies to carry them. Frank managed to bargain the number down to two men per load. 'Eventually, with many heart-rending groans, our luggage moved off,' Ethel wrote with disdain. Two hours after the first porters had set off down the track the Grimwoods mounted their horses and commenced the day's ride only to quickly find their boxes discarded by the wayside, some of them guarded by a far-from-happy cook. The coolies had all run away. More had to be found who, in due course, also vanished. 'With few exceptions our march continued like this every day until we reached Cachar,'[2] recalled Ethel.

Cachar, also referred to as Silchar, was a town 126 miles from Imphal, but just 24 miles from the Manipur frontier. The district was full of tea gardens, an Indian Army Gurkha regiment was normally quartered there, and social life for the white community included two or three race meetings every week in the winter months. The planters even had their own yeomanry regiment called the Surma Valley Light Horse.

After three days relaxation during which short period Frank Grimwood, as the new Political Agent for Manipur, was feted as a V.I.P. (Ethel no doubt basking in this adulation), the couple set off again. Two marches took them to the banks of the Jhiri River, which separated the Cachar district from Manipur. It rained all that night and the next day dawned damp and drizzling. It was here that Ethel first saw the most famous hill tribe of the area, some of whom had agreed to act as porters. These were Nagas, some of the most ferocious warriors the British had ever encountered on the Indian frontiers. Lieutenant-Colonel Alban Wilson, 8th Gurkhas, echoed Mrs Grimwood's views when he later described the Nagas as 'a fine-looking race, much resembling the North American Indians when togged up in their full war-paint.'[3] Divided into various tribes and sub-clans who often warred among themselves, about 100,000 Nagas occupied a range of hills sandwiched between Assam to the north and Manipur to the south. Each tribe was distinguishable by the way they dressed and cut their hair as well as by the style of their weapons. More than 40,000 southern Naga tribesmen also occupied the Manipur hills north of Imphal. The most warlike clan, the Angami Nagas, had gone on the warpath in 1879 in a four-month campaign that had disturbed the whole frontier. Luckily for Ethel and Frank the Nagas they encountered seemed peaceful enough (although the eastern Naga tribes necessitated several British military expeditions between 1883 and 1897). Ethel admitted that she found the tribesmen 'very alarming' in appearance. 'They wore very few clothes,' she wrote, 'and their necks were adorned with many necklaces made of gaudily-coloured glass beads. Their ears were split to a hideous extent, and in the loops thus formed they stuffed all kinds of things – rolls of paper

... and rings of bamboo, which stretched them out and made them look enormous.' Some of the Nagas had their heads shaved except for a greased ridge on top which 'gave them the appearance of cockatoos'. Others had their hair cut 'so that it stuck out all round their heads and made them look as though they had fur hats on.'[4]

Ethel was impressed by the way these tough men made no fuss about carrying her trunks. Instead they made a rush towards her bath which 'had a flat cover to it, and was easy to carry and cool against their backs.' A guard of Manipuri sepoys also marched along and helped to lead Ethel and Frank's horses through a sea of mud. It was a sticky April day and Ethel later recalled the 'legions' of horse-flies, gnats and other bugs that 'collected under the brims of our hats and stung our faces and settled in swarms on our horses.'[5]

One wonders what the tribesmen must have thought of these white-skinned strangers, one of them a woman. Frank, they knew, was an important *sahib* (gentleman). He was a civilian, a member of the elite Indian Civil Service. Political agents had a ceremonial uniform but Grimwood most likely rode to Manipur in riding breeches and a jacket, perhaps one of Norfolk serge or cavalry twill. *Puttees* – strips of cloth wound spirally from the ankle to the knee – would have given his calves extra support and protection, but he may also have worn riding boots. Ethel most certainly rode side-saddle, the accepted way of riding for English gentlewomen of her generation. *Jodhpurs* did not become fashionable for men until 1897 and women did not wear them before the First World War so she made the journey to Manipur in long skirts and a high-buttoned riding habit. The skirt was probably to her ankle and revealed low-heeled short leather boots. In the 1880s a riding habit was still designed to flatter a woman's figure, camouflage the dirt and withstand the physical rigours of long periods sitting on a horse. Ethel would not have been sewn into her riding habit, unlike the Empress Elizabeth of Austria-Hungary, a super-keen horsewoman, but with her hour-glass figure she must have still looked pretty striking. No doubt she felt hot and uncomfortable for much of the time and personally bemoaned her outfit for looking as if it had been 'designed in a rage and put on in a tempest', as Oscar Wilde wrote of a lady in *The Picture Of Dorian Gray* (published in 1890). Both Grimwoods wore gloves and *solar topees* (pith helmets) and Ethel had a veil.

Up and down the hills this curious cavalcade wound its way – the *sahib* and his lady on horseback followed by a seemingly endless line of wild-looking, almost naked tribesmen, carrying hat boxes from Harrods, London tea-gowns, crates of crockery, carpets, folding wardrobes, books and lots more. After every second pace the Nagas would expel their breath with a loud 'How' in a deep musical sound. Even noisier were the barefoot Manipuri sepoys in bright red or white jackets marching proudly along making bugle calls. Interspersed with all this cacophony were the occasional bellows from lumbering elephants, at the rear carrying the heaviest goods of all, slipping and sliding along the churned-up track. Forests of bamboo sometimes gave way at higher elevations to stands of hardwood and oak trees. From the higher crests, which rose to 6,000 feet, one earlier traveller had remarked:

The scene at sunset is sometimes magnificent. In the foreground the dark forests, and in the far distance a huge bank of golden clouds with their reflection in the watery plain, and a mingled mass of colours, green fields, purple, crimson, red and gold, all mixed up in such a way as no painter would ever attempt to copy. As the sun sinks those colours change and re-arrange themselves every minute in quick succession, and when at last night closes in, the impression left on the mind is one of never-ending wonder and admiration.[6]

Every 5 miles the Manipuris had built a *thana* (a stockade that might be used as a rest house or for military purposes), which was fortified in most cases with a palisade of sharpened bamboo stakes. Ethel was amused how the sepoys turned out at each of these posts to give a salute and exercise, 'on every possible occasion' a particular fondness for bugling.

To Mrs Grimwood's dismay, at the end of the first day's march, tired and caked in mud, she and Frank had to cross the Makru River via a rickety suspension bridge high above the waters. She was twenty years old, brave and ebullient, but recalled:

Bamboos are hung on to the wires close together to form a kind of railing on each side, and these are fastened with cane to the floor of the bridge, which is made of bamboo also, woven into a kind of coarse matting, and although they look most flimsy and airy erections they are really very strong, and can carry any number of men on them at once, and animals too, if necessary. They are a great height from the water, which you can see between the chinks of the matting as you walk across, and they have an unpleasant fashion of swinging violently when you are in the middle of them, making it very difficult to keep your footing. I did not like going over it at all, and tumbled down in the most awkward fashion more than once, much to the amusement of the Manipuris, who laughed very heartily.

The cook with his pots and pans did not arrive until 9pm and the Grimwoods ate their dinner sitting cross-legged on the floor of a *thana* (police station). For more than four more hours they waited in the steamy heat, attacked by swarms of mosquitoes and sandflies, until the elephants arrived with their bedding. One hour later a torrential downpour drenched Ethel's head through the thatch and she had to move her bed. The tropical rain continued unceasingly the next day so it was decided to remain where they were. Ethel was so exhausted that she stayed in bed all day, 'while the coolies busied themselves in making me a dooly out of bamboos, as we found that my horse had got a sore back from his long climb the day before, and my husband decided that it would be better to have me carried the rest of the way.'[7]

The sepoys became a major source of amusement for Ethel: 'We were supposed to have thirty men altogether, but I never saw more than twelve.'[8] When marching they counted themselves twice, even running on ahead and presenting arms twice. She thought them quite dotty and reckoned they only had three complete sepoy uniforms between them. Their worldly possessions were slung casually in a bundle of cloth from every rifle and at night the two men deputed to guard the Grimwoods usually fell asleep and snored loudly on the verandah.

Gradually the trek seemed easier as the British pair got used to the journey. At every Naga village the hill-people would swarm around the couple, especially Ethel, the first white woman many had ever seen. It was on the eighth day out from Cachar, near the 2,600-foot summit of Lai-metol, that Mrs Grimwood finally saw one of the great vistas of India – the trees seemed to part and revealed, like a magnificent stage-set framed by the Almighty's own proscenium arch, the beautiful green valley of Manipur, looking peaceful in the afternoon sunshine, an expanse of flat land bordered by hills and mostly covered by watery rice fields. Aeons ago it had all been one vast lake, but the waters had receded leaving this fertile valley in the mountains. 'It looked so beautiful to us after the hills of the previous seven days,' wrote Ethel, 'stretching away smooth and even as far as the eye could see, and we stopped on the top of the hill some time for the pleasure of looking at it.' The couple could detect

> ...far and away in the plain the white walls of the maharajah's palace, and the golden-roofed temple of his favourite god. Just below us stretched the blue waters of the Logtak Lake, studded with islands, each one a small mountain in itself. Villages buried in their own groves of bamboo and plantain-trees dotted the plain, and between each village there were tracts of rice-fields and other cultivation. The whole valley looked rich and well cared for, and we longed for the next day, which was to see us at our journey's end.[9]

During their journey Frank Grimwood had been thinking a great deal about his new duties at the Manipur *Durbar* (Court). He almost certainly had been reading up on the history of the state and its relations with the British Raj. Back in Shillong the Chief Commissioner had given him certain instructions, general advice, and talked of a code of behaviour as the Queen-Empress's representative in Manipur, but Grimwood knew that he would also have to rely on his instincts and learn much on the job.

Manipur (the name means 'beautiful garden'), had been a kingdom for centuries. It comprised about 8,500 square miles of territory, mainly hills, surrounding on all sides a valley roughly 25 miles wide from east to west and 35 miles from north to south. In the rainy season the valley looked green and verdant but in the dry season the grass turned brown. Glinting in the sun to the south was the Logtak Lake, 7 miles long and up to 2 miles wide, a hunter's paradise swarming with wildfowl of all kinds. All roads led to Imphal (also referred to as 'Manipur') in the north-east of the valley, though the capital was no more than a collection of villages covering some 15 square miles grouped around the maharajah's fort and palace. To the north and north-west of Manipur lay Cachar and the Naga Hills, south and south-west were the lands of the warlike Kukis, Chins and Lushais, the latter two tribes a constant source of trouble to the British during all of Frank Grimwood's time at Manipur. Away to the east lay the vast and recently annexed state of British Burma, latest addition to the Queen-Empress's dominions.

No true census had been done of Manipur but it was estimated the population stood at 80–140,000 excluding the hill tribes who numbered a further 75–100,000 people. Before the terrible Burmese invasions of the eighteenth century it was thought Manipur might have had more than 700,000 inhabitants, yet by 1825 the number of adult males had been reduced to just 3,000. The people of Manipur were properly called the Methei, a name that originally denoted just one of seven related clans, but was gradually accepted by the other six in the eighteenth century after it achieved pre-eminence among them. The Methei are of Tibetan-Burman stock 'and had the reputation of being stalwart, industrious, energetic and gifted with an aptitude for acquiring new arts,'[10] wrote a visitor. In the countryside, the Manipuris lived in villages that ran in long lines beside the banks of the rivers. Most houses, built of wood or bamboo plastered with mud or cow-dung, stood in about an acre of land and were surrounded by a brick wall. All were thatched with grass and faced east, surrounded by a large verandah. On the south side of the verandah was the mat of the head of the family. The women excelled at weaving and had a certain degree of independence; only women were permitted to be stall-holders in the capital's most famous market (this is still true in the twenty-first century). The men were considered 'not naturally courageous, but capable of fighting well, if well-led.' 'They are always cheerful, even on a long and trying march,' wrote another observer, 'and are good-humoured under any difficulties and never conscious of fatigue.'[11] The same voice also declared that the Manipuris were careless soldiers who 'neglected every rule of warfare', yet it was 'impossible' to avoid liking them. Their main defects as a race seemed to be a sphinx-like inscrutability and a rigid application of caste. Some travellers complained that the Manipuris were rather unsanitary in their habits since they did little to prevent the heavy rains sending filth into the water-tanks leading to outbreaks of cholera. The country had converted from Buddhism to Hinduism around 1720, 'after which time they looked upon their king or *ningthou* ... as the current incarnation of the god Vishnu.'[12]

The Manipuris and the Burmese had been blood enemies for centuries. In the early 1700s under a formidable ruler, Gharib Nawaz, the Manipuris and their famous pony cavalry had raided Burma time and time again, destroying whole armies sent against them and 'marching to the very walls of Ava'. Gharib's death saw the tables turn and the Burmese kings vowed to crush Manipur, which they arrogantly viewed as a particularly annoying vassal state.

Manipuri-Burmese bitterness was in sharp contrast to the little kingdom's cordial relations with Assam. The British and Manipuris had first made contact in 1762 when the latter sent an ambassador to Chittagong to try to secure help in recovering lands stolen by the Burmese. An agreement was reached granting the British East India Company – originally a purely mercantile business but now starting to flex its muscles – rent-free land in Manipur where a fort and trading factory could be set up with a view to promoting trade with China. So eager were the Manipuris to entice the British that they even agreed to pay all the expenses of any troops. So it was that in January 1763 a detachment left Chittagong, but the sepoys suffered so dreadfully from disease on the jungle march that the soldiers were recalled before they even reached the borders of Manipur.

The British and Manipuris met properly twenty-six years later when both countries provided troops to aid the ruler of Assam against a rebellion. The little state was of no real interest to the East India Company, by now the rulers of much of India, including all of Bengal, until 1824 when an ugly war took shape with the kingdom of Burma. For once it was a war forced upon the East India Company; neither the condition of their dominions nor the British Parliament was in favour of entering into a costly conflict with the large country on India's north-eastern border (though various Governor-Generals had urged it for some time). A new and young Burmese king, Bagyidaw, surrounded by sycophants, was told that he was invincible. The English, it was said, were mere traders, their successes in India attributed to weak Hindu rulers, the plunder of Calcutta alone would pay for the war, after which 'Bagyidaw proposed to march to England, the occupation of which would be signalised by the installation of his son as viceroy of all the British dominions.'[13]

The *casus belli* for war was the Burmese commander in Manipur who, in January 1824, led his war-elephants and men towards Cachar, a key state that had a common frontier with the British-administered Indian province of Dacca. It was the final provocation. Governor-General Lord Amherst declared war. The Manipuris were, of course, delighted. They at last had an ally against the hated Burmese and this new friend could wield a very big stick. The British decided that an alliance with Manipur might be most effective in this war and so threw their support behind an energetic prince called Gambhir Singh. He was licensed to raise a body of 500 Cachari and Manipuri volunteers (soon increased to 2,000), called 'the Manipur Levy', armed, trained and led by two British officers. In the meantime, a British army of 7,000 led by General Shuldham lumbered towards Imphal. This force floundered in the jungle before even reaching the frontier. Gambhir persuaded Shuldham to let him go it alone with the Manipur Levy; in a brilliant ten-day campaign they overran the Burmese stockade at Ningail, 10 miles from Imphal, killing 300 of its 1,000 defenders, re-took the Manipuri capital without a fight and chased the enemy right back into Burma. By the Treaty of Yandabo, 24 February 1826, the 1st Anglo-Burmese War was concluded. It recognised Manipur as an independent kingdom with Gambhir Singh as its ruler.

Eight years later Gambhir died of cholera and was succeeded by his two-year-old son, Chandra Kirti Singh. The stage was now set for a period of instability; a kinsman, Nar Singh, was made regent but, in a story as old as time, he usurped the throne and ruled for 14 years until his death in 1850. That year Chandra Kirti, now a virile youth, was able to depose Nar Singh's brother, Devendra, and regain his throne. Over the next twenty-six years, he had ten sons born of six queens and had to deal with no fewer than sixteen concerted attempts to seize his throne by Devendra and others of the royal bloodline. Chandra Kirti, was an amiable, thick-set man with a keen interest in science and engineering (one Political Agent was surprised to be presented with a petroleum lamp designed and made by the maharajah in his workshop). He was fair to the inhabitants whose dues to the state were met by *lalup*, a system of forced labour by which every Manipuri male not exempted by the ruler had to provide ten days free labour every thirty days. Tea became the state's main export commodity and source of revenue. All foreigners were totally excluded from Manipur unless permission had first been granted by the Durbar via application to the Political Agent. This included British tea planters since, as one Political Agent commented, Chandra Kirti 'earnestly desired to preserve his country intact and to give us no excuse for annexing it.'[14]

Loyal support to the British saw Chandra Kirti receive various honours, including being made a Knight Commander of the Star of India (K.C.S.I.) in 1880 as a reward for his help in the 1879/80 Naga Hills Expedition. The Manipur Agency was now placed under the control of the Chief Commissioner of Assam. The maharaja was delighted to receive two 7-pounder mountain guns and 1,000 stands of arms from the British. In 1884 he requested and obtained 60,000 rounds of ball cartridges to aid his troops in a course of musketry. During the 1885 Third Anglo-Burmese War the Manipuris gave great assistance and the state was rewarded with the presentation of two more 7-pounder guns.

In 1886 Chandra Kirti passed away. In accordance with the late king's wishes, his first four sons born of the first four queens in order of seniority became Maharajah (king), Jubraj (heir-apparent), Sennayak (commander) and Senapati (commander-in-chief). These were the princes Sura Chandra, Kula Chandra, Tikendrajit and Jhala Kirti. Within a few months Jhala Kirti died and Tikendrajit became the Senapati. Of the uterine brothers of the maharajah, Prince Bhairabjit took the office of Pucca Sena (lieutenant-general), while other princes were in charge of such things as the royal elephants and roads.

Uneasy lies the head that wears a crown – there was not much love lost between the various royal princes. The threat of palace revolt always hung heavy in the air. On dark nights it was almost tangible like the scent of musk on the breeze. More than once Sura Chandra had to face down a rising, either at court, or from his troublesome Kuki tribesmen. British Political Agents noted that the ruler seemed weak and vacillating but remained popular with his people alongside his more able brother, Prince Tikendrajit, the Senapati.

'The grave of fame' was how the mid-Victorian historian of British India, Sir John Kaye (also sometime secretary of the aptly named Political & Secret Department of the Government of India), described the fate of the officers who tried to make their careers on the north-eastern frontier. Assam and Bengal held none of the glamour associated with the Punjab and North-West Frontier, the areas nurtured no Henry or John Lawrence, Victorian legends of Raj rule, no young paladins such as James Abbott, John Jacob or Reynell Taylor firmly and valiantly held their frontier districts in sway with a bible in one and hand and a sword in the other. Kaye was right – but only up to a point – administering the north-eastern districts destroyed many a good man through disease, drink and depression. Yet, by 1890, some administrators had started to carve out legends for themselves, notably Thomas Lewin in the Chin Hills and George Scott in the Shan States.

The first British Political Agent to Manipur had been appointed in 1835, 'for presentation of a friendly intercourse and as a means of communication with the Manipur Government...' Roy, the historian of Manipur, wrote that the duty of the Political Agent 'was like that of an Ambassador' and strict neutrality was maintained in the internal political affairs of the state. In time Manipur became the Cinderella among political agencies. No one wanted the job and the Resident's hands seemed tied. In 1877 Captain Edward Durand, the current Political Agent, complained that he was 'in fact a British officer under Manipur surveillance. If the Maharajah is not pleased with the Political Agent he cannot get anything... The Court is almost openly hostile, though they have pliancy enough to pretend to a great regard for the Political Agent and *Sirkar* (Indian Government).'[15]

To be fair to the Manipuris there were faults on the British side too; in 1861 the Indian Government had decided to close the Manipur Agency as a cost-cutting exercise. The proposal was then dropped but the threat definitely harmed the reputation of the British Raj. Sure enough, the next Political Agent, a Dr Dillon, had to be removed for 'inefficiency' in 1865 and the post then remained vacant for some time. In 1872, and again in 1876, the Manipuri Durbar brought charges against two Political Agents, but the Indian Government refuted the accusations. One of these men, Surgeon-Major Brown, rather conveniently died while inquiries into his behaviour were being investigated. In his memoirs Henry Cotton, himself a later Chief Commissioner of Assam, recalled the doctor as 'a very quaint old type', but admitted that he had 'relapsed into what were called native ways', and it was said of him that he had registered on the Medical Civil Fund two of his children by separate women on the same day.[16] This rather extraordinary statement confirms that having sex with native women, possibly even running a *ménage a trois*, was accepted as a lifestyle choice by some political officers in remote outposts such as Manipur.

'They'll never get a good man' to take Manipur, said an Indian Government Secretary in 1877. 'Well, a good man has taken it now,' came the reply. The new Political Agent was an energetic 36-year-old ex-officer of H.M. 73rd Regiment who had seen active service in the later stages of the Indian Mutiny. His name was Captain James Johnstone. He seems to have led a charmed life. When he was in his early twenties, a man-eating panther sprang onto his right shoulder. Johnstone managed to fire his gun using his left arm. The wound was severe, but he recovered completely, and ever after was known by the Assamese as 'Bagh Khorah' or 'tiger-eater'. Johnstone arrived at Imphal in October 1877 with his wife – a woman almost as indomitable as her husband (judging by her reaction to many tribulations) – and young sons in tow. From the outset he was determined to re-assert British prestige. This determination arose as much from his own character as anything suggested or requested by the Indian Government. 'I always tried to bear in mind that I was the representative of the strong dealing with the weak,' he wrote later.

In October 1879 the Angami Nagas went on the warpath and besieged the Deputy-Commissioner of Assam at a village in the hills called Kohima. More than 6,000 tribesmen faced off against just 158 Indian Army soldiers and Frontier Police. Everyone knew that the Nagas were notoriously blood-thirsty head-hunters. A British officer once counted forty heads in a single house, 'strung together like onions.' If Kohima fell it would have meant not only a massacre, but 500 stands of rifles and over 250,000 rounds of ammunition would be in Naga hands, enough to keep the hills in a blaze for years. When news of the uprising reached Imphal, the Political Agent hastily assembled a relief column of some 2,000 Manipuri troops and Kuki auxiliaries. Doing forced marches, Johnstone led his little army, including Princes Sura Chandra and Tikendrajit, through the jungles to Kohima where they successfully relieved the garrison and about 400 natives, women and children. The Political Agent stayed on to assist General Nation who arrived with 1,200 British troops, two 7-pounder guns and a rocket detachment. The fight now had to be taken to the Nagas who had fortified their biggest village at a place called Khonoma. Five hostile villages had to be taken before an assault was launched on 22 November. The tribesmen threw spears and stones with great dexterity. Paths were booby-trapped with hidden pits of sharpened bamboo spikes. The British attack was successful but left 25 per cent of the native ranks killed or wounded. Johnstone was at the fore in all the fighting and rode back at one point to Imphal in an epic round trip of four days and more than sixty hours in the saddle.

Lauded a hero by his superiors in India and the Manipuris, Johnstone was in the fortunate position of being able to ask favours of the maharajah – and have them granted. He was allowed to start a school teaching English and get the old maharajah, Chandra Kirti, to agree to the building of a new residency. It was agreed that this building would stay in the same spot as the old one, close to the palace, but Johnstone demanded that all the squalid houses in the district be cleared away, dirty tanks of water filled in with new ones dug in their place, 'and a fine large space cleared and handed over to me.' The old residency had been a low wattle and daub bungalow, 'very dark and very full of mosquitoes'. Johnstone designed in its place a half-timbered bungalow that looked something like a thatched Elizabethan yeoman's home. It was built on a solid brick foundation with a basement 7 feet in height and designed to be shot-proof (the old residency had been subjected to a crossfire in an earlier palace revolution). The main level was approached on all four sides by flights of solid masonry steps. In total the new compound covered 16 acres, with a mud breastwork perimeter and ditch, entered by four gates. A kitchen garden was laid out, there were several flower beds and a riding track for exercise of the horses. To relieve the heat of the day and offer some shady spots for relaxation, exotic trees were planted including imported deodars. 'I spared no expense on the garden,' noted Johnstone in his autobiography, who 'covered most of the large trees with beautiful orchids, so that in the season we had a blaze of colour.' Perhaps the garden's best feature was its lake, which the Political Agent had sculpted out of a small pond, now deepened, its banks repaired. 'I never allowed a bird to be killed,' wrote Johnstone of his lake, 'it was covered in winter with water-fowls to the number of four hundred and fifty or five hundred of every kind, from wild geese downwards, and rare birds took refuge in the trees.'[18]

The Indian soldiers who formed the agent's escort were also not forgotten; new quarters were built for them in the north-east corner of the compound alongside a new tank of pure drinking water.

Johnstone left Imphal in the spring of 1886, by which time he had risen in the service and had a decidedly paternalistic view of Manipur. Within a few weeks Maharajah Chandra Kirti was dead. In Johnstone's opinion the maharajah's passing would have been the perfect time for the Government of India to institute much-needed reforms, but this opportunity was missed. In his view, the Viceroy and his council failed to replace him with anyone who had 'a real love for the work, the country and the people'. The next Political Agent, a major called Trotter, was dead within six weeks of his arrival from wounds received during the recent fighting in Burma. An infantry regiment of the Indian Army was stationed at Langthobal, 4 miles from Imphal, purposely to uphold British prestige, yet respect for the Raj seemed to be on the wane. On one occasion residency sepoys were hustled and beaten by Manipuris at a public festival. A man carrying the government mail the few miles between the residency and Langthobal was stopped and robbed. One British officer who was stationed at Imphal as Major Trotter lay dying was appalled by the lack of help provided by the Manipur Durbar:

Whatever we asked for was point-blank refused, or only given after the exercise of considerable pressure... I never knew greater arrogance or more intolerable swagger than that indulged in by the representatives of the Maharajah... instead of being at least respectful, these nincompoops appeared to think they were doing us a favour by attending at all, and so to every request the same answer was given, 'It is impossible.' Our Acting Agent invariably answered, 'It must be done, so there is an end of it,' but I own I often longed to break up the assemblage summarily.[19]

This was the state of affairs when Frank Grimwood was hastily offered what some might have called a poisoned chalice. Not that Frank or Ethel saw things that way. At the foot of the hills they were met by an escort of ten elephants and a guard of fifty Manipuri sepoys under an old soldier called Colonel Samoo Singh. Ethel thought Samoo was 'one of the most hideous old gentlemen I have ever met,' but he was 'politeness itself' and presented her and her husband with large baskets of fowls and vegetables. Elephants brightly rigged out in red cloth were provided for the Grimwoods to ride. Ethel, perhaps rather nervous, wanted to go with Frank on his elephant, but he had to explain that this was not the done thing. Samoo led the way to a final rest house where the British couple spent the night. Next morning they prepared to make their entry into Imphal. It was, of course, vital to make a good impression, especially for Frank, the new representative of the imperial power. Unfortunately in the night a rat had eaten a large hole in his hat as well as all the fingers on Ethel's right-hand glove. 'We could not get at our boxes to rummage for others, so we had to go as we were,'[20] she noted discontentedly.

Ten miles along the road and just seven from the capital, the Grimwoods were met, amid much blowing of trumpets and presenting of arms, by four of the royal princes and their escorts. Only the famous Senapati made any impression on Ethel:

> He was not a very striking-looking personage... about five feet eight inches in height, with a lighter skin than most natives, and rather a pleasing type of countenance. He had nice eyes and a pleasant smile, but his expression was rather spoilt by his front teeth, which were very much broken. We liked what we saw of him on this occasion and thought him very good-natured-looking.[21]

In all the confusion Ethel ended up by shaking hands with a sepoy, much to the man's astonishment. A reception was held in a barn by the roadside. Frank was able to converse with the Senapati in Hindustani, but the other princes spoke only Methei, so they simply 'smiled continuously' and Ethel, feeling rather sheepish, 'followed suit by smiling back'.

The speeches, smiles and present-giving at an end, the whole retinue rode on to Imphal (this time on horseback). A twelve-gun salute boomed as the Grimwoods reached the capital. Bidding the princes farewell, the couple turned into the gate of the residency compound. There was a rather bizarre half-timbered structure with low buildings either side that Johnstone had planned as a fever hospital. Ethel saw a long carriage drive, the grassland all around dotted with deodars and flowering shrubs. Next a tennis court came into view on her right side, then a hedge of brilliant cluster roses in full bloom that divided the outer grounds from the flower gardens surrounding the house. In the distance she caught sight of a lake with an island in the middle, 'where late as it was, a few wild duck were still swimming about.'

Ethel and Frank put their horses into a canter up the drive and soon reached the main flight of eight steps to the residency. The building seemed a blaze of colour since a large bougainvillea's purple blossoms 'entirely hid the thatch with which the porch was surmounted.' Mrs Grimwood immediately fell in love with the building, its walls painted white with the wooden timbers picked out in black. Dismounting, she and Frank reached the verandah, comfortably matted and strewn with luxurious rugs and animal skins. Red-coated servants were there to greet them and two Gurkha orderlies saluted. Turning to look back, Ethel saw 'a circular lawn covered with flower-beds blazing with colour', but her greatest delight, the fulfilment of all her fantasies, stood at the end of the lawn. Her heart leapt a beat. It was 'the flagstaff of my dreams and the ensign of Old England waving proudly in the breeze.'[22]

Mischievous Monkeys and Naked Nagas

Those first weeks and months in Manipur were to be a special time for Ethel and Frank St Clair Grimwood, dreamy days the former would always look upon as the most joyous of her life in a land full of surprises and delights. Mistress at last of a decent-sized house and establishment of servants, Mrs Grimwood enjoyed running the residency, and its staff in scarlet and gold with 'V.R.' emblazoned on their buttons. The building had been well designed by Sir James Johnstone and included a durbar room for receptions, separate dining and drawing-rooms, 'very airy and comfortable' bedrooms and offices. The bedrooms all had fireplaces and the sitting-rooms stoves to help take off a winter chill.

Ethel was better equipped to deal with life as a memsahib than many poor girls uprooted from a chilly England to the hotter climes of a remote station of the Raj. She had, after all, been born in India and spoke reasonably good Hindustani. Soon she was learning Methei and showed such an aptitude for it that she outshone Frank; he got into such a huff over Ethel's linguistic skill that she gave up her lessons for fear he would sulk. There were more than a few household battles, mainly fought with Moni Ram Dass, the elder of Frank's two personal bearers or manservants. He had been in Grimwood's employ since his first assignment to India and, in Ethel's opinion, 'gave himself the airs and graces of a Maharajah ... my way was not his way sometimes.'[1] Memsahib and servant particularly clashed when Dass chose one day to air all Frank's clothes, including his underwear, in the drawing-room at a time when Ethel was expecting visitors.

A properly run Raj household required a minimum of 14 indoor and outdoor servants. The Grimwoods were lucky enough to have far more. Frank had two Gurkha orderlies, a native doctor, and to help him in his office, Frank had a head clerk and assistants, a secretary and Manipuri, Burmese and Kuki interpreters as well as six general *chuprassies* (bearer-messengers) ready at a moment's notice to take his letters to the Maharajah, or even to the Chief Commissioner of Assam if necessary. To run her household Ethel could depend on the services of several native girls as maids and cleaners, a cook and kitchen staff as well as washerwomen, grooms, gardeners and water-carriers. Assuming the servants were tolerably honest and hard-working, a memsahib was expected to exercise constant surveillance and impose discipline. It was a fact that those English women who did not do so could expect only dirt in the kitchen and bad service. This was not all a matter of imposing bossy British ways; dirt in a tropical kitchen in 1890 inhabited a realm in which disease was ever-rampant and prophylactic medicine at its most primitive. A dirty kitchen could mean an early and unpleasant death. In fact *The Complete Indian Housekeeper and Cook* remarked tartly that some ladies never went into their kitchens for fear of seeing a servant, 'using his toes as a toast-rack or ... the soup strained through a greasy turban.' The answer to running a good household, according to the authors of this hefty *vade-mecum*, was to instruct the staff, 'kindly, but with great firmness',[2] and be ever vigilant.

For a memsahib life in a far-flung outpost of the Empire such as Imphal could be dull. The amount of time Ethel later stayed away from Manipur suggests that she too found the monotony of daily routine less than exhilarating, yet she glides over all of this in her memoirs. Who can blame her? It may have been a repetitive and somewhat spoiled existence but with the languid luxury came moments of intense pleasure. Twice a week the British officers of the 44th Gurkhas stationed at nearby Langthobal came to Imphal to play polo. Ethel made them especially welcome laying on 'at home' informal receptions every Thursday. Everyone enjoyed tennis on the residency court and then the Maharajah's band played light orchestral pieces, marches and waltzes from 4 to 6pm while the officers no doubt enjoyed chota-pegs of whisky and water, or gin and tonic. The musicians were, rather astonishingly, Naga tribesmen but 'dance music came easiest to them and they kept excellent time.' They were conducted by an enthusiastic young bandmaster who wore a rather weird wardrobe of white frock-coat, black baggy trousers, a red waistcoat and an 'ancient top-hat constructed in the year 1800, I fancy.' The Grimwoods sometimes went to Langthobal, Ethel being carried in a long chair due to the foul roads, and in the Gurkha officers' mess she must have been the belle of the ball, clearly the centre of attention, the only woman there. Both the Grimwoods were 'desolated' when the regiment was sent off to fight the Chins in the winter of 1888.

This sense of loss had to be compensated for somehow; in Ethel's case she made the most of her beautiful garden and a growing menagerie of wild animals. It became a ritual for her and Frank each morning after breakfast to ride around the grounds, visit the stables and kitchen garden and feed all their animals. Besides the horses there were two little otters, 'so tame they followed us about like dogs,' she recalled. 'We had three monkeys, little brown fellows, which were my delight.' The little rascals frequently got into mischief and did damage if allowed into the house, but Ethel was content to let them sleep together on a beam in the roof of the bedroom verandah where they were better than watchdogs after dark, chattering and making a great commotion if anyone came near. There was also a pair of grey and red cranes, a tame deer, and a black bear who began as a small ball of cuddly fluff, but grew up fast to be quite ferocious. One day the bear got loose in the garden while Ethel was picking some flowers. The servants ran in all directions as the beast rushed towards her. He sniffed at some dropped flowers, then came on quickly, clawing at her back and tearing a winter coat in two. One of the Gurkha orderlies managed to beat bruin away and Frank, who was understandably concerned, insisted that next morning the bear should be taken into the hills and set free.

To tend the grounds the residency staff included nine *metis* (native gardeners). These men were all Naga tribesmen who, according to Ethel, 'wore little besides a necklace or two.' Traditionally most Nagas wore a kind of kilt or narrow waistcloth to hide their private parts, but some Eastern Naga clans were referred to as 'the naked Nagas' for the very reason that they wore almost nothing. Possibly Ethel's gardeners belonged to some of these people. In his memoirs Lt-Colonel Alban Wilson wrote of one Naga tribe whose adult males wore little except a tight wedding ring of bone over the penis; its purpose was to prevent infidelity and, chortled the old soldier, the device was extremely effective! Ethel told a spinster friend about her naked gardeners and the good lady, quite horrified at the thought of all this male nudity (and apparently forgetting Adam in the Garden of Eden), despatched a gift for them – nine pairs of red, white and blue-striped bathing drawers. One fine morning Mrs Grimwood made a special presentation on the lawn to the gardeners who received their gifts with great delight. A few days later she found that one had stuck his bathing pants on his head and made a smart turban, while another had made a hole in his pair and was wearing them as a rather natty striped jacket. 'After this I gave up trying to inculcate decency into the minds of the untutored savage,'[3] wrote Ethel, tongue-in-cheek.

For company Ethel and Frank had to rely largely on the Manipuri princes and princesses. It might be said, with hindsight, that this is where their problems also began.

Political Agents, representatives at native courts of the British Raj, were not expected to act in such an informal fashion as Frank Grimwood displayed in Manipur. Subsequently his actions were to be heavily criticised, not least by Johnstone, Political Agent in the 1870s. In classic imperial fashion Sir James had exercised very subtle indirect rule. 'Whenever it became necessary for me to interfere, I did so with great firmness,' he later wrote, 'but always tried to carry the Maharajah and his ministers with me, and make any desired reform appear to emanate from him.' At the same time Johnstone allowed no infringement of what he perceived to be the rights of the British Government. Then, 'I spoke in very unmistakeable language.' An earlier Agent, Colonel McCulloch, used to tell the Maharajah bluntly, 'I don't care what you say of me, so long as you do as I tell you.' Johnstone was aware, interestingly enough, that the Manipur Durbar presented itself as independent of the British, 'but I was quite satisfied that they did not believe what they said.'[4] If this remark is true then the events of 1891 were soon to rudely shake Johnstone's *de haut en bas* confidence.

In his memoirs Johnstone had a dig at Grimwood's fondness for playing polo with the princes. He deemed this was dangerous social behaviour:

> I did not think I was justified, holding the important position I did, in running the risk of being hustled and jostled with any one with whom I played: men who I was bound to keep at arm's length. Had I done so I should have lost influence. I could not be hail-fellow-well-met, and though talking freely with all, I at once checked all disposition to familiarity, and people rarely attempted it.[5]

On its simplest level the job of a Political Agent at a native court was to be a conduit for communication between the local ruler, his ministers and the imperial government. Agents were told to discreetly advise the ruler, help him exercise good government where possible and keep the Viceroy informed, weekly, through communication with a Chief Commissioner or, in exceptional cases, directly with the Foreign & Political Department of the Government of India. Maharajahs and princes might think themselves independent and try to avoid British interference, yet it was assumed by 1890 that they understood – in the words of a later edict – that 'No Ruler of an Indian State can justifiably claim to negotiate with the British Government on an equal footing.'[6] Local rulers were allowed to retain a measure of sovereignty and various degrees of jurisdiction over their subjects (though it was rare for a ruler to try and execute one of his subjects without the permission of the British Resident or Political Agent), just so long as it was under British paramountcy.

This system of subtle indirect rule had developed since the days of Clive and Plassey 130 years earlier. It really took root after 1820 when British authority across the sub-continent became stabilised to a great extent. Generally the British did not interfere in the morals of a ruler – he could be a lecher, a miser, a rampant pederast – just so long as he remained loyal and compliant in other ways.

In 1884 the 18-year-old Nizam of Hyderabad, one of the richest rulers in India, supposedly held 'a drunken and disgraceful orgy' after a tiger shoot. The British Resident did some investigating and passed the incident off as 'boyish larking' since – the question of sexual morals aside – the young ruler was deemed politically compliant. Another ruler, Maharajah Holkar of Indore, had a nasty habit of kicking his servants in the stomach and harnessing state bankers to his carriage. In 1887 he tried to take his male lover with him to the Queen-Empress's Jubilee in London, insulted Lord Rothschild at a dinner there and was rude to officials during a tour of the Bank of England, all of which unfortunate events had to be resolved by Lepel Griffin, the long-suffering Agent to the Governor-General in Central India, even though Holkar was, as Lord Curzon said, 'a lunatic'.

It was rare indeed after the 1857–58 Mutiny for a ruler to be deposed. The most notorious case had been Mulhar Rao, the Gaekwar of Baroda, one of the most princely states. A born sadist, the Gaekwar tyrannised his subjects, flogged women, used torture and extortion on bankers, tradesmen and palace officials. In 1873 Mulhar Rao was informed that unless he improved his rule he would deposed after 18 months. Not long afterwards the Gaekwar made matters worse by attempting to poison the British Resident by offering him a glass of sherbet laced with splintered glass. The murder plot was never proven, but Mulhar Rao was duly removed for 'incorrigible misrule'. In this instance (and also in Manipur in 1891), the bad ruler's replacement was a compliant boy who could be groomed in the imperial values.

In practical terms Manipur came within the orbit of the Political Department of the Indian Foreign Office in Calcutta. Here, in a building described by one Viceroy as having all the damp charm of 'a dilapidated villa in a decayed London suburb', the Foreign Secretary (and his small team) liaised with the politicals – 'Soothing those who had been denied promotion, exhorting others to be kinder to the local ruler, upbraiding the few whose policies he thought were misguided.'[7] Manipur was very much at the bottom of the political pile and a long way behind the Residents of Hyderabad and Mysore in precedence. These top-of-the-tree posts came with a salary each of 48,000 rupees. Most political men – and Frank Grimwood was an exception – tended to be army officers. Obtaining a political rank was a plum within the Indian Army since the pay was better and the work offered far more variety than peacetime soldiering in some dusty garrison.

If one ignores Sir James Johnstone's stuffy remarks it could be argued that in some respects Frank Grimwood was not a bad choice as a Political Agent, since the Foreign Department liked its chaps to be sociable types and good sportsmen who could ride and shoot well. It was essential, as David Gilmour has written:

> To find men who could be relied upon not to make gaffes, men who would remember not to shake hands with women out of purdah but to give a salaam to a Muslim and a *Namaste* to a Hindu. They also had to know about uniforms, whether to wear spurs with levee dress, when to put on their frock coat, their Mameluke sword and their white pith helmet with gold spike and chain.[8]

Lord Curzon once said that political work required special qualities of tact, flexibility, moral fibre and gentlemanly bearing, 'which are an instinct rather than an acquisition'. An article in *The Times of India* on 7 July 1893 declared that a good Political Agent 'should possess a mind polished by social intercourse rather than that crowded with fusty learning'. In many respects (and possibly only morals aside, a matter we will examine later), Frank Grimwood fitted the bill.

He got off to a good start when a special durbar was held at the residency two days after his arrival in Manipur. Sixty Gurkhas in full uniform, their medals glittering in the sunshine, were drawn up on the front lawn. Red cloth had been laid all over the verandah, which must also have been decorated by Ethel with a colourful blaze of flowers. With a fanfare of trumpets the Maharajah arrived with all his brothers, a number of his own troops, ministers of state and their followers. Hatless in deference to the ruler, Frank met Sura Chandra by the residency gate and the pair walked together up the drive. The whole ceremony took barely ten minutes. Ethel thought she was the centre of attention. 'They all stared at me very solemnly as if I were a curious kind of animal,'[9] she wrote later, and after much shaking of hands the whole assembly soon departed.

Ethel was not all impressed by the Maharajah Sura Chandra whom she described as 'a short, fat, ugly little man', his face scarred by smallpox, dressed all in white, except for a spray of yellow orchids in his white turban, grey woollen stockings fastened at the knee with blue elastic garters and brass buckles, and 'very large roughly-made laced boots of which he seemed supremely proud'.[10] The Maharajah could speak Hindustani and some local dialects but had a very limited English vocabulary. As a young man he had seemed to James Johnstone to be 'amiable' but 'of a weak character'. Taking another swipe at Grimwood, the former Agent later wrote that Sura Chandra would have made 'an excellent ruler' if 'backed up and influenced by an honest and capable Political Agent',[11] thus implying that Frank had been neither of these things. A devout Hindu, the Maharajah tried to rule wisely. Later he declared that 'I have never neglected the duties of the State ... I have kept my dominions in profound peace and have never at any time been the cause myself, or through my subjects, of anxiety to the Indian Government.'[12]

It was not long before Frank was on amiable terms with all the princes and even Ethel 'frequently' rode with them. To the Manipuris this cheerful and attractive young British couple must have seemed like a breath of fresh air after decades of stuffy British officials. In the cold weather Prince Tikendrajit, the Senapati, 'often organised a week's deer-shooting' specially for the Grimwoods. Ethel recalled these times as 'very good fun'. Occasionally a tiger would wander down into the valley and a royal hunt was always instigated. Ethel always felt very sorry for the beast but soon accumulated 'quite a collection' of skins and claws at Imphal.

The princes were soon visiting the residency regularly and without any ceremony (Johnstone, we may guess, would have been mortified at such informality) and enjoyed examining all the Grimwoods' photographs and Frank's shotguns. On one occasion the Grimwoods organised a party on the lake in the grounds. Five boats crammed with younger members of the royal family pelted one another with big pink water-lilies to squeals of delight from the children. Strict caste meant that the visitors could not be given anything to eat or drink so Ethel and Frank presented their guests with flowers, beads and Japanese fans.

Ethel noted that the Manipuri princesses were 'very pretty' with 'long, silky black hair', relatively fair complexions and beautiful brown eyes. 'They cut their hair in front in a straight fringe all round their foreheads,' she wrote, 'while the back hangs loose, and it gives them a pretty, childish look.' She also admired the beautiful and brightly-coloured striped petticoats fastened Burmese-style under the arms. These garments were worn outdoors with 'a small green velvet zouave jacket ... a very fine muslin shawl over the shoulders, and gold necklaces and bracelets by way of ornament'.[13]

Most Manipuri girls got married between their fifteenth and seventeenth birthdays. Once wed a Manipuri bride seems to have had far greater freedom than in the rest of India. Much of the daily labour was done by the native women but they also exercised greater control in domestic matters. The Maharajah's daughter was about fifteen. Frequently she visited Ethel with nine or ten girlfriends of the same age. The Senapati used to bring them. While Tikendrajit talked with Frank, the teen princesses did the same things teen girls always like to do – they nosed all over the house, especially Ethel's bedroom, tried on her clothes and hats and brushed their lush thick hair with her best brushes while admiring themselves in a long mirror. Ethel added:

> The Senaputti generally waited in the drawing-room talking to my husband. After the party had explored my room, we used to re-join the others, and take them all out into the garden, allowing them to pick the flowers and decorate each other, and then my husband would photograph them.[14]

Those first months in Manipur, as described by Ethel, seem almost sybaritic. During the bright but cold winter weather, from October to March, the Grimwoods spent most of the time in camp, 'a month at a time', interrupted by a few days at Imphal. Often they boated on the Logtak Lake. Starting at 6am the couple went off duck-shooting, Frank doing great execution with his eight-bore, knocking over half-a-dozen birds at a time (Ethel couldn't bear to see the birds killed and called it 'butchery'). Then it was back to dinner in a lakeside village by torchlight, an inevitable bugler playing outside their tent, while the couple enjoyed an excellent dinner 'in grand style'.

Sometimes the Grimwoods went up into the hills and mixed with the Naga and Kuki tribespeople. Fifteen miles from Imphal and at an elevation of over 6,000 feet there was a hill bungalow for the Political Agent's use. The state had also given the British agents some half-dozen villages and the Naga inhabitants were quite happy since they got paid by their imperial masters and did not have to work for free under the Manipuri forced labour system known as *lalup*. Touring the southern boundaries of the state the Grimwoods visited some places where no white woman had ever been seen. They stopped off in remote villages to be greeted with presents of eggs or fowls and watch a display of native dancing. Ethel liked the simple ways of the Nagas; she did not mind that the men got drunk on fermented rice-water called 'zu', but was sickened by watching them eat a hearty meal of their favourite delicacy – roast dog. The curious Naga women would turn back Ethel's sleeves at the wrists and gasp to see that her arms were also white! Always a fashionable lady, Ethel was wearing a steel bustle frame at the back of her riding habit (bustles having returned to fashion), on one occasion, but the next day rode without it. To her amusement the villagers asked what had happened to her tail! Back at camp she showed some of the women the steel frames and the locals – some might say very wisely – thought it a very funny and weird European fashion indeed.

The letter arrived in December 1888. It looked like any other official document but the contents devastated both of the Grimwoods who met the news with 'hopeless silence'. Frank had been re-assigned to a posting at Jorhat in Assam. Despite their disappointment the pair must have realised that this kind of news was commonplace in the Political Department; promotion was largely on seniority (rather less on merit) and officers were shunted about quite regularly. In Frank's case it appears that 'a number of senior men were returning to India after furlough who needed to be provided with districts ahead of the junior officers.'[15]

It was two months before the Grimwoods departed. Frank's successor, a bachelor named Heath, had to travel from the far side of Assam and according to Ethel he was 'as loath to take the place as we were to give it up.' She confessed to being heartbroken at having to leave her freshly planted rose bushes, specially imported from Calcutta, along with an asparagus bed she had just laid out. 'I almost felt inclined to destroy everything,' she wrote, 'but my husband was more magnanimous, and even went so far as to say he hoped Mr Heath (our successor) would enjoy it all.'[16] The couple made the most of their last two months; two more shooting expeditions to the Logtak Lake and a journey to Cachar for the Christmas race meeting helped occupy the days, then it was time to start packing up all their belongings.

Mr Heath duly arrived to a welcome by the same crimson-covered elephants that had greeted Ethel and Frank. Grimwood was there to greet his successor, but Heath 'hadn't a good word' to say about Manipur and 'seemed to dread the loneliness terribly'. The Gurkhas had left Langthobal and it was true, thought Ethel, 'how the solitude will weigh on him'. He also looked like a sick man. The night before her departure she took Heath on a walk through the women's bazaar and across the polo ground. He later seemed 'in a happier frame of mind and the band playing whilst we were at dinner cheered him up considerably.' Next morning, however, as the Grimwoods said their goodbyes to favourite servants, orderlies and beloved pets (though Ethel refused to be parted from her trio of mischievous monkeys), everyone was gloomy. Later Ethel admitted that she was partly to blame and 'could not put on a pleasant outward appearance'.[17] She and Frank rode slowly up the drive to the gate. Then, as if thinking the same thought, both spurred their horses and galloped for 4 miles until Imphal lay well behind them. Neither spoke much for the rest of the day.

Jorhat was 200 miles away in the Assam Valley. The route would take the Grimwoods over the Naga Hills, past Kohima, scene of the fighting ten years earlier. Ethel was cheered by the magnificent scenery along the way, especially forests of oak in the high Naga country. After Kohima the path led eight more days to Golaghat via the Namba Forest, a wilderness of dense jungle and redwood trees interspersed with valleys and swift flowing streams where each morning the couple saw the muddy tracks of numerous animals including bears, deer, wild elephants and leopards.

No sooner had the Grimwoods arrived at Jorhat than a telegram had them on the move again. Frank had been posted to a rather better sub-division at Gauhati on the mighty Brahmaputra River. It was early April when Ethel and Frank got there and she was dreading the sticky Assamese heat. One week after their arrival, while still unpacking, news came that Mr Heath was dangerously ill with dysentery. Within a few days he was dead and Frank Grimwood was re-assigned once again to Manipur. He was delighted, but Ethel no longer wished to return. This may sound strange but she later claimed to have a 'presentiment of evil' about Manipur, a premonition of bad things to come. In her memoirs she claims to have kept these thoughts to herself, but the length of time it took her to return suggests that she and Frank must have, at the very least, exchanged words and possibly argued over his re-assignment. Ethel says that she told Frank to take the job but was exhausted by all the travelling and feared returning to a house in which a man, a friend, had just tragically died with 'rooms that were full of his things'.

When the Grimwoods reached Shillong it was decided that Ethel would stay there some weeks until the hot weather had subsided. Frank was back in Manipur by mid-May. His wife did not join him until mid-November – a full six months apart. Her long absence was noted. Thereafter she also made several visits to Cachar and Shillong, which became the cause of society gossip. She was seen on the arm of a handsome officer in Shillong. Few people realised that this was her half-brother, 30-year-old Alan Boisragon, now a captain in the 1st Battalion, Royal Irish Regiment. Neatly moustachioed, prematurely going bald, but a good athlete, Alan had served in the 1884–85 Nile Expedition. It was quite natural for Ethel to want to spend time with Alan. They had been close since childhood and he was perhaps the only man besides Frank in whom she could confide, possibly even more so. Yet hill stations, such as Simla or Shillong, were always rife with mischief-makers and tongues were soon wagging that Ethel Grimwood seemed a little too fond of Captain Bosiragon's company.

Any modern reader of Ethel's memoirs cannot fail to notice her occasional references to ill-health yet she never tells us what her trouble was. Two things come to mind – she may have suffered intermittently from one of India's many debilitating, fever-ridden sicknesses, or she may have had a miscarriage.

The Americans spent years trying to solve the mystery of yellow fever, but the Indian Army can take the prize for discovering an antidote to malaria. It was a doctor in the Indian Medical Service, Ronald Ross, who isolated the crucial malaria-mosquito link in his laboratory at Begumpet on 20 August 1897. This was a few years after Ethel had left India.

Victorian women were supposed to start a family within a year or two of marriage. This was crucial in India where children often died in infancy, so better to try early on. Ethel was less than twenty when she married, in theory a perfect child-bearing bride. Frank was already in his thirties but apparently virile. It seems inconceivable that they did not want or try to have a child. Ethel avoids the whole matter in her book and, of course, if a miscarriage had occurred she most certainly would not have mentioned it. There was a native doctor at Imphal (Mrs Johnstone had delivered a child there in the 1870s), but one can imagine the terrors of childbirth for a memsahib in such a lonely outpost. A complication in pregnancy or labour would have been a nightmare, a Caesarean birth unheard of. A contemporary textbook claimed that metritis (inflammation of the womb), was most likely caused by masturbation, coitus, ice cream, abstinence, alcohol, tea, wearing corsets too tightly and the reading of saucy French novels. It is worth remembering that axis-traction forceps for a difficult delivery were not invented until 1877 and it is doubtful if any hospital closer than Shillong had them. Possibly the couple had discussed the whole matter and decided against having children, either as a lifestyle choice, or until they were based in a place not so remote as Imphal. The Manchester Church Congress in 1888 had slammed contraception as an 'awful heresy'. Even so, Frank could have worn a 'French letter' or 'instrument of safety' – 'condom' was a dirty word at the time and not used in polite society – made of sheep's intestines (apparently very reliable), or of the new vulcanised rubber introduced into Britain after 1876. These India rubber sheaths cost two shillings and sixpence (about £9 today).

Leaving Ethel in Assam, let us return to Frank who had a nightmarish journey back to Imphal. All his servants went down with fever and he ended up having to cook his own meals, groom the horses, set up camp at night and re-pack in the mornings.

His return to Manipur was, of course, a joyous event for the Maharajah, his brothers and the residency staff. Office work aside, he was free to indulge in his twin passions – polo and amateur photography.

Manipur was sometimes called the Land of Polo. The game had developed here in the 16th century (though a similar game has long been played in Gilgit and Persia). From Manipur the sport was exported by British officers into India; the first polo club was formed at Cachar, Assam, in 1859. Twelve years later it was being played by H.M. 9th Lancers and 10th Hussars. Within a decade it had become an obsession within both the Indian and British armies, most especially and naturally, though not exclusively, among cavalry regiments. Polo Manipuri-style (then as now), was and is a most exciting game to watch. Hurlingham rules do not apply. Indeed, the only rules, as one army officer remarked, are that there is a goal at either end of the field, 'and the ball has to get there anyhow.' The princes and Frank Grimwood played on eleven- and twelve-hand ponies equipped and protected by a special saddle, head-stall and crupper:

There is no offside, no objection to fouling, crossing, or hooking sticks. Play is at full-speed all the time, and if a player or pony is tired or injured a fresh one takes his place. The only pause occurs when a goal is hit or the ball goes off the ground. The game is watched by a crowd of partisans, who keep up a continuous roar of comment, advice, and encouragement, above which is heard the thudding of the ponies' hoofs, with the rattle of the sticks or clicking of the ball, not to mention the continuous drumming of the players' heels on the big leather shields, which is supposed to encourage their own ponies, whilst making most of their opponents shy off. Each player, too has his puggri tied over his head and ears, round his neck and under his chin to prevent his head being injured, for nothing is thought of hitting the man or pony if it is impossible to hit the ball. Seeing that all Manipuris ride entirely by balance and not by grip, it is astonishing how very seldom anyone is hurt or takes a serious toss.[18]

For complete relaxation Frank Grimwood liked to take pictures (amateur photography and bicycling being the two greatest social crazes in England during this period). It seems that he had his own studio and darkroom in the residency grounds. Sadly, all his plates, prints, cameras, alongside all the evidence of what he did – or did not – photograph were destroyed during the 1891 war. He was certainly following in a grand tradition; photography began in India just after the invention of the salt print process in Europe in 1839. A lithograph based on a photograph was published in Calcutta one year later. The first commercial photographer opened his shop in 1844. During the 2nd Anglo-Sikh War 1848–49 a Bengal Army surgeon, John McCosh, used the calotype process to make prints at Lahore, Multan and other parts of the Punjab as well as photographing leading British and Sikh figures. 'They are the earliest photographs taken in connection with a war anywhere in the world.'[19]

India was in many ways a perfect laboratory for the development of photography; its plentiful sunshine helped to compensate for the long time exposure it took the chemicals to absorb an impression. In the 1850s and 1860s the development of albumen-positive prints, using a mixture containing egg-whites, suddenly allowed copies to be reproduced cheaply from an original glass-plate negative. The economic feasibility of making multiple high-quality copies saw a surge worldwide in commercial photography. Increasingly it became a hobby for keen amateurs. Hobbyists such as Frank Grimwood in Manipur (or even professionals like John Burke in Rawalpindi), had to tread delicately since producing a negative was 'still akin to alchemy'. Any mistake handling a glass plate or mixing the chemicals would ruin the exposure. It was also highly dangerous since each plate had first to be coated in a mixture that included an explosive material called collodion. The plate was then slipped into a light-tight frame and inserted into a box camera on a tripod. An exposure of 30 seconds or more was made by removing the cap from the lens. Next came the really tricky part – before the collodion dried the exposed glass-plate negative had to be developed on the spot. We can imagine Frank rushing off to his residency darkroom, or perhaps on tour he used a tent near the Logtak Lake. The albumen prints could be made later. It is likely that a keen amateur such as Frank had designed his darkroom with a retractable roof or some special opening to control the sunlight that was passed through a negative to expose the paper positive. Each positive had to be processed individually. It was a time-consuming process. The prints were made on very thin paper and usually attached to a thicker material or pasted onto an album page to make them stay flat. Often they faded under the Indian glare or turned yellow.

Grimwood continued to invite the teen princesses and daughters of high-ranking Manipuris to be photographed by him during Ethel's long absence. These modelling sessions may have been entirely innocent, but rumours started circulating that other things also went on.

Frank's main friend when Ethel was away seems to have been the Senapati, Prince Tikendrajit. It is time to turn our spotlight on him and other members of the Manipur Court. Of all the players in the crisis of 1891, Tikendrajit is the most important precisely because the image of the prince set down in print seems to be like someone viewed through a distorting mirror, or the wrong end of one of Frank Grimwood's camera lenses. His opponents, such as the Viceroy, Lord Lansdowne, or former Agent, Sir James Johnstone, have not one good word to say about him. For them he is a villain of the deepest dye. This sadistic cad is at variance with Ethel and Frank Grimwood whose description of Tikendrajit is of an admirable man and loyal friend.

In photographs Tikendrajit Bir Singh stares out at us with a rather arrogant look befitting a royal prince. His lips are firmly closed so we cannot tell if he had the bad teeth claimed by Ethel, but a light moustache gives him a slightly rakish air, while expressive almond-shaped eyes of the kind British people associate with the Burmese mark him as decidedly good-looking. A British signaller who observed the prince under arrest in 1891 described him, rather unflatteringly, as 'Middling height, light complexion, black eyes, very flashy in dress, eats beetles (sic) all day, has a looking-glass in front of him all day, admiring himself every 5 or 10 minutes, slight moustache.'[20] A Gurkha officer, Lieutenant Henry Senior, writing at the same time, thought Tikendrajit's face showed 'an air of resolution. The deep pitted frown that scars his forehead and the thin lips show his determined but fiery temper.'[21] It seems that Tikendrajit, who was born on 29 December 1859 (some accounts say 1858), grew up a rather spoiled but energetic royal child. Like many intelligent children he seems to have been a show-off and at times a bully with an arrogant disregard for those he thought lowlier than himself. One can imagine this youngster looking down rudely on a strange foreigner apparently living off his father, the Maharajah's, largesse and called 'the British Agent'. Colonel McCulloch, the Agent who preceded Johnstone, told him that as a boy the prince used dirty language and was disrespectful. No doubt what he heard coloured Johnstone's perceptions, but something else must have happened, something serious, for the ex-Agent's hatred of Tikendrajit ran deep. The assumption must be a serious insult. In his memoirs Johnstone called the prince 'always a bad character, cruel, coarse and low-minded'. Tikendrajit led the Manipuri troops to Kohima in the 1879 Naga Hills Expedition yet even this bravery did not stop him being anathema to the Political Agent. In 1882 Johnstone tried to have Tikendrajit banished from Manipur for having – in the Political Agent's words – 'three men so seriously beaten that one had died, and two were dangerously ill.'[22] The Senapati was thus branded a murderer in reports to the Indian Government. The Maharajah refused to go along with Johnstone's request and Prince Tikendrajit was banished for one year to an island in the Logtak Lake where his life continued much as normal.

The blood-thirsty sadist described by Johnstone stands in stark contrast to Ethel Grimwood's description of Tikendrajit as 'manly and generous to a fault, a good friend and a bitter enemy. We liked him because he was much more broad-minded than the rest.'[23] The truth seems to be that Tikendrajit had a magnetic personality. He was clearly a man of strong emotions yet also, as one might say in the twenty-first century, 'a fun guy', and the young British couple were automatically drawn to him. One can guess that the prince's nine wives and also his servants all found it best not to upset him, yet he seems to have learned to control his temper and improve his manners.

One of Frank Grimwood's first tasks on arrival at Imphal was to investigate an incident in March 1888 when his predecessor, Mr A.J. Primrose, had reported to Calcutta that Tikendrajit had ordered two men to be flogged until both fainted, then had them partially roasted over an open fire while he watched the proceedings. Primrose concluded:

Complaints of petty oppression committed by this man are endless... The Senapatti has been guilty of crimes which warrant the passing on him of the severest sentence of the law. The least that the Indian Government can do in the present case is to order his deportation as a political prisoner.[24]

This case sounds bad indeed, but Grimwood found that the true situation was rather different; on 27 April 1888 he wrote to the Chief Commissioner of Assam:

I sent for the two men who were beaten, and questioned them... From my inquiries, I consider that the placing of the men before the fire was not intended to torture them... As soon as the men said they felt the fire, they were taken away from it. There was certainly no roasting ... the hospital assistant tells me that when he first saw the men ... there were no traces of burns ... the Senapatti himself left directly the beating was over, and was not present when the men were held before the fire... I may add that Mr Primrose ... is now of the same opinion. He wrote to me from Kohima on the subject and said, 'I am now inclined to think that the roasting was intended merely to revive the men'... I am told that the Senapatti's men are in the habit of seizing and taking ponies for their own use when out on their master's orders, and it may be that because Bapu Chand objected to his pony being taken and took it away, he and his brother were seized and beaten like this for daring to resist a servant of the Senapatti.[25]

Despite Grimwood's findings a letter arrived from the Foreign & Political Department in Calcutta saying that while they would not insist on Tikendrajit's banishment it should be suggested to the Maharajah as a punishment. The rumpus faded away and Tikendrajit got away scot free for his supposed misdeeds. Right up to his own death Frank Grimwood would stay loyal to his admittedly hot-tempered friend, while Ethel bluntly refused to blame him either for the rebellion or her husband's murder. 'If he promised a thing, that thing would be done,' she wrote of the prince, 'and he would take the trouble to see himself that it was done... He was always doing courteous acts to please us ... Another time I had been very ill, and when I was getting better, kind inquiries came every day from the Senaputti.' Above all else she remembered him on the polo field:

> He was very strong; in fact, the Manipuris used to tell us that he was the strongest man in the country. He could lift very heavy weights and throw long distances, and to see him send the ball skimming half across the ground with one hit was a very pretty sight. He could do strokes that few Manipuris knew, which is saying a great deal, for an average player at Manipur can beat most Englishmen. The Senaputti was a magnificent rider, and he was always mounted on beautiful ponies. He wore a very picturesque dress for polo – a green velvet zouave jacket edged with gold buttons, and a salmon-pink silk Dhotee, with white leather leggings and a pink silk turban. He had long hair which he used to twist up into a knot at the back of his neck, and he always looked very nice on these occasions.[26]

The Jubraj, or heir to the throne, Prince Kula Chandra Dhuj Singh, was a very different man. Ethel summed him up as a 'second edition' of the Maharajah, 'only stouter and uglier'. He was about thirty-five years old, 5 feet 8 inches tall, with swarthy features and a small moustache. At the time of his arrest in 1891, Kula Chandra was described by one newspaper correspondent as 'strong and robust, not too fat for work, with a very villainous cast of countenance, rather Chinese, very small pig's eyes, with a slight squint.'[27] This unflattering portrait is even borne out by Johnstone who called the Jubraj boorish and stupid, a man unworthy of becoming Maharajah.

A third prince was Bhairabijit Singh, known as the Pucca Senna, or Commander of the Horse. A full brother of the Maharajah, born of the same queen, it was said that Manipuris found him to be a dangerous man, often bad-tempered and with a jealous disposition. The Grimwoods thought him lazy, though Ethel admitted that he was a fine marksman with a gun, and James Johnstone dismissed him entirely noting only that he was a good polo player. For a time the Pucca Senna came to the residency for English lessons, 'but, it was suspected, more probably to ingratiate himself with the Political Agent.'[28] Certainly, it seems that the tutorials were not a great success; Ethel recalled that the prince liked the word 'goodbye' so much that he used it also on arrival and it was 'a little embarrassing to meet him ... and be welcomed by a shake of the hand and a solemn "goodbye".'[29]

Kesarjit Singh, known as the Samoo Hengaba, was the prince in charge of the Maharajah's sixty or so elephants. On grand occasions, when the Maharajah was forced to ride an elephant (something he disliked doing because of his weight), Kesarjit acted as his *mahout* (driver). Most times the Maharajah used an ornately gilded *doolie* (a covered litter suspended at four corners by a bamboo pole and carried by four men). Another brother, Prince Gopal Senna, was Dooloroi Hengaba in charge of the royal doolies. Tall and stout, Prince Angao Senna was supposedly in charge of the road between Imphal and the Burmese frontier but in reality he did no work. Ethel remembered him as always having 'a large piece of betel-nut in his mouth', giving him a swollen face, 'he never cared for anything but eating and drinking and watching pigeon-fights,' on which he gambled excessively until the Maharajah refused to sanction his debts.

Youngest of the eight brothers was Prince Zillah Singh, a youth of about seventeen whom the Grimwoods nicknamed 'the Poem' because he seemed ethereally slight and graceful. 'He used to ride a tiny mite of a pony,' wrote Ethel, 'and never troubled himself with many garments.' On the polo field 'his turban was always coming off and his long black hair streamed in the wind as he flew all over the ground.'[30] One suspects she rather liked this bare-chested and long-haired athletic young man. Did it make her Anglo-Saxon heart flutter as she watched Zillah or 'strong' Tikendrajit race about the field? It seems hard to think that she did not find it all stimulating in some way.

The officers of the Durbar, known as the 'Top Guard', were also men Frank Grimwood had to deal with on a regular basis and handle with care, though only one of these was a major player in the drama soon to be enacted. This was Kungaba Tulinaha Major, better known to history as 'the Thangal (or Tongal) General'. He had been born around 1817 and so was in his mid-seventies. Brave, cruel, cunning, the old warrior with a grizzled face had become something of a living legend by 1890. There was even a rumour in

British army circles that he was, in fact, Nana Sahib, the notorious Indian ruler who had massacred the men, women and children at Cawnpore in 1857. Nana Sahib had vanished into the jungles of Assam, but had he really re-surfaced in Manipur? A local legend said that the Thangal General was a Naga, but researchers John and Saroj Parratt have concluded that this theory 'is very unlikely'. They think he got his name by leading a punitive expedition against the Naga village of Thangal during the reign of Chandra Kirti. As a young man he had accompanied Chandra and his mother into exile and over the decades proved his loyalty to them as well as demonstrating his skill as a soldier. Johnstone clearly liked the old rascal who had been at the forefront of the fighting at Kohima in 1879. The Agent described him as 'unscrupulous' and bloodthirsty, but insisted 'nothing could have induced him to join in any plot against our rule in India.' What Johnstone does not say is how the Thangal General might have reacted in an emergency, when his blood was up, or he was under pressure. He admitted simply 'a straightforward and abrupt manner ... he was what circumstances and education had made him.' Interestingly enough, Johnstone noted how the Thangal General, though ignorant of the English language, 'knew our ways well and soon took a man's measure.'[31] Did the old man, in fact, take Frank Grimwood's measure – and did he find something lacking, something he didn't like ?

Ethel thought the Thangal General was like an old eagle:

He had the same keen, rugged expression and deep-set glowing eyes. Few things happened without his knowledge and consent, and if he withheld his approbation from any matter, there would invariably be a hitch in it somewhere. He was credited with more bloodshed than any man in the kingdom. If a village had misbehaved itself, raided on another, or refused to pay revenue or do Lalup the Tongal General would travel out to that village and wipe it off the face of the earth. Men, women and children were cut down without the slightest compunction ... the Tongal had, as he expressed it, 'nautched [danced] through many villages' in the style described, and brought desolation into many a hill man's peaceful home.

The old tyrant was also fond of building bridges and improving roads about the capital. For Frank the Thangal General's chief difficulty was that he could be obstinate. Then again, as Ethel said in a sentence pregnant with possibilities: 'Once he had promised to get anything done, he did not go back from his word.'[32]

The general had several children. His favourite daughter we will meet anon, but of his sons, Yaima, the eldest, was 'a nice young fellow and very hard-working', often accompanying Frank on tour, while a second son, Lumphel, was the Maharajah's favourite aide-de-camp and given charge of road maintenance between Imphal and Cachar. 'At durbar he used to stand behind the Maharajah's chair with a very magnificent uniform covered with gold lace and a gold turban'[33] recalled Ethel. Frank Grimwood thought that Lumphel would one day be chief minister of the state.

These, then, were the principal Manipuris with whom Frank spent his time before his wife's return in November 1888. Once back home Ethel found the residency grounds even prettier than before her departure. Yet from her bedroom window she could see the grave of Mr Heath. It lay next to two others, those of Major Trotter who had died from wounds received fighting in Burma, and a young lieutenant named Beavor whose life had been cut short by fever as he passed through Manipur. To Ethel her once beautiful garden was turning into a graveyard. Heath's death in particular came to haunt her.

Some gaiety returned at Christmas thanks to the Senapati who decided to organise a gymkhana similar to the sports he had seen the 44th Gurkhas enjoy at Langthobal. In one feat a bare-chested man laid out on the spikes of several bayonets without them seemingly piercing his flesh. There were wrestling matches in which some of the princes took part, even foot races, with prizes, mostly money, awarded by Tikendrajit. The Maharajah's three jesters, faces painted in multi-coloured streaks, their heads shaved 'like the back of a poodle', impressed some of the audience to join them in a funny play. Slowly this burlesque grew more rowdy with men dressed as women and various scuffles. The Manipuris laughed loudly at what sounds like a stream of dirty jokes.

The Grimwoods left at this point embarrassed somewhat by the vulgarities. Lewd references to women losing their clothes and sexual innuendos were not acceptable entertainment for a sahib and his lady. Next day the princes told Ethel and Frank 'that it had been a very good play and the only pity was that we had witnessed so little of it.'[34]

Christmas festivities aside, Ethel could not shake off her premonitions of an approaching disaster. She particularly kept turning over in her mind what a friend had once said to her: 'What an unlucky place Manipur is! I have seen so many political agents go up there and something always seems to happen to them!'[35]

Uproar at the Palace

The trouble began over a girl. Not for the first time in history a shapely female form, in this case a 16-year-old called Maipakbi, was to rock a royal dynasty to its foundations, though to be fair to her, she simply provided the lure for those twin horns of machismo – lust and pride.

The fair-skinned Maipakbi had attracted two suitors – the Senapati and his brother, the Pucca Senna. Both of them had determined to ingratiate themselves with the Grimwoods and each became jealous of the other – 'if one came more often than the other, that other would get annoyed and refuse to come at all for some time,' recollected Ethel. Then they argued over the attentions of Maipakbi, supposedly the most beautiful girl in Manipur, though Ethel thought she was not as pretty as some of the princesses. She was tall for a Manipuri, with thick tresses of black hair, always very well-dressed, with gold bracelets on her arms 'and some necklaces of pure gold which weighed an enormous amount'.[1] These trinkets helped advertise the fact that she was not royalty but the daughter of a wealthy goldsmith who served on the state council.

The Grimwoods were in the habit of holding *nautches* (dances) at the residency and Maipakbi came one night as chief dancer. 'Every child in Manipur learns to dance,' wrote Ethel, 'they cease when they marry, but up to then they take great pride in their nautches.' Manipuri dancing is subtle – no facial expressions, eye or belly movements – using only the palms, arms, legs and feet. The dancers wear 'spectacular dresses: bell-shaped skirts, twinkling with tiny mirrors which are sewn into them, are stretched over hoops and have gauze over-skirts like a ballerina.'[2] The Manipur dances developed out of ancient rituals, integrated with the country's Vaishnavite Hinduism, which welcomes dancing. Often the dances tell folk tales. At the residency the dancers seem all to have been girls and they used their entrancing skill, alluring costumes and tempting style to mesmerize the men first and foremost. Nautches were usually performed before male guests in India and the lissom Maipakbi, a dazzling vision flashing her multi-coloured skirts and gold jewellery, made sure that the two rival princes for her hand got the full exotic, sensuous and sinuous message.

One night the Senapati seemed very cheerful (we can guess he was currently Maipakbi's favourite beau), while the Pucca Senna was gloomy. Shortly afterwards the two men had a terrible quarrel and the Maharajah had to intervene. Tikendrajit vowed never to speak to his brother again, 'an oath which he kept to the letter.' Frank told Ethel that the two princes must never be invited again to the same event.

Shortly after this it seems that the eight royal brothers split into two factions – the Maharajah, Pucca Senna, Samoo Hengaba and Dolloroi Hengaba on one side, while the Jubraj, Senapati, Angao Senna and young Prince Zillah Singh made up a second group. More jealousy developed when the Maharajah raised the status of the Pucca Senna giving him jurisdiction over all civil and criminal cases in the state, a function traditionally held by the Jubraj. Matters started to come to a head early that September; Zillah Singh was arguing 'over everything and anything' with the Pucca Senna. The elder brother persuaded the Maharajah to forbid the youngest prince to sit in the durbar. Rubbing salt into this wound, Zillah was further humiliated by being deprived of some small offices of state that he held along with the traditional 'honour and distinction' of having a bugle sounded when he went around the palace. 'Subjected to insult on various occasions, and made to suffer in silence,' the young prince turned to his powerful brother, Prince Tikendrajit, for help.

The storm of jealousies, recriminations and quarrels finally burst over the palace on the night of 21/22 September 1890. The Pucca Senna falsely declared that the Angao Senna was planning a revolt against Maharajah Sura Chandra. The ruler, without making any inquiries, gave orders for his half-brother to be arrested with

Zillah Singh. The two young princes 'resolved to die fighting before the throne of their ancestors rather than to suffer the disgrace of either banishment or death.'[3] Sometime after midnight, when all in the palace were asleep, save some friendly guards, the two disgruntled men led a small party of followers to the walls leading to the Maharajah's private apartments. Here they used a ladder to get a good view, then started firing their rifles through the open windows. Bullets splashed about the rooms and ricocheted off the walls. The royal ladies were screaming for their lives and the Maharajah, never very brave, later recalled how 'I was trying on my turban when it was pierced by a bullet.'[4]

The Maharajah later claimed that the firing was so intense that he thought his palace had been 'treacherously seized' and so he made an escape. Based on Frank Grimwood's first report of the incident it seems that the Senapati was not present during the initial attack but once he arrived on the scene, he quickly took charge. It is likely that after the first few shots Sura Chandra thought he had better get dressed and beat a hasty retreat. He did not even rouse his loyal guard to repel any invaders but simply crept out of the back entrance of the palace with his three loyal brothers and headed for the British residency. Following in his wake were some loyal retainers and sepoys, armed with rifles, swords, daos and other weapons, among them the old Thangal General.

What happened over the next 36 hours is open to interpretation. 'What exactly followed is complicated,' wrote an eminent Indian historian, 'it is not easy to disentangle the truth from the conflicting versions.'[5] Ethel's account, given in her memoirs, for instance, has been quoted many times but in fact she was not even in Manipur. What Sura Chandra later wrote conflicts sharply with Frank Grimwood's account.

The first Frank knew was when he was woken at 2am by a bearer saying that a fight had broken out at the palace. He was not even properly dressed, probably wearing only a dressing gown, when the Maharajah arrived in great agitation. Frank had to go off and put his trousers on. By now some shots from the palace were humming over the residency. Just as the Agent's detachment of 44th Gurkha Rifles arrived from the nearby cantonment, the grounds began rapidly filling up with the Maharajah's supporters. Sura Chandra claimed he had 2,000 men with him of whom 400 to 600 were armed. Frank later told the Indian Government that there 'may have been 400 at the outside, of whom 40 to 50, certainly not more, were armed.'[6]

Grimwood told Sura Chandra to go and rest in the durbar room but, according to Ethel, 'he refused any comfort, though he was told that he need have no fear, even though the Ghoorkhas were marching in from Langthobal, and as many as were needed could be got down from Kohima in four or five days to retake the palace which the rebel princes had got possession of. But all to no purpose.'[7] Frank tried all he could to get the Maharajah to 'brave the matter out' but Sura Chandra blankly refused to leave the residency. He refused all that day of the 22nd right through until his departure from the state on the evening of the 23rd. 'After some hours spent in fear and terror,' wrote Ethel, who clearly loathed Sura Chandra, 'he signified his intention to my husband of making a formal abdication of his throne for the purpose of devoting the remaining years of his life to performing a pilgrimage to the sacred city of Brinhaband on the Ganges.'[8] Sure enough, on the night of the 23rd, under a strong escort of Gurkhas, Sura Chandra – no longer a maharajah – left for Cachar never to return.

It is generally accepted that the Jubraj, Kula Chandra, spent most of this period at Bishenpur, 17 miles from Imphal. The palace operations were overseen by Prince Tikendrajit who 'took possession of everything'. Much later, after the war, a senior India Office civil servant would admit to the Secretary of State that this 'commendable action' had 'the practical result that there was no bloodshed, no plundering, no disturbances after the Maharaja's flight.'[9] Tikendrajit later said himself:

> The subjects immediately commenced rushing into the palace, and a vast number (over ten thousand men) all cursed Pecca Sing for his evil intrigues and designs, and applauded Angao Sing for his valour and success in becoming a khatri or warrior.[10]

Despite Tikendrajit's fine words it appears that all the royal council, save one man, had followed the Maharajah to the residency. This implies a degree of loyalty to the Maharajah at the outset that might have gained momentum if he had taken the offensive.

Grimwood was criticised at the time – and also by historians – for not doing enough to help the Maharajah. Later Sura Chandra would claim that Frank disarmed his loyal sepoys, thus preventing him from staging a resistance, but Ethel insisted that this was a lie; she stated that the senior Gurkha (a Nepali) at the residency, in consultation with Frank, thought it best if the Maharajah's troops stowed their weapons away on the verandah since 'they were under no sort of control, and they were ready to fire without any provocation at all.'[11] There was the danger that if they had begun shooting at the palace from the residency, the Senapati might have replied with one or all of the four mountain guns in the royal arsenal. If Ethel is to be believed then her husband's action possibly saved a lot of bloodshed.

Frank denied that he had prevented the Maharajah from fighting to regain his throne or sent the loyal sepoys home 'disheartened and humiliated'. 'The Maharaja had no wish to fight and his troops had the whole day to fight if they wished to, as the disarming took place late in the afternoon,' he wrote (meaning the 22nd). He claimed to have collected 30 guns when 'the Maharaja objected, and I at once gave them all back on condition that the armed men went into one of the villages nearby, which they did.'[12]

Meantime Grimwood had contacted his superiors. His first telegram to the Chief Commissioner of Assam, Mr J.W. Quinton, read: 'Maharaja's brothers attacked palace during night. Maharaja fled to Residency. Shall defend him as long as possible if attacked.' Next he wired:

Senapatti and two brothers in possession of palace. Jubraj and three brothers with Maharaja at Residency; only 65 rifles besides escort. Please instruct how to act. Do not anticipate attack on Residency at present, but Maharaja and brothers preparing to attack Senapatti if they can collect men. No loss of life as Maharaja has fled.

This telegram clearly states that the Jubraj was at the residency before he quietly left the city.

On the 22nd the Chief Commissioner wired instructions:

Protect the Residency. Endeavour to mediate between the parties, and if necessary wire for troops to Kohima. Commanding officer has been authorised to send you 200 rifles. Defend yourself but do not assume the offensive without informing of the reasons on which you recommend it, and obtaining orders.

Quinton's advice was sound; the residency – British property – took priority. Grimwood was not allowed offensive action without more instructions from Assam but he now knew that 200 soldiers were on their way and would arrive in four to six days. On the 24th Grimwood probably surprised Quinton with another telegram:

Maharaja has formally abdicated in favour of Jubraj and goes to Brindaban as a fakir. This is his own wish. I told him I could guarantee his personal safety at the Residency, but refused to allow him to collect armed men in Residency grounds; also told him if once abdicated he could not return to Manipur. This seems to me best solution. Jubraj has held aloof from both sides and could therefore be acknowledged as Maharaja *if you approve* (my italics). Maharaja leaves tonight.[13]

In their different versions of events both Ethel and Frank suggest that before he was able to go to the palace on the morning of the 23rd to speak with the Senapati, the Maharajah had clearly made up his mind to abdicate. In other words Grimwood had been faced with a *fait accompli*. Even so, the Indian historian, R.K. Majumdar, critical of Grimwood's actions, complained that he 'did not ask the troops of Kohima to march, nor evidently inform the Maharaja that he could count upon their help.' Having done this he could then have negotiated with the Senapati. Majumdar wrote:

He did neither ... knowing full well that the recognition of Maharaja Sura Chandra as the king of Manipur by the Government of India gave him full authority in speaking on his behalf, he did not intercede on his behalf, in any way, nor even asked for an explanation of their conduct from the rebels.[14]

The plain truth was that Frank Grimwood was inexperienced. It is also clear that he had forged what the historian, Caroline Keen, calls 'an unwisely close relationship with the Senapati'. What Grimwood ought to have done was ascertain from Tikendrajit the reasons for the disturbance, convey this information to the Chief Commissioner and await his instructions before agreeing to Sura Chandra's departure. By not doing so he laid himself open to a charge of 'tacitly accepting the success of the revolt.' Later the Viceroy, Lord Lansdowne, was to pen a sharp rebuke when he wrote: 'A political officer has no power to accept the abdication of a Native Chief. Mr Grimwood's actions greatly prejudiced the case, and was the cause of much subsequent trouble.'[15]

In a confidential letter sent to Quinton from the Indian Foreign Department on 24 January 1891 it was even suggested that the palace revolution occurred with Frank Grimwood's connivance. This is over-stating the case. Frank's position, of course, is that he had fully intended to ask the Chief Commissioner for more instructions until the loose cannon that was the Maharajah insisted he wished to abdicate. This was a *fait accompli*, but, Grimwood suggested, it was all to the good. In his full report on the palace revolution and abdication crisis, written on 25th September, he explained:

I have no doubt that the departure of the Maharaja and three of his brothers will be at any rate beneficial to the country. A Maharaja and seven brothers, over whom he had little real authority was too many for a small country like this, and their reduction by half will be a relief in more ways than one. The Maharaja personally was popular, but he was a weak ruler and paid little attention to public business, and spent hours every day worshipping in the temple. He was not at all the person to keep order amongst his brothers, and he is a man who will be much happier, I imagine, as an ascetic than as a ruler. The Jubaraj, who I hope, will be allowed to succeed to the 'Gaddi' has the reputation of being much more active and business-like. The Senapatti has more than once incurred the censure of the Government, but ... he is popular amongst all classes; he is the only prince who is said to be poor owing to his generosity. He is also on good terms with the Jubaraj; and if the latter is allowed to succeed to the 'Gaddi', the Senapatti, as Jubaraj, would assist in making his rule strong and popular.[16]

During his forty or so hours at the residency Sura Chandra's nerves were so shot to pieces that he refused any offer of food.

Frank started to make arrangements for the ex-Maharajah's departure for Cachar under an escort of thirty-five Gurkhas. A large number of Manipuris flocked to the residency after word was whispered around town that Sura Chandra was leaving, many of them offering their ex-king sums of money for his pilgrimage. Grimwood wrote: 'To judge from the way people wept ... everyone seemed sorry at his departure,'[17] though some others were happy to see that the ill-tempered Pucca Senna was leaving too.

Quinton at Shillong telegraphed to Manipur that subject to the sanction of the imperial government, Kula Chandra could be appointed regent. Early on the morning of the 24th he entered the palace and the former Jubraj formed his council. The new Jubraj or successor to the throne was Prince Tikendrajit. The Manipur Court Chronicle, known as the *Cheitarol Kumbaba,* was emphatic that a new reign had begun:

> Shri Kulachandra Singh became king at the age of thirty-seven years. At four pung hours he entered the royal palace ... at three pung hours after the noon yuthak he was enthroned. At the night yuthak the eldest wife of the king was brought from her parental residence. On that day the one who was also called Chinglen Lanthaba (Sura Chandra) left for pilgrimage to the sacred places.[18]

Ethel Grimwood was away from Manipur during the palace revolution and did not return until two months later. She admitted that it was obvious in court circles that Tikendrajit was 'ruler of the roost'. Yet several changes for the better had happened in the state since the revolt. Roads around the capital had been repaired and in the country new bridges erected, all clearly the effects of Tikendrajit's energetic administration. 'The people seemed happier and more contented' noted Ethel. Her husband now found it easier to work with the durbar and there 'were no more petty jealousies and quarrels among the princes,'[19] all things to the good, which bore out Frank's report of two months earlier.

That Christmas of 1890 it seemed to the Grimwoods that the past was behind them and the future looking brighter. They laid on a magic lantern show to entertain the court. Frank had arranged for a lantern projector to be shipped over from England. He had taken great time and trouble to make the glass slides himself from photographs he had taken around Manipur. These included groups of subjects and some of the princes. His royal guests found it all a lot of fun, though Frank made a bit of a *faux pas* by inserting a slide of the ex-Maharajah which was greeted by an embarrassing 'dead silence', but otherwise the show was deemed a success. Frank had no way of knowing that he had exactly three months left to live.

Early in January 1891 the Grimwoods went to Kohima to meet with the Chief Commissioner who was touring the Naga Hills with his daughter. No doubt Frank must have discussed the recent troubles with his superior and the talks left him with no idea that the Indian Government was unhappy with the situation. Whatever the Chief Commissioner knew of the Indian Government's feelings he kept those feelings to himself. The couple invited Quinton and his daughter to visit Manipur but the Chief Commissioner declined on the grounds of his tight schedule.

Next Ethel and Frank headed to the far north of Manipur on their first visit as a couple to Burma or, to be exact, the Manipur-Burmese border country. Frank had toured the area in 1890 but Ethel had been too ill to accompany him on that trip. She noticed, as they headed towards Burma, that the forests were not so dense as around Cachar:

> Range after range of mountains rise gloriously around you, as you wend your way among the leafy glades and shimmering forests which clothe their rugged sides. Cool and green near you, growing purple as you leave them behind, and becoming faintly blue as they outline themselves on the far horizon, these mountains fill you with admiration. Forests of teak rise on each side of you as you get nearer Tummu, and the heat becomes much greater.[20]

The couple stayed for a time in a pagoda surrounded by Buddhist statuary. Ethel loved the bright colours of the Burmese dresses and the way all the women smoked cigars.

At Tammu, 68 miles from Imphal, just over the Burmese border, they learned to their surprise that there was an English officer living there. 'We had no idea when at Manipur that we had any neighbours nearer than Kohima ninety-six miles away,' said Ethel. One day she and her husband surprised the officer, who had his shirt sleeves rolled up and was casually dressed. He was just as surprised to run into an Englishwoman 'spying on him unawares'. His name was Charles Grant, a lieutenant in the 12th Regiment (2nd Burma battalion), Madras Infantry. He rushed back to his bungalow, changed his clothes and returned in evening dress for dinner. It is hard to imagine without a smile the fact that the Victorians, even in the steamy jungle, did such things, but formalities helped to discipline their lives and also remind them of the way life was lived back home in Britain, Ethel sweating in her tight corset and full-length dress, the two men uncomfortable in tight starched collars and shirts.

Grant was delighted to meet the Grimwoods and during their four days at Tammu he invited them over to his small bungalow. Ethel especially adored his jokes and jolly manners – so much so that she and Grant decided to bake a cake together. Their cookery lesson was not a success and the cake came out of the oven 'burnt to a cinder'. Frank, rather sarcastically, joked that they would not need to buy charcoal for some time to come. Ethel, undaunted, perhaps stung by Frank's cheeky words, carved into the cake with Grant's help and found that its middle was quite edible, 'which my husband also,' she wrote, 'condescended to try after some persuasion and pronounced fair.'[21]

On their way back to Imphal the couple learned that they were to have two visitors – Lieutenant Walter Simpson, 43rd Gurkhas, and Mr William Melville, Superintendent of the Assam Telegraph Department.

Ethel and Frank had originally met Simpson in Shillong. He may also have visited Frank during some of Ethel's absences from Manipur. Thirty years old, Simpson, son of a Lincoln's Inn barrister, had been educated privately at Cheltenham followed by Rugby and Sandhurst; appointed to the 39th Foot in 1880, three years later he transferred to the Bengal Staff Corps, then joined the 43rd Gurkhas in time to see action in a small expedition against the Aka tribe on the north-east frontier 1883–84, followed by punitive operations in Burma 1886–87. He was adjutant of his regiment and thus it was his duty to inspect some stores left behind at Langthobal. Ethel, a keen pianist, admired the lanky Simpson's versatility as a musician, especially the way he loved to play the piano for hours without interruption. Frank knew him as a good shot and sociable fellow who, as he guessed, would make excellent company at shooting parties with the Manipuri princes.

Melville was a 42-year-old Scot from Dumfries who had served 21 years in the Indian telegraph service. He stayed just three days, promising to return and spend more time with the Grimwoods after touring the Tammu area.

Simpson arrived the day after the Grimwoods got back to Imphal and made himself at home. Everything seemed normal. Nothing was amiss. Ethel and Frank had not detected what one Indian historian called 'an ominous silence' from the Indian Government.

Everything changed on Sunday 21 February – ironically five months to the day since the palace revolution – when a telegram arrived from the Chief Commissioner. It read: 'I propose to visit Manipur shortly. Have roads and rest-houses put in order. Further directions and dates to follow.'[22] Ethel described the reaction to this telegram as like being given an electric shock. Her premonitions and fears were now to prove well founded; life in Manipur for the Grimwoods and all its inhabitants would never be the same again.

Servants of the Great White Queen

Some things never change. A modern tourist in Kolkata – the imperial Calcutta – who peers through the railings at the palatial white Georgian mansion close to the grassy maidan sees much the same sight as someone would have done in 1891. Back then the Raj Bhavan, as it is called today, was known to all as Government House, home of the lord sahibs, Governor-Generals of India since 1803 when Lord Wellesley, one of the grandest of them all, had made the East India Company pay £63,291 for its construction, a sum the directors thought 'excessive'. Britons who had made their fortunes in India – the notorious 'nabobs' – disagreed; the building had been modelled on Kedleston Hall in Derbyshire and was, said one of them, 'a noble structure', money well-spent since 'India is a country of splendour, of extravagance and of outward appearances ... the Head of a mighty Empire ought to conform to the prejudices of the country he rules over.'[1]

The building did not please everybody; Lady Canning in the 1850s complained of the oppressive indoor heat, with lizards and bats in her bedroom. The building often seemed damp, there were no lifts, only countless stairs and staircases, the kitchens were in another building altogether. Even in the 1890s it was not unknown for civet cats to climb the drainpipes and get into the rooms. The building's chief occupant in 1891, after his arrival, told his mother in a letter:

Words cannot describe the hugeness of this place or the utter absence of anything like homely comfort – my study is tolerable – business-like and fairly cheerful, but oh! the bedroom with its height and cold distempered walls, and colossal bed large enough for half a dozen couples and enveloped in a vast tent of mosquito netting running all the way up to the ceiling which is so far up that one can scarcely see it. Then the crowd of black servants oppresses me. I told them to go to bed (if they ever do such a thing) an hour ago, but I know I shall find the whole gang outside my door including a six-foot specimen who is always there standing to attention, and who I am beginning to think is stuffed, for he never moves or changes his position, whereas Gholam something or other (who is my personal attendant) and his myrmidons think it necessary to salaam and play other heathenish antics every time I go by. I have come across the remains of a corkscrew stair (now disused) from this floor to that above, which was I am convinced contrived by one of my predecessors with the sole object of escaping from Gholam the all-pervading.[2]

The man who so wittily and gloomily disliked Government House had succeeded Lord Dufferin as Viceroy in 1888. His name was Henry Charles Keith Petty-Fitzmaurice, 5th Marquess of Lansdowne. He was, like his predecessor, another member of the Anglo-Irish aristocracy, a career-diplomat who had followed in Dufferin's footsteps as Governor-General of Canada (1883–88) and now did the same in India. He was forty-three years old, a dapper, small-boned man, prematurely balding with a high, domed forehead, long sideburns and an elegantly curved moustache. Happily married for 19 years to Lady Maud Hamilton, youngest daughter of the Duke of Abercorn (a former Viceroy of Ireland), the patrician Lansdownes arrived in India accompanied by their two teenage daughters and personal staff.

Since so many events in the Manipur Rising were instigated by Lansdowne it is worth pausing for a moment to examine the man. His family had for generations owned vast estates in Ireland and England. They had been the lords of Kerry since the 13th century. His principal seat was Bowood, a Robert Adam masterpiece in the rolling Wiltshire countryside, but 'Clan', as his friends called him (after his boyhood title of Lord Clanmaurice), also owned Dereen House and 120,000 acres of Kerry; Meikleour

House, by the banks of the salmon-stocked Tay in Scotland; and Lansdowne House, Berkeley Square, a sumptuous London mansion hung with in excess of 200 Rembrandts, Gainsboroughs and Romneys. The first Marquess had been a Prime Minister under King George III, the third Marquess had turned down a dukedom and the premiership under King George IV. 'Clan's' mother, whom he adored all his life and remained close, was a daughter of a French Napoleonic general – an illegitimate son of the great Talleyrand and an aide to the Emperor at the Battle of Borodino. People who met Lansdowne remarked that he seemed rather French to them; he dressed with the cultivated ease of a French aristocrat and spoke the language perfectly, honed after long summer holidays with his maternal relatives, the Comtes de Flahault. With polished grace and the kind of courtesy bred of generations that allowed him to discourse widely while discouraging intimacy, Lansdowne was a classic *grand seigneur*. Privately he hated pomp and show, yet was unselfconsciously viceregal as to the manor born. Strangers never quite knew what to make of this little man as they stared at his French face with its 'fine bone-structure, an aquiline nose, rather piercing, twinkling eyes beneath dark eyebrows'.[3]

At Eton his tutor noted that Henry was 'talented without imagination, clear-headed but rather uncertain'. He was praised for being modest, unselfish and having a good sense of humour. All these traits remained with him at Oxford where he scored only a second in Greats. He almost immediately entered politics and became a Liberal peer. By March 1870, he was sitting on the front bench as the new Lord of the Treasury. The ever-dutiful Lansdowne went up to Oxford for a dinner about this time, got drunk, and with some friends took part in the 'mad freak' of wrecking the Dean of Christ Church's garden. This event, which could have ended 'Clan's' political career, was hushed up, though it stopped him from collecting his degree for several years. Lansdowne toiled away in the Lords during the 1870s but after six years he split with the Liberals over their Irish policy. The 1880s saw a hardening of the divide in Ireland between tenants and landowners. Matters grew especially grim after the assassination of the Secretary of State and his assistant in Phoenix Park, Dublin, in 1882. Bad harvests coupled with the agitation of the Irish Land

League meant that Lansdowne's tenants were constantly in debt. To try and save some of his salary he agreed to the Governor-Generalship of Canada.

To his surprise 'Clan' found that from Quebec to Vancouver he was something of a success. French Canadians especially warmed to a man who spoke their language so fluently and with such passion. 'Clan' liked the Canadians and was extremely happy that his duties were not too onerous and he could go fishing – in four summers he and his friends pulled 1,245 salmon out of the streams. The average fish weighed twenty-four pounds. During all this time he despatched Canadian boatmen to take part in the Gordon Relief Expedition in the Sudan and put down a rebellion in the North-West led by Louis Riel, a Metis of mixed blood. This rising was quickly extinguished by troops under the command of Major-General Sir Frederick Middleton, Riel was captured, tried and condemned to death. A reprieve then followed and an appeal to the Privy Council in London. The sentence was confirmed and Riel was hanged on 16 November 1885. Lansdowne had advised the Queen 'that it was desirable that the prerogative of mercy should not be exercised.'[4] It was not to be the last time in his career that he demanded the death penalty for political prisoners. Using words that have an ominous inference when Manipur is borne in mind, the Governor-General told Her Majesty that it would be wrong to extenuate the guilt of a man who made his grievances a pretext for bringing upon his country the calamity of a war. Riel, he concluded, 'has had a fair trial' and the renegade had, after all, been a thorn in the Canadian moose hide for more than 15 years.

On his return from Canada 'Clan' found that his financial situation was, if anything, worse. His Kerry estates, nominally worth £23,000 per year in rents, had sunk to a return of barely £500. Things were so bad that he seriously considered selling the Bowood estate. It was while he was turning over all these thoughts in his mind that he was offered the plum job in the Empire – Viceroy of India. So it was that this well-bred man, with his equally well-bred wife and daughters, set off for the Far East. He was to prove to have a high sense of duty, a good sense of the ridiculous, a man quite free from colour prejudice because he was simply above such petty nonsense. Yet he was also to show that he could be manipulated by stronger men, that once he made up his mind on something it was not easily changed, in short, an obstinate man and also, as some contemporaries and several historians have commented, a fellow without 'the faintest spark of imagination'.

Things got off to an embarrassing start; at the Bombay quayside a steam launch snorted and figuratively blew its nose over the Vicereine's lovely white frock, showering poor Lady Maud in a mixture of coal-dust and steam. Soon the Lansdownes were on their way across India on the viceregal train. 'Scenery, trees, crops, people, animals, birds, all very new and interesting,' noted his lordship in a letter to his mother. The train was the height of luxury with a carriage and bed each for Clan and Maud, 'to say nothing of a full-sized bath' and an army of perspiring cooks who produced 'elaborate repasts'.[5]

Lansdowne was the ninth Viceroy since the Crown took over from the East India Company in 1858. In the same year as the Manipur disaster, a once-a-decade census was taken so we know that he had in his care precisely 287,223,431 souls (who was the odd one, I wonder). From Government House, Calcutta, the Viceroy was expected to move through India, 'resplendent with all the colour and dash of the vast Empire at his feet, with his superb bodyguard jangling scarlet beside his carriage, silken Indian princes bowing at his carpet, generals quivering at his salute and ceremonial salutes of thirty-one guns – independent Asian sovereigns were only entitled to twenty-one.' The Viceregal life came with all the trimmings befitting a monarch:

He had a pleasant country house at Barrackpur, twenty miles up the Hooghly River, with moorings for the Viceregal yacht; and when the summer came, and the heat of the Indian plains became incompatible with the imperial dignity, up he went with his army of attendants to the hill station of Simla. There on a hill-top his summer palace awaited him, scrubbed and gleaming for the season, its major-domos, secretaries, chefs and myriad maidservants immaculate and expectant in their several departments – a sprawling chalet set in a delicious garden, where a Vicereine might stroll in the mountain evening spaciously, as a great chatelaine should, and the pines, streams and crispness reminded visitors that these were the rulers from the distant north, sent by royal command to govern with such grandeur the sweltering territories of Asia.[6]

The Lansdownes took all this in their stride; Lady Maud was to become famous as a great hostess at formal dinners where she sparkled in more ways than one, thanks to the famous Lansdowne pearls and other jewels. A State Ball meant almost 1,600 guests, a State Evening Party, an event usually reserved for native Indian guests, saw the Lansdownes greeting 1,500 people. A typical winter month at Calcutta might see two Levees, a Drawing Room, a State Ball, a State Evening Party, a Garden Party and lesser balls, official dinners and a dance or two. During most of these occasions the Fitzmaurice plate and solid silver candelabra, dragged over to India by Maud, gleamed across the huge table, 'interspersed with massive silver bowls, each filled with fragrant flowers' that reflected about the room. At the centre of Government House was its Marble Hall and Throne Room. For almost a century these magnificent State apartments had regularly hosted visits by Indian maharajahs and rulers. From his throne, in the words of one Viceroy:

He looked down the long vista of the Marble Hall with its gleaming white pillars, absolutely empty save for the Bodyguard in their magnificent uniforms, standing like statues on either side. In the distance could be heard the music of the band playing upon the great exterior staircase. An intense silence prevailed, broken at length by the crunch of wheels on the gravel and the horse-hooves of the Bodyguard, as they escorted the carriage containing the Prince to the foot of the steps. At that moment thundered out the guns from the distant Fort, giving to the Chief his due salute. One–two–three– up to the total of seventeen, nineteen or twenty-one, the reverberations rang out. Not until the total – carefully counted by the Chief himself – was completed, did the procession that was being formed on the terrace at the top of the staircase, attempt to move forward. Then he would be seen to advance along the crimson carpet laid outside and to enter the Marble Hall in all his panoply of brocades and jewels, the Foreign Secretary leading him by the hand. As they approached at a slow pace along the polished floor, not a sound was heard but the clank clank of the scabbards on the marble.[7]

The Indian potentate and his nobles came through the great doorway of the Throne Room and bowed. Depending on his visitor's rank the Viceroy either descended from the steps of his throne to greet him or awaited him on the dais. A *nazur* (token offering) of one or two gold mohurs was presented by the prince for the Viceroy to touch and remit. A short conversation ensued, important staff were introduced, the Viceroy offered his guest the traditional hospitality of rose-water or betel-nut. Within fifteen minutes the ceremony was all over; the native ruler walked backwards to the end of the Throne Room, bowed and departed. Some Indian princes could have been forgiven for thinking they had been in the presence of a living god. Even the most cynical and British-hating of them realised that they had seen the magnificence of a great imperial power.

The historian, Thomas Pakenham, suggested that Lansdowne was much influenced by General Sir Frederick Roberts, his bright, energetic, C-in-C of the Indian Army. This mutual admiration must be set within what we know of Lansdowne's obstinacy once his mind was made up on any matter. Three men helped shape his opinions on things military: Roberts; General Sir George Chesney, Military Member of the Viceroy's Council, and Sir Mortimer Durand, Foreign Secretary of the Government of India. Roberts's chief obsession was Afghanistan and a fear that Russia might advance on India. Early on, Lansdowne decided that the Afghan Amir, Abdur Rahman, was 'a spoilt child', lectured him on his admittedly repressive regime and generally thought him 'a very unsatisfactory neighbour'. With Roberts blessing he re-instituted a frontier 'forward policy', pushing telegraph and rail lines up to the Afghan frontiers and opening a high road to the independent state of Chitral in the heart of the North-West Frontier tribal belt. Naturally, Abdur Rahman viewed all this British activity with alarm. He was deeply suspicious – quite rightly so – of both his Russian and British neighbours and determined to preserve his country's independence.

When Lansdowne wished to send Roberts to Kabul to discuss the whole frontier question, the amir refused to accept a visit from a soldier who had played such a pivotal and controversial role in the Second Afghan War of 1878–80. Instead the mission was led by the Indian Civil Service's master-diplomat – Sir Mortimer Durand.

His crowning achievement was to be the 1893 'Durand Line' that demarcated then – as it still does – the boundaries of Afghanistan, India (and modern-day Pakistan). For almost a decade from 1885, Durand was Foreign Secretary to the Government of India, a powerful role he conducted with great skill. Highly intelligent, much admired, he looked not unlike a taller version of Lansdowne with the same domed forehead, receding hairline and handsome curled moustache. His opinion on native states such as Manipur was that they deserved courteous treatment, but should never be under any false impression of where the real power lay.

An ally of both Roberts and Durand was General Chesney who had been the Military Member of the Viceroy's Council since 1886. The role was 'approximately the counterpart of a war minister', the Viceroy's advisor on all things military. Real executive action lay with the C-in-C who was also an extraordinary member of the council. This 'dual control' was a policy that led on occasions to conflict, but not so with Chesney and Roberts, who worked together harmoniously and agreed on everything from martial race policy to princely states contingents and counter-defensive measures against a possible Russian invasion. Chesney, an elderly Royal Engineer who had seen fighting at the Siege of Delhi thirty-four years earlier, was an efficient controller of the Military Department whose responsibilities covered Indian Army pay, fortifications, hospitals, ordnance, military education, clothing, the marine service, transport, horse-breeding and the illegal sale of ammunition.

The Viceroy's Council of about a dozen men met once a week in Calcutta and invariably rubber-stamped whatever Lansdowne proposed. There was the occasional dissenting voice, raised politely, but a viceroy could override his council anyway. Kipling cynically described them as: 'Earnest, narrow men. But chiefly earnest ... And end up by writing letters to *The Times*.' Some cynics noted that if one aspired to the ultimate I.C.S. job – a Lieutenant-Governorship and 100,000 rupees a year – it was wise to be subservient to a viceroy. Lansdowne's Council, however, did contain some men of real note. Sir Charles Elliott, a staunch imperialist, had arrived in India in 1856 after Trinity College, Cambridge, then fought as a magistrate during the 1857–59 insurgency and rose through the service to become an expert on famine relief. In January 1891 Lansdowne officially recognised the Indian National Congress as a legitimate political movement, an action opposed by Elliott who feared that government officials might start to support independence. Another council member, Sir Andrew Scoble, had led the prosecution of the notorious Gaekwar of Baroda; on the very eve of the Manipur crisis in March 1891, his Age of Consent Bill was passed. This raised the age of marriage in India from ten to twelve years. Both Elliott and Scoble would have opinions on events in Manipur as they unfolded.

It seems that an opinion, once formed in Lansdowne's mind, turned into cement. He, no doubt, listened to advice from Durand and his council, read a digest of events covering the recent palace revolt and his eyebrows were raised by all he learned of Prince Tikendrajit's behaviour ever since he was a youth. Then came the pleadings of the now exiled ex-Maharajah and his staunchest ally, the former Manipur political agent, Sir James Johnstone.

Sura Chandra never made his pilgrimage to Brindaban. Instead he made his way to Calcutta and tried to convince the Indian Government that he had never intended to abdicate. He maintained that Grimwood had misconstrued his abdication statement pointing out that 'had I intended to, it would have been by a more formal act, and with some stipulation that provision should be made for me and my family by the State. As it was I came away without a single *pice* in my pocket, or even a second suit of clothes or bedding, being dependent for everything upon the assistance of the Government.'[8]

Johnstone wrote: 'The case was a simple one, a palace revolution had occurred and our nominee whose succession and whose throne we had guaranteed, had been deposed. The course to be adopted by Government was as clear as the day, Soor Chandra Singh should have been restored at once and the usurper severely punished for insulting the majesty of the British Government. Nothing of the kind was done.'[9] Tikendrajit, roared Johnstone, in letters to newspapers and influential friends was, 'always a bad character' who would be 'the ruin of the State'.

In retrospect it seems clear that Sura Chandra was intent upon a game. Even the Indian historian, R. Majumdar, who usually took an anti-British stance, wrote: 'Either he at first really intended to abdicate and later changed his mind or played a very dirty trick for getting out of Manipur.'[10]

Turning all these matters over in his brain, Lord Lansdowne came to a decision; Tikendrajit might be a prince of Manipur but he was as much a rebel from authority as the Canadian half-breed, Louis Riel. Such men unchecked could not be allowed to act with impunity before the imperial government.

During December 1890 the Viceroy received a long report on the palace revolt and recent developments in Manipur from the Chief Commissioner of Assam. Quinton defended Grimwood's actions and pointed out that despite Sura Chandra's assertions, he had given up the Sword of State and keys of office quite voluntarily. If the ex-maharajah was allowed to return to Manipur, the Indian Government would need to back him with a show of force. Hostilities might re-occur and the soldiers would need to stay in the country so long as Sura Chandra occupied the throne. The Chief Commissioner rather naively failed to see that the Indian Government's recognition of Sura Chandra as successor to his father had some bearing on his case. In Quinton's words it was merely 'a family quarrel'. He backed Grimwood's assessment that the country had improved enormously (though he personally had never visited the place), since Kula Chandra assumed the Regency. He held to the view that 'the administration has been successfully and thoroughly conducted, and the Political Agent expects no opposition to it.'[11]

What sort of man was Quinton who was so shortly to quite literally lose his head? After the Manipur rising it was suggested, and has been trotted out by historians ever since, that James Wallace Quinton's problems stemmed from a lack of knowledge of how things should be done on India's north-eastern frontier because he was new to his job. A portion of the blame for the Manipur disaster rests squarely on his shoulders, but Quinton's mistakes were basically plain human errors of judgment compounded by a too-cheery optimism, which gave him a false sense of security and a mistaken view of human behaviour. These defects had little to do with north-eastern India and he had, in fact, served two years in Burma as judicial commissioner in the 1870s. He had been Chief Commissioner of Assam for eighteen months prior to the Manipur outbreak.

An Ulsterman from Enniskillen, Quinton had been born in 1834, son of a wine merchant. He was bright at school and finished his education at Trinity College, Dublin, where he was secretary and president of the university philosophical society. By 1891 he had served thirty-five years in India having entered the Indian Civil Service in 1856. He spent his first two decades toiling up the promotions ladder in sun-baked Oudh and the North-West Provinces, before getting sent to Burma in 1875. In 1877 he returned to the north-west as magistrate and collector of Allahabad. One year later, he added civil and sessions judge to his duties. In July 1878 he was appointed to be a member of the North-West Provinces famine commission. Next came his elevation to commissioner – first of Jhansi, then Lucknow. His rise seemed unstoppable; during the 1880s he served four years on the Viceroy's Council under the progressive Lord Ripon and his successor, Lord Dufferin. In 1887 he had been gazetted a Companion of the Star of India (C.S.I.).

Fellow civil servants liked the good-natured Quinton; Henry Cotton, chief secretary to the Lieutenant-Governor of Bengal, praised this Irishman with his soft County Fermanagh brogue, delightful smile and short, wavy hair as a man 'of high character and sweet disposition'. Sir Andrew Scoble who served with him on the Viceroy's Council thought he was the kind of man who listened to others and did not act rashly. Quinton had been a supporter of Ripon's attempts to give Indians a larger role in their country's affairs – offering peasants a greater security of land tenure, appointing a commission on primary education, trying to ease the conditions of factory workers, pushing for greater self-government and – most notoriously – allowing Indian magistrates to try British offenders (a measure that proved a step too far). It is not surprising then that this likable, easy-going and progressive-thinking Chief Commissioner of Assam supported the new regime in Manipur since, as Frank Grimwood stated, the land was at peace and the people seemed content.

In Calcutta the die had been cast; on 24 January a confidential letter was sent to Quinton that made clear the Viceroy and his advisors did not approve of the status quo in Manipur. In their minds the usurpation of an Indian ruler appointed by the Government of India could not be allowed to go unpunished. There seemed to be a fear that what had happened in Manipur might set some precedent for the future (though this was not directly stated in the letter). Sura Chandra had abdicated in 'a state of terror'. There was 'no reason to believe that events were the result of popular feeling against the Maharaja or of any deep or widespread discontent with his rule.' Sura Chandra's flight, though a ruse, was excused on the grounds 'that his mind was at the time so engrossed ... in the difficulties of the moment that he was incapable of taking account of his actions upon the future.'

It was clear that Prince Tikendrajit would now wield the power in Manipur (this was true), but he had 'more than once incurred the displeasure of the Government of India' and the matter could not any longer be viewed 'with indifference'. Perhaps thinking of a short war less than three years previously with the Kingdom of Sikkim, or the disturbed state of Burma, the letter went on to say: 'We have now a stronger interest in Manipur than we had in past years, and the toleration of such disorders may be expected to have a mischievous effect upon the lawless tribes adjoining the State.'

Quinton was told that the Viceroy wished him to visit Manipur and assess the situation. He was to go with 'a small body of troops' from Cachar or Kohima. If it seemed likely that Sura Chandra's return might be supported by a majority of the people, then Tikendrajit was to be banished for 'his violent and lawless conduct'.[12]

James Quinton must have sighed when he read this letter. To what extent its contents were put together by Lansdowne or Durand we will never know. It is possible that Sir Mortimer had advised tightening control over 'frontier states such as Sikkim, Kashmir and Manipur, which were to be employed as buffer zones against foreign aggressors.'[13] Lansdowne was later criticised for waiting four months after the palace revolt before laying his cards on the table, but he was not a man to make quick decisions and possibly wished to evaluate the matter. He also had an extremely busy schedule that winter, and in January 1891 had the headache of entertaining the Tsarevitch of Russia (the future Tsar Nicholas II), who was on a grand tour with his 'great, good-humoured' friend, Prince George of Greece.

It was nine days before Quinton got the Viceroy's letter and he spent, as he admitted, one more week thinking over the matter 'very carefully'. Then, on 9 February, from his stateroom on the Chief Commissioner's official yacht, the *Sonamukhi*, he replied that the restoration of Sura Chandra 'would not be for the benefit of good government in Manipur'. Quinton pooh-poohed the ex-Maharajah's 'state of terror' by pointing out that he had taken 'part of a day and a whole night to think over his determination and adhere to it'. Three of Sura Chandra's brothers, noted the Chief Commissioner, went into exile with him and none of them did anything to stop him leaving. Showing good common sense, Quinton suggested that an inquiry be made into Tikendrajit's conduct before any decision be reached on him. In his opinion the whole Manipur affair was 'a mere family dispute'. He told Lansdowne that he was on his way to Calcutta for talks. In March he would visit Manipur but he ended his reply with a clear – and as it turned out very accurate – warning that 'inquiries such as those suggested must have the effect of upsetting men's minds and disturbing the tranquillity which now prevails.'[14]

At Calcutta there can be no doubt that Quinton stuck to his guns; he reiterated his objections to Sura Chandra and once more laid them out in a letter to his superiors dated 19 February. To be fair to the Chief Commissioner, he did not mince his words. By this date he must also have been apparent to him that Lansdowne wanted Tikendrajit removed from Manipur. Yet he told the Viceroy, once again, that since the Manipuri princes revolt there had been 'no cause for complaint to us, or so far as I can ascertain, to their subjects.' Quinton pointed out how popular Tikendrajit, now Jubraj or heir-apparent, was with his people. He warned that any attempt to remove the prince might be resisted, or Tikendrajit might then 'use his utmost efforts to stir up disaffection and rebellion.' In Quinton's views British bayonets would be needed to enforce Tikendrajit's removal and the Manipur garrison reinforced. 'Constant interference will be no less necessary than in the internal affairs of the country,'[15] he warned. Once again, the Chief Commissioner urged his plan of holding an inquiry into Tikendrajit's behaviour and reporting his findings back to the Indian Government.

It was all to no avail. On 21 February James Quinton was informed of Lansdowne's decisions; the Viceroy now accepted that Kula Chandra should ascend to the throne, but 'it will be desirable that the Senapatti should be removed from Manipur and punished for his lawless conduct.' Quinton was ordered to go to Imphal and enforce the imperial edicts, taking with him 'sufficient force' as he thought necessary, though it was inexplicably and naively thought that 'opposition may not be expected.' The Chief Commissioner was given leeway to decide on the 'amount of restraint' to be placed on Tikendrajit along with any allowances for his maintenance. He could also decide if the two younger princes who began the palace revolt ought to be banished or if the three princes now in exile with the ex-maharajah might return.

Removal of Tikendrajit from Manipur seems to have been Lansdowne's chief objective. Punishment of the prince was a minor issue and the very fact that Quinton was to work out some allowances for Tikendrajit makes this clear. Banishment was viewed as punishment enough. Quinton's rational suggestion of an inquiry was totally ignored. Tikendrajit 'was already found guilty and his punishment awarded without giving him an opportunity to answer British charges and to explain his conduct.'[16] In hindsight it seems that the Indian Government simply wanted to assert authority over Manipur in some way. No one anticipated any violence in a State that had always been friendly to the Raj. Four days after writing to Quinton the Viceroy told his Whitehall master, Viscount Cross, Secretary of State for India, that 'the recognition of the present Regent shall take place under circumstances which will show the Manipur people that he has been accepted with our full concurrence and we shall deport a ruffianly brother ... who was, I believe, at the bottom of the late cabal.'[17]

Somewhat ironically, on the same day – 9 February – that Quinton had set out his case for non-intervention, Sura Chandra had written to Lansdowne declaring that he was not 'some priest-ridden imbecile', as others had reported, but a ruler whose departure was met with 'universal regret' by his subjects. Lansdowne and Durand may have read these words with a pinch of salt, but the ex-Maharajah may have rubbed a little of that same salt into their pride when he declared:

My case is being watched with interest by Native Chiefs, as well as by my people to see whether the paramount power will allow a successful conspiracy to deprive a people of its Prince, instead of calling upon the rebels to lay down their arms and not disturb by force the possession of a Prince who ruled, recognised and protected by the British Government.[18]

These were the same kind of words that Johnstone and some others had uttered. Lansdowne undoubtedly thought that by at least removing Tikendrajit he was taking a cancer out of Manipur and demonstrating the power of the imperial government. It was all so simple – flex the imperial muscles a bit, show British authority but avoid bloodshed, give recognition to a new ruler and banish a truculent prince. Who could possibly object? It was, after all, the way the Raj skilfully operated and had done so for many years.

Thus it was that James Quinton was given the job of doing the empire's dirty work. One can guess his reactions, yet 35 years in the I.C.S. had taught him that duty came before all private feelings. The situation was worrying and he had laid out the difficulties to his superiors, but with his usual cheery outlook on life Quinton probably thought that he could stay in control of all events: a small sized escort; a sensible durbar at Imphal; the quick arrest of Prince Tikendrajit; then a fast march over the frontier and back into Assam. He had no way of knowing that the job Lansdowne had tasked him with was to go horribly wrong. Soon blood would be flowing in Manipur, including his own.

Arrival of the Chief Commissioner

In the days that followed Quinton's telegram to Frank Grimwood at Imphal a sense of unease in the Manipuri capital would ratchet up to one of palpable tension. This changing mood among Manipuris of all classes, unaware that Prince Tikendrajit was the main cause of the Chief Commissioner's visit, was a fear that the British intended to restore Sura Chandra at the point of the bayonet. Thus uncertainty for the future of Maharajah Kula Chandra, still officially referred to by the British as 'the Regent', helped fuel a sense of paranoia most especially among the courtiers and royal family. The Indian Government must be held culpable for this behaviour. If it had declared its views earlier on the royal succession, then this mood of unease would have evaporated. Even the ex-Maharajah was kept wondering about his status and not informed of Lansdowne's acceptance of Kula Chandra until the very eve of Quinton's visit to Manipur on 21 March 1891.

Ethel first got wind that something was up when she asked a local *shikari* (sportsman or hunter) to shoot some wild duck for the residency dinner table. 'He said that he was not able to shoot,' she wrote, as Tikendrajit 'had ordered him, as well as all the other men in his village, to bring their guns into the palace arsenal, and that all the villages in the neighbourhood had received similar commands.' When she told this story to her husband, Frank remarked that 'it looked as though preparations were being made to resist the ex-Maharajah, should he return to Manipur.'[1] Curiosity on the part of Tikendrajit, the Thangal General and others was at fever pitch. Frank found the Manipuris constantly asking his opinion on the possible restoration of Sura Chandra. Ethel later wrote that: 'From private sources we had heard that arms, ammunitions and food were being collected ... inside the palace' on the orders of Prince Tikendrajit. The Grimwoods were as much in the dark as the Manipuris about the reasons for the Chief Commissioner's visit, a fact that the locals, quite understandably, found hard to believe. A telegram had been received from Calcutta stating that 'a big tiger will shortly be caught in Manipur.' It did not take much intelligence for the Manipuris to guess at a hidden meaning since Tikendrajit's nickname was 'koireng' or 'tiger hunter'. The mood in Manipur was perfectly captured by Ethel in a letter to a Lieutenant Williams of the 43rd Gurkhas on 12 March:

> Excitement is tremendous here. The Chief Commissioner is to arrive on the 22nd and Col. Skene, six officers and 450 of the 42nd with him. We have not been told what they are coming for, but of course can guess. The Manipuris are in no end of a funk; but they say they mean to resist sooner than let the Rajah return. Today we hear that one of the Princes with 1,000 men is going out to Sengmai on the way to Kohima to meet the Chief Commissioner and force. What this means we cannot tell; but it looks like resistance, and if so, there will be a small battle on the road.[2]

During this period Ethel quite innocently added to the air of growing paranoia by letting it be known that she might soon be leaving for England. The Grimwoods had been planning a furlough for some time. Frank now urged his wife to leave earlier than originally planned so as to be 'out of danger, in the event of anything serious happening' following the Chief Commissioner's visit. Ethel was reluctant to go and told a friend that she wanted to stay and 'see the fun'. The Resident's attempts to hustle his wife away were duly noted by the Durbar and Tikendrajit. It was concluded by them that this was an unlucky omen with a 'very serious meaning' – she was 'flying from danger'. Messages were sent from the Maharajah, the Thangal General and the princes asking Ethel not to leave. It was explained to all of them that a passage had been booked on a steamer, a ticket had been paid for, but the entreaties continued. Frank wrote to a friend about this time:

My wife leaves for England on April 9, and I hope to be home for September. I am expecting every day now the Viceroy's decision whether the Maharajah is to come back or not. His brothers, who turned him out, are rather uneasy as to what the result may be. If the Viceroy decides he is to return, there will be a small scrimmage. I hope he won't come back. Not that the present lot are much better; a native Administration is a dreadful thing to have to do with. It seems impossible to improve it.[3]

Eventually Ethel's determination won out and her husband agreed that she could remain until after Quinton had left.

Mrs Grimwood had quite a lot on her dinner-plate since preparing a feast fit for a Chief Commissioner and his large escort was no easy matter in a strictly Hindu country – beef was an impossibility, mutton equally unprocurable. Meat in Manipur invariably meant wildfowl. While wondering what to do a solution was sensibly suggested by Ethel's native bearer – serve the guests goat. So a billy-goat was bought, tethered to the kitchen garden, and fed 'every day and all day.' The animal, blissfully unaware of its intended fate, grew to an enormous size, eating as much as it wished, when not sleeping, 'which was his favourite occupation.'

While Ethel Grimwood worried over her goat and cuisine, matters military were occupying the minds of officers worried by the size of the Chief Commissioner's escort. Quinton was later much criticised for intending to visit Manipur with just 150 military police, yet the Indian Government had initially suggested taking as small an escort as possible, so he was merely following orders. Brigadier-General Henry Collett, General Officer Commanding the Assam District, was appalled and wired Quinton on 14 February: 'My advice is that if you go via Kohima you should take 200 of 42nd from Dibrugarh, with Colonel Skene in command... We cannot afford to have mistakes, and a scratch force of police under a subaltern not suitable escort for Chief Commissioner.'[4] When a small escort was mooted before the Viceroy's Council during Quinton's Calcutta visit, General Chesney declared 'that it would be madness' to go with less than 400 men. The generals got their way and an escort was agreed of 200 men of the 42nd Gurkha Rifles (G.R.) and 200 more of the 44th G.R. all under the command of Lieutenant-Colonel Charles Skene. These troops were to be reinforced by 200 rifles of the 43rd G.R. under Captain J.W. Cowley who would march separately and slightly later from Cachar. The soldiers of the 43rd would reinforce the 100 men of their regiment who formed the Resident's small escort at Imphal. Trying to distance himself after the uprising, Collett admitted to the Adjutant-General of the Indian Army that he had under-estimated the scale of military support needed:

> The universal opinion in this province was that the Chief Commissioner had an escort of overpowering strength, and no one dreamed of the terrible disaster that has occurred. It seemed that an escort of 400 Gurkhas added to the permanent garrison of 100 Gurkhas, and supported by 200 Gurkhas en route from Silchar, would be ample to overawe malcontents... I would also draw attention to the fact that an escort of 400 men appeared to be considered sufficient by the Governor-General's Council sitting in Calcutta. That we were all mistaken is now too terribly evident.[5]

Quinton's visit was shrouded in such secrecy that the Commander-in-Chief of the Indian Army, General Sir Frederick Roberts, later complained that he too was not told all the details – an astonishing admission – on the composition and strength of the escort. He later confessed to an old friend that: 'The whole business was kept a secret, and Skene apparently did not know what Quinton meant to do.'[6] This may have been so at first, but Roberts's assertion is refuted by Lieutenant Gurdon, assistant commissioner of Assam, who wrote: 'Colonel Skene knew all about the objects of the march to Manipur; he was shown the whole of the confidential papers in Golaghat dak bungalow on the 6 March.'[7]

It was 'common knowledge' that the Manipuri royal arsenal contained some 7-pounder guns, four mountain guns and 200 of the latest Lee-Metford rifles (adopted by the British Army in 1888 but not by the Indian Army). Lieutenant J.W. Chatterton, staff officer of the escort, recommended to Skene that two mountain guns belonging to the 43rd G.R. at Kohima ought to be taken along, but Quinton, possibly fearing that his mission might soon take the shape of an invading army, rather than a peaceful visit, declared that they were unnecessary. The 400 men of the 42nd and 44th G.R. were armed with the old Snider rifle and the 200 men of the 43rd G.R. with the Martini-Henry, main firearm of the British Army for most of the 1870s and 1880s. Originally it was intended that each soldier would carry 40 rounds of ammunition in his pouch along with a box containing a further 50 rounds. This order was countermanded by Collett on hearing that there were 13,000 rounds of Snider and 6,000 rounds of Martini-Henry ammunition at the Manipur residency. The result was that each man marched with just the 40 rounds in his pouch. As an after-thought, the general ordered that the police at Kohima should provide the Gurkhas with as many rounds of Snider ammunition as they might require, but the escort left the place without making use of this source of bullets. Collett and Skene, both of whom had served in Burma, knew that troops in Assam generally marched with 40 rounds of ammunition. The large amounts of bullets stored at the Imphal residency seemed, under the circumstances, to be more than sufficient.

The senior military man of the escort was Charles McDowell Skene. He was a kinsman of the Duke of Fife and had been born in Aberdeenshire in about 1844. Skene had completed his education at Addiscombe, the East India Company's training academy in Surrey before joining the 43rd G.R. in time to serve in the final stages of the hard-fought Umbeyla Campaign against fanatical tribesmen on India's north-west frontier in 1863. Eleven years later he took part in a bloodless expedition against the Daflas on Assam's northern frontier. During the subjugation of Burma, following the Third Anglo-Burmese War, he led what was termed 'the Ruby Mines Expedition', getting mentioned in despatches and winning a D.S.O. On 27 January 1890, during the 1889–90 Chin–Lushai Expedition, Skene led a brilliant charge against a heavily fortified stockade, an event watched by Sir George White V.C., the general commanding in Burma. In a series of actions that winter Skene's Gurkhas, assisted by the Norfolk Regiment, were in the forefront of the fighting in the northern Chin Hills. His departure for Imphal coincided with the handsome colonel's transfer as commanding officer of the 42nd G.R. Generally, Skene was considered by his colleagues to be a brave and competent soldier who had served more than twenty years on the north-east frontier of India and knew as much about its various tribes as any white man. Along with Quinton, Skene 'did not anticipate much opposition' at Imphal. If security had not been so tight it is probable that he would have been told that one native officer and thirty-three men of the Resident's escort, with 3,800 rounds of Martini-Henry ammunition, were actually at Langthobal, outside Imphal, and not at the residency. A further eleven men of Grimwood's escort (with, we must assume, another 440 bullets in their pouches), were *en route* to Cachar with a prisoner.

Quinton set off for Manipur via Kohima on 7 March. He took with him 414 Gurkhas, a contingent of 9 native officers, 7 buglers and 398 sepoys under Skene's command. To assist him in his civil duties was Quinton's assistant secretary, William Henry Cossins; a long-faced, rather lugubrious-looking young man of twenty-six, Cossins had served in Assam since 1885, his first posting on joining the I.C.S. straight from Balliol (Lansdowne's old college). With neatly parted short hair and a trim moustache, Cossins looked every inch the diligent junior civil servant. It was in his blood. His father was in the consular service and young William had been born during a posting to Marsala in Sicily. Also serving in civil capacities were two assistant commissioners: Lieutenant P.R.T. Gurdon, formerly of the Devonshires, a renaissance kind of young man with a Bachelor of Science degree, with a junior I.C.S. man, Lieutenant Albert Woods, seconded from the Madras Staff Corps and going with the escort to Imphal as the quickest route to take up a post as divisional sub-inspector at Hailabandi.

In order of rank, Skene' immediate deputies, Captains G.H. Butcher of the 42nd G.R. and T.S. Boileau of the 44th G.R. had never seen action before, a matter which later was to take on some significance. Both Lieutenants J.B. Chatterton and E.J. Lugard of the 42nd G.R. had served in Burmese operations as well as the recent Chin-Lushai Expedition. They were accompanied by regimental surgeon J.T. Calvert. Boileau had with him Lieutenant Lionel Wilhelm Brackenbury of the

44th G.R. A distant cousin of the famous army reformer, General Sir Henry Brackenbury, Lionel had only recently lost his father, Major-General Sir Charles Brackenbury, who had died of a sudden heart attack on a train. The 'Wilhelm' in his name was a result of his father's fondness for things Teutonic (he had been *The Times* correspondent with the Austrian army during the Austro-Prussian War of 1866. He had fought in the Crimea and later served in the intelligence branch at the War Office). Lionel had been born in 1868 and entered the army in 1886. Manipur was to be his first real taste of danger.

The stand-out among these young officers was Lieutenant Edward James Lugard. He already held the Distinguished Service Order (D.S.O.) awarded to him during the recent Chin-Lushai fighting for 'conspicuous gallantry and intelligence leading his men on several occasions during the operations'.[8] Edward – known as 'Ned' by close family and friends – was the younger brother of a man destined to be far more famous than anyone connected with Manipur; this was his adored sibling, Frederick (later Lord Lugard), the man who added Uganda and Northern Nigeria to the British Empire. Edward had been born on 12 June 1865. Three months later his mother, Mary Jane, passed away. Though surrounded by a clutch of adoring elder sisters, the loss of their mother at so early an age – Fred was only eight years old – forged a close bond between the two Lugard brothers. Named after a famous fire-breathing dragon of an Indian Army uncle who fought in the days of the Great Mutiny, Edward tried after school to make a go of farming in western Canada. This venture failed and so he followed his elder brother into the British Army and transferred into the Bengal Staff Corps in 1888. Aged only twenty-seven and with a D.S.O. already on his chest, the future for 'Ned' Lugard looked bright.

It was not until 18 March and deep in the Naga Hills that Quinton telegraphed his plans to Calcutta. He expected to reach Imphal on Sunday 22 March. On meeting with the Regent and members of the Durbar on arrival he would reveal the Indian Government's decision to arrest and exile Tikendrajit. The prince would be informed that the length of his exile and his return would depend on his good behaviour and the tranquillity of Manipur. Kula Chandra was going to be ordered to place a 7-pounder gun at the disposal of the Chief Commissioner during his stay of less than 72 hours. A departure with Tikendrajit in tow was intended by 25 March. Quinton advised his superiors to exile the prince a long way from Manipur, preferably on the sub-continent, and not in Assam. The Chief Commissioner also made suggestions for the maintenance of the ex-Maharajah and those members of his family who had gone into exile. The future stability of Manipur was also addressed and the new ruler was going to be told to accept certain conditions:

> Three hundred troops were to be located in Manipur and a site given for their accommodation; the Maharaja must accept the advice of the Political Agent in all matters; the Pucca Senna was not to be allowed to return to Manipur, and the younger brothers were to be permitted to remain.[9]

Once well into his journey, Quinton decided – at last – to inform Frank Grimwood of the reasons for his visit. Not trusting the telegraph to keep his secrets, the Chief Commissioner sent on ahead Lieutenant Gurdon, his bright assistant seconded from the Bengal Staff Corps. 'These Staff Corps acted as pools of officer manpower,' writes T.A. Heathcote in his administrative study of the Indian Army, 'from which officers were drawn to fill either civil posts, military departmental posts, army headquarters and staff appointments, or regimental appointments.'[10] So nervous was Quinton of his telegrams to Imphal being read any other than Frank Grimwood that it has been rumoured (and is probably true), they were written in either Italian or the favourite language of the Victorian public schools – Latin.

Gurdon reached Imphal on the evening of 15 March and quickly went into a private room to reveal the purpose of Quinton's trip to the Resident. Frank, according to Gurdon, was 'astonished' and 'hinted' that Tikendrajit 'might give us some trouble'. As the two men talked long into the night Grimwood grew more emotional and defended his princely friend, warning that the Indian Government would only get 'his dead body' since he would sell his life dearly. After reiterating the argument of the Indian Government, Gurdon asked how the prince could be taken without offering forcible resistance. Frank remained unhelpful and his attitude seemed to have hardened by the time the two men met after breakfast on the next day. According to Gurdon in his report, Grimwood 'showed that he was greatly annoyed at the decision of Government with regard to Manipur affairs not having been communicated to him before. He more than once said to me that as he had not been consulted, he would wash his hands of the whole business.'[11] Frank pressed his guest for information of how exactly Tikendrajit was to be arrested, but the assistant commissioner pointed out that he had no idea and this information would have to be imparted by Quinton. The Resident advised Gurdon that the prince might agree to deportation if he was given some assurances of an eventual return to Manipur. The two men agreed that the younger princes who had started the palace revolt could be left in Manipur while the brothers-in-exile should on no account be allowed to return.

On the 17th Gurdon set off back towards Quinton. He was thoroughly dispirited and felt his mission had been, in his own words, 'a failure'. The Resident had so strongly defended Tikendrajit that Gurdon was now left wondering if 'perhaps Mr Grimwood was right.' When the lieutenant met Quinton on the next day the two men realised that the Resident had sent only brief notes, 'little more than "yes" or "no" to certain queries'. They discussed Grimwood's unhelpful and rather strange attitude; Gurdon reported how Frank had argued that Tikendrajit should not be deported (though he had done this only verbally and not in writing). The lieutenant urged the Chief Commissioner to meet with the Resident 'and hear himself what he had to say.' Quinton agreed that it sounded a sensible idea and a message was sent to the residency requesting that Grimwood attend on his boss.

As soon as Gurdon had left Imphal on 17 March, the Resident did a most curious thing. He went out shooting that day with the very same man that he now knew his government viewed as a criminal and had sent troops to arrest. What was Frank Grimwood thinking of? Did anything happen while the two friends talked? Did Grimwood say anything to alert Tikendrajit? Even if he had held his tongue, did Frank's demeanour give the game away? We can never know, yet it was an extraordinary thing for a British official to do and, it might also be fair to say, demonstrated great loyalty to his friend.

On the 21st Frank got up early and rode out the 10 miles to Sengmai, the last halting post on the road to Kohima. Here he met James Quinton and the pair talked privately for some time. It must have been a most difficult discussion for both men. Then, for half-an-hour, they were joined by Cossins and Skene. Gurdon later insisted (although we do not know on what authority) that the Resident 'never definitely stated the amount of resistance we might expect. All that he said was that the Senapati, personally, would fight to the last. To the best of my belief, the Political Agent never told the Chief Commissioner and Colonel Skene that the fort was full of armed men.' Lieutenant Gurdon saw Grimwood break away from this group and wander off in contemplation. He was, noted the lieutenant, looking 'annoyed'. Next it was Gurdon's turn for a private talk with the Chief Commissioner; he was informed that Tikendrajit would be arrested in Durbar, 'and that after his arrest, it would be my duty to at once proceed with him that same afternoon from Manipur.'[12]

It must have been a very dispirited Frank Grimwood who rode back to Imphal that night. He now knew that the British authorities intended to arrest and swiftly deport Prince Tikendrajit in a rather shady way. Clearly he felt that it was a betrayal of his own sense of honour and the fact that he had not been informed until the last hour hardly reflected very well on the Indian Government. He may well have guessed that those in authority considered him too intimate with the Manipur royal family.

That evening, as Frank trotted home from Sengmai, Ethel, in company with Lieutenant Simpson, had gone for a ride. Both of them noticed as they rode back into Imphal that 'a great number of Manipuri sepoys were met, hurrying into the citadel. They swarmed along the road, and on getting near the big gate of the palace we had some difficulty in getting our horses through the crowds which were streaming into the fort.'[13] A despondent Frank returned about 7pm, 'very tired and much worried'. Privately he told Ethel about Tikendrajit's fate and made her promise not to breathe a word to either Simpson or Melville (the latter having returned to Imphal), their residency guests. Later, alone in their bedroom, it seems that the Grimwoods talked further. Ethel was acutely aware that the friendship she and her husband had shown the Manipuri royals was 'infra-dig' in certain quarters. In her memoirs she defended Frank who had been told to establish friendly relations with the Manipuris and learn their language. He had, she declared, only ever given 'praise where praise was due', but balanced this with a strong reproof if it had been necessary to discipline the Maharajah, princes or the Durbar. Yet now, at last hearing what was in store for Tikendrajit, whom she considered a good friend, Ethel felt 'very sorry' for him.

The Manipuris had, despite their misgivings, lavished the usual hospitality on the visit of so illustrious a personage as the Chief Commissioner. He was met at Mao just inside the state by an escort of 700 sepoys under the Thangal General's command. British officers noted that most of these soldiers were bearing arms. It was noticed that some of the Manipuris kept inquiring: 'Have you brought your guns? Aren't they coming too?'[14] When Quinton got to Sengmai he was met by the Angao Senna with a further 50 sepoys. The prince was given a letter to Kula Chandra pointing out that the Chief Commissioner wished to have a Durbar immediately after his arrival at Imphal. The reason given by Quinton for this rushed meeting was that he was on a special march to Tammu on the Burmese frontier. Twenty men of the 44th G.R. under a *havildar* (sergeant) was left at Sengmai, with an additional 80 kits, intended to be used by the men who it was planned would rush from Imphal under Gurdon with Tikendrajit.

Four miles closer to the capital, the Chief Commissioner reached the steep banks of a river to be met by none other than Prince Tikendrajit in command of two regiments of Manipuri sepoys. Rather ominously the soldiers were all drawn up in a long line on the far bank. It was at this point that Quinton ought to have got wind of the way things were moving. A wooden bridge, a bit rickety, but built on wooden spars across the river, had mysteriously been destroyed during the previous night by 'a jungle fire' according to the Manipuris. British officers stared at the burnt embers while the acrid smell of smouldering ashes polluted the morning air. It seems highly likely that the burning of this bridge, with the large number of soldiers that Tikendrajit had brought with him, were acts intended to prevent the return of the ex-Maharajah. Of course, once it was obvious that Sura Chandra was not with

Quinton, the situation changed. Some of the Gurkhas, however, attuned to omens, may have realised that indirectly the Manipuris were wishing Quinton and his escort to go back.

Inexorably the British marched on, carefully negotiating the banks of the stream, while getting everyone and everything across to the other side. Quinton then had a short conversation with the man he was intending to arrest on the morrow. Tikendrajit was being carried in a litter. He looked unwell and complained of gallstones. Quinton dismounted and chatted briefly and respectfully before the prince made his departure.

One mile from the palace the British came across a long line of Manipuri sepoys guarding the route on either side of the road. The Court Chronicle noted:

> Plantains, sugar-cane and torches which were to be lit were planted in front of all the houses along the road where the Sahep was to pass, to show that he was the Commissioner Sahep. Shrijut Kulachandra Maharaj along with all the noble and brave men of the land welcomed him at the Sna Keithen, the Royal Market. A thirteen cannon salute was fired.[15]

The time was about 10am. It was turning into a hot day. Ethel later recalled it as a beautiful morning:

> The place had never looked more lovely. Clusters of yellow roses blossomed on the walls of the house, and the scent of the heliotrope greeted me, as I went into the veranda to watch my husband start to meet Mr Quinton. There was a delightful sense of activity about the place, and one felt that something of more than ordinary importance was about to take place; white tents peeped out from amongst the trees surrounding the house, and the camp prepared for the Sepoys stretched along under our wall at the end of the lake. Mr Simpson and I strolled down the drive, out into the road, to see the preparations in honour of Mr Quinton's coming. Chairs were placed near the principal palace gate, and a carpet, and a table with flowers on it; and there were a great many Manipuri Sepoys lining the road by which he was expected to arrive.[16]

After the formal courtesies and introductions the Chief Commissioner wasted no time in telling Maharajah Kula Chandra that a durbar would be held at the residency at 12 noon. He and all his brothers were expected to attend. We can guess the Maharajah's nervousness on receipt of this news. He pointed out that it was a Sunday and also, according to the Hindu religion, an *ekadasi* (fasting day). Would not a postponement be better? Frank Grimwood now spoke, possibly in Methei, and pointed out that the Chief Commissioner's order had to be obeyed.

While Mrs Grimwood was watching this ceremony news reached her of a personal drama back at the residency – her goat, pride of place at the dinner party she was planning for that night, was dying! She rushed back to find Billy breathing his last, 'and with his departing spirit went all my dreams of legs of mutton, chops and cutlets.'[17] No amount of beer or brandy would revive the animal and Ethel felt close to tears. Luckily, Percy Melville and Walter Simpson saw her distress and made such a big joke of the whole thing that it banished her depression, just in the nick of time, as the thirteenth cannon boomed out and Quinton, Skene and Frank were at the residency steps.

For a few minutes the seriousness of the day gave way to hearty laughter and light conversation as the British officers sat down to breakfast. Ethel recalled how the conversation 'flowed merrily'. She could see that her husband seemed troubled but the pair had no time for private conversation. After breakfast was over Frank went off to change into his ceremonial uniform. On important occasions the Political Agents at native courts wore a dark blue jacket with gold embroidery, black velvet lining its collar and cuffs, worn with dark blue cloth trousers, a gold and lace stripe two inches wide running up the leg. This whole rather splendid ensemble was finished off by a beaver-skin cocked hat decorated with a black silk cockade and ostrich feathers, and a ceremonial sword. Quinton must have worn a similar kind of uniform but in his case it is likely that he wore his decoration as a Companion of the Star of India (C.S.I.), the lowest grade of the highest honour of the Indian Empire. A white-edged light blue sash was worn over his right shoulder to the left hip. Around his neck the Chief Commissioner would have displayed his decoration on a similarly coloured silk ribbon; this was a small oval effigy of the

Queen-Empress surrounded by a light blue ring bearing the motto of the order. The decoration was suspended from a five-pointed star illuminated by brilliants (and for more exalted persons with diamonds).

While he changed his clothes, Ethel had a few moments alone at last with Frank. She heard with horror how, at the end of the durbar, it was her unhappy husband who had been deputed to arrest Tikendrajit! Ethel wrote: 'To be obliged to arrest a man himself with whom he had been on friendly terms for nearly three years, and see him treated as a common felon, without being able to defend himself, was naturally a hard task, and my husband felt it bitterly.' Only Skene, Gurdon (and possibly the other civilian, Albert Woods), along with the Grimwoods knew exactly what was to take place. The other officers were kept completely in the dark. They joked with Ethel, 'trying to find out whether I were in the secret or not'. [18]

Two office clerks and the Burmese interpreter were deputed to translate the Indian Government orders into Manipuri. Each clerk had a Gurkha sentry placed over them and they all had to swear an oath that they would not divulge one word to anyone of the contents of the papers given to them to translate. The minutes ticked down to 12 noon but the work was not done. The sweating translators led by Rassick Lal Kundu, Bengali head clerk of the Political Agency, did not finish the work until ten minutes past noon (some sources say twenty minutes past the hour). Skene had ordered all his men to remain under arms and told Lieutenant Chatterton to station 70 men at the rear of the durbar room. He then posted a further 20 soldiers, forming a double line of Gurkhas, on the residency steps and ordered all doors except the main one to be securely locked. 'With the 80 men warned to be in readiness to march back to Sengmai and with the customary guards mounted in the compound and the camping-ground adjoining it, practically all the sepoys were under arms,'[19] noted *The Pioneer* newspaper correspondent.

Meanwhile, the sounding of conch shells and bugles told everyone inside the residency that the royal procession was on its way. Grimwood hurriedly told an interpreter to go and tell the Maharajah to delay his arrival. A request was sent back that Kula Chandra wanted to bring three regiments with him as an escort (it is not difficult to guess why), but Frank sent a message back that one regiment was sufficient.

It is not clear if Skene and his officers were in dress or undress (service) uniform, most likely the latter, but all of them now took up positions at the foot of the residency steps to receive the Maharajah. The one person who was conspicuously absent was the Chief Commissioner, James Quinton. When Kula Chandra reached the building, closely followed by about 100 of his retainers all armed with rifles and shields, it was Frank Grimwood, no doubt looking very dashing in his Political Agent's clothes, who stepped forward saying: 'Rajah, you were asked to bring the Jubraj [Tikendrajit] – why has he not come?'[20] Kula Chandra said that his brother was unwell but on his way.

Perhaps at this point it is worth mentioning one of the great myths of Manipur. This relates to Ethel who is a person of legendary status in Manipur. It is said that she sent a servant with a gift of flowers to Tikendrajit. Hidden in the present was a message warning him of the dangers at the residency. The story is probably apocryphal but like all such tales it may well contain the germs of truth.

At his trial after the uprising Tikendrajit explained what had happened; he had not felt well that morning yet still made his way towards the residency alongside his brother, the Angao Senna. On reaching the gate the two princes were kept waiting for more than half an hour. 'This was against etiquette and the defendant, being on horseback exposed to the burning sun, became annoyed and disheartened.' Seeing large bodies of armed Gurkhas in the grounds, Tikendrajit sent one of his servants named Dasu Sardar to inquire about the delays. Dasu 'brought news of the armed sepoys being placed in front and rear of the Residency bungalow, and that the officers were fully equipped and on horseback. The suspicion which the defendant so long entertained, was thus confirmed, that the Durbar was a trap to make his arrest.'[21] Claiming later that he felt 'exhausted', tired of waiting and no doubt very angry, Tikendrajit (with the Angao Senna), returned to the palace.

As the midday sun beat down on the Maharajah in his loose flowing robes and the Political Agent in his stiff uniform the pair held a long conversation. Around 1.30pm a message was sent to

Tikendrajit saying that he must appear. One hour later a reply came back that he was too ill to attend but sent his apologies. He was not, apparently, the only invalid; the old Thangal General had been unwell for several days and Ethel now found him asleep on the floor of the residency drawing room. Taking pity on the old fellow, she got him to lie down on the sofa and put a pillow under his head.

The durbar was postponed until 8am on the following day. It was impressed upon Kula Chandra that all his brothers must attend. The Maharajah and his followers left the residency about 3pm, 'with great mortification and disappointment', according to a witness. Kula Chandra had tried to explain that he was powerless to make his sick brother attend the next day, 'but he would do his best'.

During his time at the residency, a period of almost three hours, the Chief Commissioner had ignored his royal guest and not put in an appearance. It may seem remarkable, in hindsight, but Quinton had not even bothered to say hello for a few minutes. This extraordinary and foolish behaviour, according to historian Caroline Keen, 'only exacerbated matters'. The Indian scholar, R.C. Majumdar, noted how Kula Chandra returned to his palace 'a sadder but wiser man'. Two days later the Maharajah wrote to Lord Lansdowne explaining the insult:

> According to previous custom, Chief Commissioners would come down to the Residency bungalow, and having shaken hands with the Maharaja, would welcome him to the darbar. But in the present occasion I could not see the Chief Commissioner even after entering the darbar house. Instead I saw numerous troops ready with arms in the front, back and below in the darbar bungalow: in its stairs and even within the darbar house. Such an unusual arrangement gave rise to suspicion in my mind. Notwithstanding as I was eager to hear the intimation that was sent by the Governor-General, I waited in the darbar house, having born all the indignities and dishonour.[22]

Another account, ignored by the official British records, described how the Maharajah stood on the verandah 'for an hour and a half' before he complained of tiredness and 'then Mr Grimwood allowed him to sit in another room.' It was while inside the building that some courtiers looked out of a window and saw all the Gurkhas gathered on the residency back lawn. They reported all of this to Kula Chandra who, according to Captain Boileau, 'stamped his heel on the floor in annoyance.'

The cat was out of the proverbial bag. Now, at last, the Manipuris realised why the Chief Commissioner had come with such a large military force at his disposal. 'There is little doubt that, from this moment, some inkling of what was intended penetrated the minds of the princes and their ministers,' wrote Ethel, 'just as all the officers guessed it was the Jubraj [Tikendrajit] who was "wanted".'[23] Before he left the residency Kula Chandra stopped on the verandah to converse again with some of the officers. He seemed outwardly to show 'no signs of resentment' at his treatment, wrote *The Pioneer* correspondent, ' asked one subaltern how many years' service he had, witnessed the guard-of-honour go through the manual exercise and departed in high good-humour, shaking hands with all who were near him.'[24]

'Such was the reception of the independent ruler of Manipur State in his own capital city,'[25] fumed Majumdar. Another historian, Jyotirmoy Roy, thought that Quinton's 'utter lack of courtesy and tact' contributed hugely to the dramatic change in Manipuri attitudes towards the British. News of the Maharajah's treatment filtered down to the populace who, it must be remembered (as the British officials somehow forgot), saw their king as a living god. Not only was the ruler humiliated and insulted but, in effect, so too were the Manipuri people. What made James Quinton so stand-offish that he failed to show even basic cordiality to the ruler of the state, a man he surely needed to have on his side, is hard to fathom. His actions including the military stage-management of the durbar itself turned the Manipuris against the British Raj. Possibly he felt that Kula Chandra was somehow in league with Tikendrajit and thus felt insulted by the Manipuri ruler? Whatever the reasons, his fit of pique was to have dire consequences.

The Chief Commissioner was, however, quite sanguine about achieving his goal. In a telegram to Lord Lansdowne that afternoon he referred to the 'delicate nature' of his business and wrote that despite Tikendrajit's failure to attend the Durbar,

'I still hope to avoid a resort to force, which, however, must be used in the long run if he holds out.'[26]

In an effort to defuse the tension at the residency the Grimwoods tried to return things to the social events calendar that they had planned for Quinton's visit. The soldiers strolled the grounds and admired the lake or, as one officer later called it, 'the duck pond'. During the late afternoon they walked into the open-air market. Women, then as now, ran the famous bazaar. Hundreds of them sat in their uniquely styled dresses of bright fabric wound around their body from the bosom to their heels and offered their wares for sale – cloth, fish, foodstuffs and jewellery. Quinton even came out of purdah and joined Frank Grimwood for a stroll through the bazaar. Officers and men, acting like tourists everywhere, 'moved freely amongst it, purchasing cloths etc.,' according to Lieutenant Lugard. The Maharajah's band had been booked to play at the residency that evening. Ethel later claimed that she felt 'rather forlorn', being the only lady present, but she probably enjoyed all the attention and flattery. It was, she said, 'a bright and cheery evening', this assembly of fifteen Britons, the officers in uniform, medals sparkling on their breasts in the lamplight, while red-coated residency servants bustled with the plates and poured the wine. Ethel, one suspects, was dressed fashionably, a decoration in her hair, her best jewels off-setting the décolleté of her gown. Much later in her life, a much-prized diamond and ruby ring was pawned to pay some medical bills. Did she wear it that night, its facets twinkling as she moved her hand? While the officers smoked their cigars and enjoyed a brandy, the sound of waltzes and light orchestral pieces floated across the gardens on the still night air. 'Little we knew,' wrote Ethel, 'that it was the last evening we were to spend in peace there all together.'[27]

In the nearby palace it is likely that the evening was a far more serious affair. Almost certainly the Maharajah and his brothers, notably Tikendrajit, decided that they would resist British attempts to seize the prince. Prevarication would be their main weapon. Physical violence a last resort.

All were up early next morning at the residency. The durbar room was prepared for its 8am ceremony, but at the appointed hour no Maharajah appeared, while Prince Tikendrajit sent a message excusing himself due to sickness. News came that even more Manipuris were pouring into the palace compound and large numbers were seen manning the walls. Quinton decided to write to the Maharajah; with the cat out of the bag he bluntly stated that unless Tikendrajit was handed over he would have to make an arrest. He tried to put a gloss on things by saying that the proposed exile would not last forever, but it would be determined by Kula Chandra's good behaviour as ruler.

During the early afternoon Frank and Ethel Grimwood stood on the residency steps and waved goodbye to Percy Melville, who was setting off back to Kohima. 'Watching the coolies loading his luggage, they felt a sudden fear for him, not liking the present feeling of uncertainty. He was slightly crippled, and the thought that he was leaving without an escort to protect him bothered them, although he couldn't be persuaded to stay on.'[28]

Around 2pm Grimwood, Simpson and Rassick Lal Kundu set off to the palace to deliver Quinton's note. Very early that morning, about 6.30am, the Resident and Kundu had tried to see Tikendrajit, but the prince refused to see them at so early an hour. Now the trio saw Kula Chandra who claimed that Tikendrajit was unable to go to the residency on account of illness. The Maharajah insisted, however, that his brother 'would make preparations for leaving Manipur in two or three days', though he did not specify how long the actual preparations might take. A contemporary Indian account of the uprising tells a rather different story; it says that the Maharajah told Grimwood that he could not arrest Tikendrajit without first consulting his ministers. He was allowed 30 minutes to organise this meeting, which the prince attended, but the ministers refused to give him up without a further appeal to the Chief Commissioner. Grimwood then demanded an arrest warrant from Kula Chandra but he refused to sign such a document.

Frank felt hugely frustrated. He now decided to try one last time to speak personally with his old friend. At Tikendrajit's house in the palace compound they found the prince looking decidedly seedy. He even fainted once during the conversation. Kundu, who was no great fan of the prince, wrote later: 'He certainly seemed to me to be ill. He hadn't bathed and was not dressed, and his face was half covered up.'[29] Frank was convinced that his friend was genuinely sick, yet he did his utmost to try and convince him to give himself up quietly. The Resident tried to soft-soap Tikendrajit by saying that if his behaviour was good he would return one day to be ruler of Manipur (this had most certainly *not* been decided by the Viceroy). Despite all Grimwood's entreaties the prince, who was steely enough to be unmoved by flattery and fine words, would not budge.

After three hours at the palace Grimwood, Simpson and Kundu returned to the residency. Frank told the Chief Commissioner and Colonel Skene that the palace was a 'veritable hornets' nest' filled by between 5,000–6,000 Manipuris. They had seen large quantities of ammunition in piles or being moved about by the sepoys, hundreds of troops now lined the palace walls and more were massing on the polo ground (within the enclosure). Frank told Quinton that Kula Chandra was 'in a very nervous state'.

He was not the only one getting panicky. About mid-afternoon Skene, who was clearly losing his patience, readied Lugard using 80 soldiers, to go and arrest Tikendrajit with Butcher supporting him with 100 more troops. The order was never carried out. Now, after Frank's abortive mission, Skene, Quinton and the Resident sat down to decide on a course of action. Political negotiations had clearly come to an end. There seemed no other course but to militarily enforce the orders of the Indian Government. Later, Quinton would be heavily criticised for rushing things at this point. Perhaps Tikendrajit in a few days might have been more amenable to exile? The British could have bluffed things out, talked more with the Maharajah and the Durbar, played it cool. Quinton clearly wanted to keep to his dates and schedule, which he saw slipping away, along with British authority. So it was time to use force.

At sundown pickets were posted and hourly patrols marched around the residency grounds. Imphal was, for once, ominously deserted. No evening market took place. Rumours reached Captain Boileau that 'there would probably be a rush made on the lines that night and, perhaps, all buildings set on fire.'[30] He reported these fears to Skene and it was agreed to order the Langthobal troops to march to the residency and reinforce the garrison. Ethel, too, noted how 'a number of the servants had taken French leave and departed, scenting danger.'[31] She needed to lecture the remainder that dinner would be served as usual to her guests.

It must have been a very strange dinner party. Ethel had made a large quantity of soup and had extra fowls cooked, thinking that the food might be handy the next day. She felt 'very lonely, quite out of place amongst those men whose profession it was to fight.' The meal was eaten largely in silence as everyone concentrated on the morrow. Frank blamed himself for allowing his wife to stay. She wrote:

> Even then we did not dream of any really serious ending. We expected that the Jubraj [Tikendrajit] would fight well – in fact, the officers and Sepoys were hoping that the resistance would be strong, and my husband was afraid that the house might get knocked about, and some of our property destroyed; but serious alarm for our own safety never entered our heads.[32]

A special dance display to entertain the Chief Commissioner had been arranged for 9pm but the girls failed to make an appearance. Quinton, who seemed remarkably unaffected by the impending danger, played a rubber of whist before dinner. A concert of sorts was provided by Lieutenant Brackenbury who sang comic songs to amuse everyone and accompanied himself on the banjo.

Just before dinner, as if to set the mood for what was to follow, a terrific thunderstorm broke the dark clouds that had built up during the afternoon. The night was now lit by 'brilliant flashes of lightning'. The storm cleared the stuffy air and forced the clouds away leaving a brilliant moonlit night. Guests went to their bedrooms fairly early as all knew that they had to be up by 3am. Ethel and Frank strolled out together into their garden. She felt very 'restless and unhappy'. He, using his famous charm, despite what had been a long and disappointing day, gallantly tried to cheer her up. Near the residency gate a sentry approached and said a Manipuri from the palace was asking if they still wanted the dancers. The Grimwoods had intended to show Quinton a demonstration of the Manipuri *Ras Lila* (the Maharajah had also lavished 'considerable expense' on this entertainment). It was an historic and highly stylised dance portraying the love of Krishna for his consort. Under the circumstances the nautch now seemed 'altogether inappropriate' and the couple agreed that the man was probably a spy so he was sent away.

Once in bed Frank fell into a deep slumber, 'knowing not that it was his last night upon earth,' wrote Ethel sadly in her memoirs. She simply could not sleep, but lay awake hardly closing her eyes, tossing in her pillows as she listened to the night hours slip by, a mournful gong being sounded down in the guardroom to knell the passing of each one.

Day of Disasters

Early on the chilly morning of 24 March 1891 the officers of the Chief Commissioner's escort prepared to carry out Skene's plan to arrest Prince Tikendrajit. Before we examine this scheme and what happened when the British tried to execute it, we will pause for a moment to consider the soldiers involved on both sides and the layout of Manipur Fort, a huge compound that included royal quarters, a polo ground, native villages and a well-stocked arsenal of weapons and explosives.

All the British soldiers, except for a small group of officers, were Gurkhas, the hardy race of hill men from Nepal who, after a hard-fought war against the Raj in 1814–16, had become first an irregular and then accepted arm of the imperial power fighting against the Sikhs in 1849, helping defeat the mutineers at Lucknow in 1857 and taking part in numerous expeditions on the Indian frontiers. The 42nd, 43rd and 44th G.R. were originally the Assam and Sylhet Light Infantry localised in Assam, a regiment that had some of the frontier tribes in its ranks mixed with a large proportion of Gurkhas. British officers in Gurkha regiments were expected to learn Gurkhali and were known to be fiercely loyal to the men under their command. Alban Wilson who served with them in Manipur describes them thus:

Soldiering was the only thing which induced the Gurkha to leave his own hills, for he loves a military life of adventure, besides being keen on all sports and games. They will eat almost anything except beef, yet many of them raise no objection to buffalo, as they say it is not of the cow tribe, and therefore not sacred, but the food they love most of all is fish, and they do not care how high it is. Their great vice is gambling; this, drink and women are the most frequent causes of punishment in a regiment. In spite of their independent character, they are very amenable to discipline ... and bear no ill-will towards any officer who is strict with them, so long as he is just and consistent. Their fighting qualities are too well-known for me to enlarge on them. In seven campaigns I have never known or heard of a Gurkha not standing by his British officer, for one of their proverbs is, 'Is it better to die than live like a coward.[1]

James Willcocks who also fought in the Manipur campaign had this to say about Gurkhas:

The Gurkha's pluck is proverbial, his nature generous, and he will not brook insult or wrong. A Gurkha regiment is a body which most men would sooner fight along with than against. In sickness he is more sullen, and requires less comforts than any Native soldier I have met; he is active beyond all the races of India, and can help himself under difficulties probably better than any fighting man in the world.[2]

The 42nd and 43rd G.R. were armed with Sniders, as stated earlier, the 44th with the Martini-Henry rifle. The .577 Snider-Enfield was a breech loader adopted by the British Army in 1866. It used a metal-cased cartridge called a Boxer (named after its inventor, Colonel Edward Boxer of the Royal Arsenal). Despite later rifles, the Snider had its fans who admired the old gun's stopping power. Kipling eulogised the Snider in his poem, *The Grave of the Hundred Head*:

> A Snider squibbed in the jungle –
> Somebody laughed and fled,
> And the men of the First Shikaris
> Picked up their Subaltern dead,
> With a big blue mark on his forehead
> And the back blown out of his head.

The British used the Snider effectively during the 1868–69 Abyssinian Expedition where it cut down the wild warriors of mad

Emperor Theodore. Generally the rifle had a rate of fire of 10 rounds per minute, was effective to about 600 yards (550m) and had a maximum firing range of 2000 yards (1,800m).

During the mid-1870s the Snider was replaced by the Martini-Henry, which went through four improvements from 1871 to 1889. The weapon used a brass cartridge filled with 85 grains of coarse black powder and was notorious for its heavy recoil on firing that left soldiers with bruised arms and shoulders. Generally it had a rate of fire of 12 rounds per minute, was effective to 400 yards (370m) and had a maximum firing range of 1,900 yards (1,700m). This was the famous infantry weapon of the Zulu War and Gordon Relief Expedition. Indian Army regiments had been given the Martini-Henry as the British Army, always one weapon ahead in sophistication, were given the Lee-Metford rifle.

Gurkhas also fought using their famous curved knives known as kukris. These are essentially chopping tools, but in a Gurkha's hands a kukri becomes one of the world's deadliest weapons. The foot-long (23–36cm) blade is made of sprung steel, held by a bone or hardwood handle. A magnificent slashing weapon, the angle of the blade allows the user to slash as he chops. With a penetrative force disproportionate to its size, the user can inflict deep wounds and easily penetrate bone. For a Gurkha soldier in 1891, as in 2018, the kukri is also functional; it can be used as a smaller knife, an axe and even a shovel.

Facing Skene's troops in the Fort at Imphal were twelve times as many men as he had at his disposal. Less than half of these, however, were regular sepoys, the majority being able-bodied villagers summoned over several days by Tikendrajit. The sepoys wore a mixture of white and red jackets with white turbans and *dhotis* (loin cloths). Some men possibly had green jackets or khaki similar to the Gurkhas (whose regimental uniforms were deep green with black facings, though they fought wearing khaki). Their leather belts, pouches and shoes (if they wore any) were lacquered 'very nicely in black'. Manipuri officers tended to wear comic-opera creations as jackets – blue was a favourite colour – 'with one or two rows of brass buttons on the breast, sometimes additional buttons on the cuffs.' Distinguished officers might wear a specially decorated turban, perhaps with feathers. Bead necklaces were worn, 'the precise number perhaps serving as an indication of rank.'[3] A senior officer might also wear epaulettes.

By 1890 the famous Manipuri light cavalry of the 1820s was a thing of the past. All troops including the villagers rallied by Tikendrajit used the spear, dao or some other kind of sword. Less than half the Manipuri troops had guns but the prince seems to have tried to train them in rifle practice. Their musketry had been noted as being of a fairly high standard for a native army even by the time of the Naga Hills Expedition of 1879. The marksmen were armed with a mixture of weapons, mainly old muskets, but also some Sniders, a few Martinis and a small consignment of the latest Lee-Metford rifles. When the British seized the royal arsenal after the war they found 940,000 rounds of unused ammunition (including 250,000 rounds of British Government issue) and 872,000 percussion caps for muskets, as well as 180 barrels of gunpowder. When the 7-pounders and mountain guns owned by the maharajah are added to this tally it must be concluded that the Manipuris, though far less disciplined than the Gurkhas, were a formidable opponent with excellent fire-power.

To apprehend Prince Tikendrajit, the British had to enter Manipur Fort. It covered a huge area in comparison to the 25 acres of the British residency, which was situated at the south-west corner of the enclosure. The residency itself had very little protection; a mud wall 3 feet high ran around the north, south and west sides of the grounds, though it was 6 feet high on the eastern side where it faced the fort. This wall could absorb bullets, 'but was not loopholed and was never intended to withstand attack.' It was completely commanded by the rampart of the fort to the east. A shallow ditch also ran around the residency grounds, 6 feet deep and 12 yards wide on the sides nearest the city. About a foot of water normally lay in the ditch but in March large stretches were dry. The quarter-guard building at the residency gates was built of brick and two other buildings close by, the school and the hospital, had solid brick foundations.

The great enclosure or *pat* of the fort was an irregular parallelogram. On its western side it ran past the residency compound in a smooth line for another 1,400 yards. The distance on its north and south faces was about half this length. On its eastern flank the fort followed the contours of the Manipur River which flowed in a wobbly 'W' shape at this point. The maharajah's palace, a small part of this huge *pat*, lay close to the river in the short 'peak' of the 'W'. The fort's first line of defence was a wet ditch or 'moat'. It had some water near the residency but was dry for most of its three sides. An earth rampart ran around the enclosure 8 feet high, 'faced on the outside by a brick wall which rose 4 feet about the rampart to form a parapet'. A second moat led to an inner rampart of 8 feet 'also faced with a brick-wall parapet, and small circular bastions providing flanking defence to the inner wall.'[4] This second defence line led into a wide area filled with parkland and a large *bustee* (an area of close-built native huts). Main gates of sun-dried bricks linked these inner and outer enclosures. Tikendrajit's home and personal temple lay in the north-west sector of this second enclosure near the houses of his brothers (excluding the maharajah). The reduit of the fort was called the 'citadel'. It was entered by what was called the 'Lion' Gate (some contemporaries refer to the Dragon Gate), guarded by two weird beasts called '*nongsa*', 10 metres in height and 30 metres outside the gate. They were stone lions and bore 'a remarkable likeness to the Burmese *chinthe*, mythical creatures which guard Burmese pagodas, on which they were presumably modelled.'[5] Once past this gate a visitor would see a polo ground on his right and in the distance, near the actual palace, the durbar hall. The palace was built of brick covered in white plaster. The citadel was built on slightly higher ground than the rest of the *pat*, 150 yards long on each side with small bastions. Its walls were the highest of all, at least 15 feet high, faced on the outside by a brick wall which rose a further 3 feet to form a parapet from which defenders could, if necessary, command the inner or second line of defences. This parapet had a flaw; despite loopholes it was only effective on the north-east, eastern and southern sides as trees and houses obscured the view to the north and north-western end. This was the direction of the princes' enclosure where most of the fighting would take place, though fire could be directed towards it some 500 yards away.

It was known on 24 March that the outer west gate was held by only a small guard of Manipuris. Tikendrajit's home in the enclosure was a thatched house, not unlike the residency. The building was built of wattle and mud like most Manipuri houses. Close by stood a number of smaller buildings, grouped around a brick temple some 50 feet high crowned with a corrugated iron roof.

Skene's plan was relatively simple and sounded, at least on paper, to be effective. Captain Butcher, with Lieutenant Simpson as a guide, was ordered to take 70 soldiers of the 42nd and 44th G.R., cross the ditch where it was dry on the west side of the fort and rush from the south of the enclosure towards Tikendrajit's home, hopefully while the prince was inside and asleep. A second group of 30 Gurkhas under Lieutenant Brackenbury, assisted by Subardar Hima Chand of the 44th G.R., were to go along the entire western wall, turn east and then south into the enclosure by its northern entrance to prevent Tikendrajit from making a fast escape down the Kohima road. The wall at this point 'was in ruins and the moat dry'. Brackenbury's party thus had to go almost a mile to get into position while Butcher's men had barely one quarter of a mile to cover. Once the two groups had set off Lieutenant Lugard with 40 rifles (20 men each of the 42nd and 44th G.R.), was to take up a support position. Fifty men of the 42nd G.R. and 50 more of the 44th, with 100 men, 2 native officers and 2 buglers of the 43rd G.R., forming the Political Agent's guard, were to stay at the residency under Captain Boileau. Slightly outside the residency grounds, and a short distance further away from the fort on its western side, Colonel Skene was in readiness with 100 soldiers kept in reserve. Captain Chatterton with 50 rifles 'was detailed to capture and hold the west gate of the outer enclosure facing the Cachar road and commanding the ground on which the Chief Commissioner's escort was encamped.' Once this was accomplished Chatterton was ordered to keep a strict watch upon the next gate in the inner wall directly facing his men inside the fort. Skene had ordered in the detachment from Sengmai, but his instructions were misunderstood, and only 10 more men arrived. To every sepoy in camp armed with a Snider, 20 extra rounds were served out from the large store at the residency, 10 rounds being left in reserve for an emergency. The 43rd also got extra rounds for their Martinis. In theory all agreed that it seemed a fine plan. 'No one doubted of success,' wrote *The Pioneer* correspondent.

At 4.45am in a cold half-dawn Brackenbury set off. He was followed about 15 minutes later by Butcher's party. All officers had been told by Skene that morning not to fire unless fired upon. Lugard and his 40 men were the last to leave. All the soldiers moved stealthily. They seemed to have no trouble in getting past the Manipuri guards at the west gate who were probably fast asleep.

So much for success. From that point on, everything went wrong. Brackenbury reached the north entrance to the fort where his men saw that many armed Manipuris were on the walls. A soldier with a drawn sword approached him and Brackenbury, perhaps deciding to bluff things out, demanded to know the whereabouts of Tikendrajit. The sentry quite correctly replied that he and associates were servants of the maharajah and advised the British soldiers to withdraw. Brackenbury repeated his demand. This led to a noisy and heated discussion by the Manipuris out of sight on the other side of the wall. Hurriedly, and just in time, the lieutenant ordered his men into an extended firing line as bullets started splattering all around them. The British troops were fired on from the fort and also natives hidden on the other side of the river. Volleys spattered back and forth for some time until about 6am when a heavy gun also opened up on the Gurkhas. The Manipuri firing was intense with bullets kicking up a veritable dust-storm. Brackenbury remained in charge of things until about 8am when he was wounded in the ankle. A havildar and two privates were soon wounded and when Subadar Hemarchand and an orderly, Dhup Chand Thakur, tried to drag away Brackenbury, the native officer was also hit. Three of the Gurkhas (we must assume nearest the compound) were taken prisoner. Despite this heavy fire the British troops successfully fought off a Manipuri attack on their rear just as Butcher launched his attack from the south on Tikendrajit's compound. Skene, of course, had no idea that things were starting to go wrong and he did not hear of Brackenbury's problems until Lieutenant Simpson stumbled back to the residency about 8am and announced to everyone's horror that 'Brackenbury's party were completely surrounded and in dire need of assistance.'

Butcher and his 70 men had entered the fort by crossing the dry ditch and half-ruined wall about 200 yards beyond the west gate. Approaching the princes' compound the captain was challenged in English by a sentry. Failing to reply, the British troops now came under a heavy fire from defenders in the nearby houses as well as

on the walls. Bullets were soon zipping in all directions. Shouting
to a native officer, Butcher ordered 20 men to take up positions
behind the outer wall of the fort and cover the advance of the rest
of his party. In a rush these soldiers inflicted heavy casualties on the
Manipuris as they worked their way, grimly yet steadily, towards
Tikendrajit's house. The fighting was at close quarters with much
bloody use of the bayonet and kukri. Near the prince's thatched
'palace' the Gurkhas came under fire from the inner wall of the
citadel and some men were wounded. They held their ground, the
kukris proving as deadly as their Sniders, until Lugard's support
troops arrived. Then Butcher posted 'a number of rifles along the
wall facing the inner lines of the fort to keep down the attack'.[6]

What happened during this initial assault on Tikendrajit's
compound is not entirely clear. The residency scribe, Rassick Lal
Kundu, later said that British troops 'destroyed idols, mounted
on top of the temple, and polluted it, killed several women and
children and consequently regular fighting commenced on both
sides.'[7] On the following day Maharajah Kula Chandra wrote to
the Viceroy and complained:

A large number of armed troops suddenly entered the palace ...
having killed eleven keepers of the gate, entered the house [of
Tikendrajit], cut the heads off two boys, killed three boys by
shooting. Having entered the temple, smashed the idol and all the
articles with it; set fire to a village in the neighbourhood of the
palace, and having set fire to a Brahmin's house, burnt the idol,
the cows and everything else. Having tied up the hairs of two
girls together, threw them into the fire and got them burnt. One
woman was flying away through the panic, who was seized and
her hands and ears mutilated; she is still alive. The hands and legs
of a man were first cut off, and then he was killed with cruelty.
Although there was so much cruel treatment, we did not act in
opposition, but at last they attacked my palace and set fire to it.
And then when it could not be borne any longer, and my subjects
turned mad and lost my control, they began to fight to protect
their wives and children and religion.[8]

There are inconsistencies in Kula Chandra's remarks and some
actual lies – the British did not attack the palace itself for

instance – but it does seem that some bad behaviour was going on. Buried in the India Office files the present author found a never-before-published letter written three months after the uprising by Major W. Hill commanding 1st/2nd Gurkha Rifles who were then stationed at Imphal. Hill told a friend, Lt-Colonel Ian Hamilton, the Indian Army's Assistant-Adjutant General for Musketry:

> My men are on excellent terms with the Manipuris (men *and women !!),* and the events that took place on the 24th March are pretty well known... The *probable* story is all I will guarantee: on 24th March Captain Butcher was sent to arrest the Jubraj in his house. The chances were fifty to one that he did not find him. Apparently he did not ask for, nor receive, any orders for his next move, so he did nothing... He remained in the Jubraj's enclosure for several hours, *looting! – n*o doubt about it!
>
> They took all the jewels and ornaments and silver cups from the temple, the ponies from the stables, etc. In the meantime the Manipuris began to fire, and the Fort (which up to then had few men in it) began to receive many hundreds of reinforcements from the east gate. If Butcher had advanced 100 yards across a dry ditch and up a small mud wall (not held in force), he could have been master of the situation. Skene could have advanced to the west gate without opposition if Butcher held the north face. However he did nothing. Nobody did anything apparently except the Manipuris and they came swarming into the fort, occupied the west face and north face of the inner enclosure. In the meantime, Brackenbury was missing, and eventually found on the river bank outside the Jubraj's enclosure... Butcher did not know where Brackenbury was, and the two parties were firing their rifles, it is quite possible they fired at one another. Then a desultory sort of fire, with no definite scheme of attack or cohesion went on till dark, or rather till 8pm.[9]

The above letter thus suggests a reason why events with Butcher's party, especially during the early hours of the attack, sound confused in later military accounts. It also suggests quite reasonably that the two groups of Gurkhas, amid all the dust and madness of battle, may have been firing at one another for at least part of the time. A soldier testified after the war that during the assault on Tikendrajit's compound, 'a Muhammedan woman was shot in a hamlet ... two or three children were also hit in the same volley.' We will never know the real details but clearly some atrocities took place.

One thing was sure; there was no sign of Tikendrajit. He may not even have been in his house that night or got away at the first sign of trouble. After the seizure of the temple, shell casings and dead bodies littered the enclosure. Butcher 'placed his wounded, seven in number, in the temple, and sent a detachment to the upper storey to fire volleys against the men holding the bastion and the walls of the inner enclosure of the Pat. This party enfiladed one wall and soon cleared it, and at the same time kept down the fire on the other which was at right angles to them.'[10] Surgeon Calvert described the temple, despite its religious significance to the Manipuris as a holy building, as a *'pukka'* (excellent) place for a dressing station. The doctor had arrived at about 10.30am with Simpson, 50 more troops and hospital orderly Hariban Tiwari, along with two *doolies* (covered litters). It was Butcher who had commandeered the temple as a suitable place to rest his wounded men. The seven injured Gurkhas were bandaged, then given stimulants or opium to alleviate the pain.

No one was quite sure where Brackenbury was or what exactly had happened to him. At great personal risk Surgeon Calvert set off with a *doolie* to look for him. Lieutenant Lugard, meanwhile, had found the wounded *subardar* (senior native officer) of the 44th and also an injured Gurkha private, so he led Calvert to them as the two officers dodged swarms of bullets.

The only British success of the morning had been led by Lieutenant Chatterton who, with 30 Gurkhas, crossed the dry ditch where Butcher had entered the fort and rushed the Manipuris holding the west gate from the rear. This tactic caught them completely unawares. Several men dropped 'panic-stricken' from the parapet onto the roadway where they were shot down by the reserve troops on the nearby camping ground. Chatterton pushed open the fort's heavy wooden gates as the men cheered. Two Manipuris had been killed according to the official report (but this estimate seems low) and 2 native officers and 17 men were captured and led back to the British lines 'and treated very well' (according to Captain Boileau).

Around 10am Colonel Skene, with Frank Grimwood as a guide (who, it must be remembered was not an army officer and under no orders to take part in a military assault), went with a further 80 men from the 42nd and 44th G.R. to assist Butcher and Lugard's troops. They were able to march through the captured west gate and took with them a number of scaling ladders and a further five boxes of ammunition. They found the area between the temple and inner citadel walls was a maze of small alleys and thatched huts giving excellent cover for the Manipuri defenders. The situation now got even worse in this area as 'armed Manipuris in large numbers were seen dropping from the wall of the inner enclosure and plunging down into the bed of a very small winding stream with steep grass-grown banks and sinuous course':

It was at first supposed they were beating a retreat, but on the contrary, they soon re-appeared in the jungle to the eastwards, and from below a long low wall opened a heavy fire. It was some of these, it was believed, who took shots at poor Brackenbury as he lay wounded on the west bank of the river.

Volleys were fired at them from time to time, but these failed to dislodge them. In the neighbourhood of the Regent's [Kula Chandra's] Palace the Senapatti [Tikendrajit] now brought his battery of four 7-pounders into action, firing at his own temple, which was a good mark, being of white masonry, topped by a corrugated iron roof with gilded eaves. The practice was good, as the walls were repeatedly struck, but no serious damage was done. It was difficult to see the exact position of the guns owing to the mud huts and trees about the Palace: the range was probably 500 yards. The shelling continued all the morning, but was intermittent.[11]

Skene realised that Tikendrajit was probably in the palace directing the artillery fire. To storm the building would require crossing a road and shallow ditch in plain view of the defenders' guns before trying to scale walls 15 to 20 feet high. The other alternative seemed to be the storm the gateway of the citadel in a classic *coup de main*. Such an assault seemed out of the question because the British had no explosives or artillery.

Below the guns of the fort Calvert was meanwhile trying to deal with the wounded Gurkhas found lying in the river. The surgeon later praised the way his *kahars* (medical orderlies) crossed a road with bullets fired all around them to get to the wounded, then had to advance under an enfilading fire since there was no shelter. Having done all they could for the injured men the whole group waited patiently. They hoped that when a main assault on the palace was made they would be able to get back to the residency unnoticed. The hours ticked by. About 4.15pm, hearing no news from Butcher, who failed to keep in contact with Calvert, it was decided that an attempt must be made somehow to get back. During this journey that took almost four hours the surgeon met up with Lieutenant Simpson who had been ordered by Skene to clear the left bank of the river with 50 men. Unfortunately, even this sortie had met ill-luck and Simpson felt isolated. The return to the residency had its hazards, as Calvert reported:

> As we were passing some houses to the west of the Polo ground, we saw considerable numbers of villagers standing by. Suddenly a shot was fired from their direction, it was very close, very sudden, and apparently startled everybody. The men of Lt. Simpson's party turned round in a rage, abused people and fired a couple of vollies (*sic*) into the houses before Lt. Simpson could stop them. Lt. Simpson was very angry with the men who belonged to both the 42nd and 44th for firing without orders and wasting ammunition. I noticed that the telegraph wire was cut, and torn down near the Polo ground and within a few hundred yards of the Residency.[12]

Later it was discovered and admitted by the British that Simpson's men had killed three women hiding in the long grass.

Things were not going well at headquarters; some officers noticed that Skene seemed to be getting increasingly despondent. In a conversation with Lieutenant Chatterton he replied that 'we had got into a nice fix.' He said he wished we had brought the guns (from Kohima) as they would have been invaluable and, pointing to the residency, he said, 'I don't know what we are to do, the place is perfectly untenable... We have got no men, we have got no ammunition.'[13]

It seems that Skene advised Quinton that the residency was not a suitable base; he wanted to concentrate all the troops and make a fighting retreat or march to Langthobal. As the two men were debating all of this, a heavy fire suddenly opened up for the first time that day on the residency itself. The rear face of the building was splattered with hundreds of shots zipping into the plaster and crashing through the shutters.

The residency's only female occupant, Ethel Grimwood, had been through a hazardous morning. She had risen early, like the others, and put on a warm, tight-fitting, winter dress. A scratch breakfast followed of eggs and bread and butter at 3.30am. Later in the morning she was unhappy to see Frank going off to war with Skene and it seems likely (being hinted at in her memoirs) that the couple argued. Earlier she had gone with Quinton and Cossins to the residency telegraph office situated down the drive about 300 yards from the main building. Whilst there and just as dawn was fully breaking the trio heard the first shots of the day. Not long after this the Chief Commissioner was about halfway through sending a wire to Calcutta telling the Indian Government of the state of affairs when a bullet smashed into the room, scattering glass from the window and burying itself in the opposite wall. Ethel's heart 'went to [her] mouth with fright'. Later that morning, as she and Quinton stayed protected to some extent by the building's stone basement, Cossins made several trips to the residency roof to see what was happening at the palace but had no success. Some of the Gurkhas kept running outside the residency gate to see what was going on, but they had no more luck than poor Cossins. Then the telegraph was cut so all contact with the outside world was lost. Finally Ethel and Quinton returned to the residency where Mrs Grimwood, every inch an Englishwoman, decided that everything would be better after a nice cup of tea. She had been cutting bread for sandwiches when the midday fusillade began.

It took a time to organise a party of Gurkhas who could remove the Manipuris infiltrating the residency grounds via the Naga village which lay near the river. Eventually, about 1pm, soldiers sallied forth under Captain Boileau. They set fire to the Naga huts and drove the attackers back at the point of the bayonet and kukri. Frank Grimwood tried to get his wife down to the basement for safety but Ethel refused. She was nevertheless 'heartbroken' to see the state of the place – 'The windows were broken, and every now and then bullets crashed into the rooms, smashing different things – first a picture, then a vase, then a photograph. All my beloved household goods seemed coming to grief under my very eyes.'[14]

About 4pm word was sent to Captain Butcher to withdraw his men back to the residency. It was around this time that Brackenbury was finally discovered lying badly wounded on the west bank of the river that flowed north of the palace, 'though how he had managed to crawl so far will never be known.'[15] The Manipuris were able to fire at will along this stretch. Into this hailstorm of bullets went *Naik* (Corporal) Singhia Lama and Sepoy Jaimana Thapa of the 42nd G.R. with *Havildar* (Sergeant) Dhup Chand of the 44th G.R. These brave Gurkhas went down the bank, lifted up Brackenbury, tied a rope around him, and by hauling and lifting carried him along. Occasionally they had to pause to catch their breath while bullets peppered the ground all round them. Eventually they got to the temple where it was seen that poor Brackenbury now had six wounds. After getting Skene's orders to withdraw, Butcher started back with his men carrying the British officer, a *jemadar* (an Indian officer equivalent to a lieutenant), a havildar and seven more wounded sepoys. It would be close to 8pm when this band arrived back at the residency, tired and dusty. A few minutes later, Calvert, Simpson and his band also staggered into the grounds. Brackenbury was too weak to say much. Condemning his suffering the C-in-C, India, General Roberts, later stressed 'his especial regret that from 6am until the afternoon no effectual effort was made to reinforce Lieutenant Brackenbury's party or to rescue this gallant young officer and his wounded comrades from their isolated and perilous position.'[16]

During that late afternoon it seems that Calvert and Simpson had been forgotten by Skene and Quinton, 'a severe lapse in duty'. Chatterton holding the main gate was also told to withdraw. He was not impressed explaining later that 'It had been Colonel Skene's intentions to hold the main gate permanently and to occupy the palace wall behind the wet moat in front of the Residency; and orders were given to Captain Boileau to make bamboo rafts to enable men to cross the moat. These rafts were made from green male bamboo, no other materials being available; but they were useless, as green male bamboo does not float.'[17]

It is clear in hindsight that Skene had in his mind to bring all the British troops into the residency and possibly plan a major fighting retreat. Yet by giving up the west gate he severely weakened the defences in that direction. It was a foolish blunder. Clearly the enemy would not let this chance to dominate the residency grounds as well as the camping ground go amiss. From the west gate and walls nearby they would be able to fire at will on the British buildings and troops – which is exactly what they did.

Within minutes of the Gurkhas evacuating the west gate it was retaken by the Manipuris, who now placed two heavy guns facing the residency. Soon shells were whistling across the grounds and hitting the building. Everyone made hastily for the cellars where a rough hospital was created. Sheets and blankets were dragged down from the bedrooms. Most of the shells ended harmlessly in the lawn or in the lake with a splash. The tanks and ornamental waters were churned into foam. Exhausted and dejected, Skene, with Quinton, now seemed to lose the will to fight or even dream up a new strategy. Skene especially needed time to think, to re-charge his batteries, but he was winded. There was no time. Later the Adjutant-General of the Indian Army, Major-General W. Galbraith, would castigate Skene and the valuable hours 'lost in indecision; and even when it was resolved to concentrate for defence, there was inexplicable delay and want of concerted action.'[18]

About 7.30pm Frank Grimwood managed to arrange for a ceasefire to be sounded by one of the buglers. This was played several times. Finally a shout came from the fort. It was a taunt, at once insulting, swaggering and apt: 'You came to fight us,' yelled a Manipuri, 'now you want to stop. Are you women and children?'[19] Fifteen minutes later a gong sounded from the fort. The firing died down and finally ceased.

Now the remaining wounded could be taken down to the makeshift hospital in the cellar. The Gurkhas and their British officers had been fighting without a break for 14 hours. Nerves were shattered. People were exhausted, dehydrated and starving. For a few minutes all were happy just to bask in the silence. It had been a day of awful disasters. Few could have imagined that the coming hours of darkness would unleash on them all horrors beyond their imagination.

Night of Horrors

A blood-red sun slowly fell in the western sky. Ethel Grimwood later recalled how its strange glow seemed to illuminate the landscape and the faces of her husband and Colonel Skene, who were talking in low tones in the cellar doorway, their faces a mix of physical exertion and despair. The brick basement was now filled with people including the Grimwoods, Quinton, Skene, Cossins and Gurdon. In a letter to one of Frank's family she described the scene:

> I pray that I may never see such a sight again. There were crowds of them: some dying. Poor Mr Brackenbury was the first, shot all over, both legs broken, both arms, bullets in him all over the place; and yes, poor lad, he was alive and perfectly conscious the whole time, and in awful agony. I did what I could to help, but it seemed almost impossible to do anything. In one corner was a poor fellow with his brain shot out on the top of his head, and yet alive. Another with his forehead gone, and many others worse. Luckily, I am rather strong-minded and so I was able to help in bathing some of the wounds and bandaging them up.[1]

Surgeon Calvert moved among the wounded doing his best to work with the aid of one dimmed lantern. He was later full of praise for Ethel's ability to remain strong and help the injured men:

> The brave woman had been under fire all day, her own room had been wrecked by shell fire. She came down amongst the wounded,

after herself preparing soup, beef-tea, etc and administered it to them, having been without food all day. This enabled the medical officer and the hospital assistant to dress the wounded and begin operating.[2]

Sometime after 7pm Frank Grimwood had gotten a few minutes alone with his wife and told her that the plan was to evacuate the residency and make a fighting retreat towards Cachar and the expected 43rd Gurkha troops of Captain Cowley. While Ethel was digesting this news, a further consultation was held between Quinton and his advisers; it was decided to send a letter to the palace asking for terms. The Chief Commissioner argued strongly that the troops should remain; Captain Butcher later testified that Quinton felt a withdrawal would be 'a terrible political disaster'. It was while a letter was being drafted that the cease fire had been sounded. Quinton signed the document which said simply: 'On what condition will you cease firing on us, and give us time to communicate with the Viceroy and repair the telegraph?'

A Manipuri (Keen states that this was one of the prisoners, Mrs Grimwood says it was a soldier called from off the wall of the fort) agreed to take the letter to the palace under a flag of truce. On reflection it might seem astonishing, but the Chief Commissioner's letter was written in English and not Bengali or Methei. When it was opened by Tikendrajit he remarked to one of his Top Guard officers named Lukramba: 'I cannot read this; but if the sahibs want to stop fighting let them give up the prisoners they captured this morning in my compound and let them come to a durbar to talk matters over.'[3] Lukramba was quickly despatched to the residency with a verbal message inviting Quinton for talks. A farce of sorts now took place at the palace where Kula Chandra and his ministers passed around the Chief Commissioner's note but none of them could read English. Eventually a Bengali court secretary, Bamon Mukherjee, was able to read and explain its contents. The maharajah drafted a reply. This arrived back at the residency not long after Lukramba had delivered his invitation for talks.

By this time Quinton, Skene, Cossins and Grimwood had gone down the residency drive to await events at the Resident's office near the gate. Lieutenants Chatterton and Simpson followed a few minutes later. Ethel asked Frank if she might come, but 'he said I was safer where I was, and bade me goodbye, telling me to have a brave heart, that the firing was at an end and peace about to be restored.'[4] He also told Ethel that she looked terribly tired, 'and should try and get some rest.' Whether or not the pair kissed in the moonlight Ethel does not say, but with so many other people around this would not have been the done thing. The British observed the proprieties and norms of class behaviour even when facing death. Thus with that famous stiff upper lip, Frank Grimwood parted from his wife. Their relationship may have had its ups and downs, as we will examine in a later chapter, but clearly there was a deep attachment between the couple. She would never see him again.

The palace farce now went into its second act at the residency where Cossins and Grimwood worked on the Bengali translation; the maharajah had written that he understood the British wanted to stop fighting, which was agreeable to him, but if they laid down their arms in one minute, then his troops would not resume hostilities. The two civil servants now argued over the exact meaning of the Bengali phrase, *'jadi astra shastra pheliya deba'*; Cossins thought it meant 'surrender arms', while Grimwood held out for 'cease fire'. It was a tricky matter of context.

Historians cannot agree on whether it was Grimwood, 'in a move that appeared to defy all rational thought', (Keen) or Quinton, 'under the mistaken impression that the Jubraj [Tikendrajit] was at the west gate' (Parratt & Parratt), who suggested going outside the residency grounds towards the fort's west entrance. Quinton did ask Grimwood if he thought it was safe. Frank, ever the optimist, replied that it was. After all, he knew the Manipuris and was not Tikendrajit his friend? He asked Lukramba to take an oath of safe conduct and the Manipuri officer replied in his own language, 'Why should we harm you, who are like gods to us?' (Chatterton later recorded this as 'Why should we harm you who are our God?') Lanky Lieutenant Simpson, his young good looks catching the moonlight, then turned to Quinton and said, 'Will you come out, sir – we think terms can be made as the Jubraj [Tikendrajit] says he has had enough of it, and that he will meet you on the road.'[5] These were positive words and probably welcomed by the Chief Commissioner although they were quite misleading and Simpson really had no idea – none of them did – if Prince Tikendrajit was ready to stop fighting. Quinton, Cossins and Grimwood now set off for the palace gate. Frank had already asked Simpson to tag along. Then, almost as an afterthought, Colonel Skene remarked that he 'might as well go too'. The five men set off slowly, the moon above showing the way although it kept disappearing behind banks of clouds. Following behind was just one Gurkha, a bugler named Gunna Ram of the 44th G.R.

Before setting off the group divested themselves of their swords and pistols. One modern Methei historian, writing on the web, sees this as a sign of British arrogance, but most people might view the act as one of submission and conciliation, not to say foolishness. Later Quinton, Grimwood and the others would be severely criticised by the British Government for going to the meeting unarmed. Yet bearing in mind that they had no reason to expect foul play at this stage – it was, after all, a meeting on the road – is it fair to blame them? Even later, taken deep inside the citadel and passing through several sets of gates, they could not have fought their way out. The simple fact is that Quinton was hoping his show of peace might impress the Manipuris.

The party walked in silence. About 10 yards from the west gate a palace official, Hoabam Dewan, came out to greet them before disappearing inside to announce their arrival to Tikendrajit. 'The night was clear, with few clouds, and the faces of the group near the gate and the Manipuri sepoys on the wall were clearly visible to those watching from the Treasury Gate in the Residency.'[6] Lieutenant Chatterton ordered a soldier to take a few chairs over to the group, but the Gurkha was turned back by the Manipuris because he had a rifle slung over his shoulder. Chatterton saw a court official, Nilamani Singh, known as the Ayapurel, talking with the British officers. Several other Manipuris joined them.

The parley lasted two hours. We have no idea of what was said exactly but the debate was clearly an intense one on both sides. The Manipuris no doubt accused the British of an unprovoked attack on the palace and we must assume that Quinton and Grimwood tried their best to defend the position of the Indian Government. Suddenly there was a shout and the watchers from the residency gate saw the small party move forward and into the fort. It happened in seconds and came as a nasty surprise, yet the British had clearly entered the enemy enclosure of their own accord.

Watchers saw the gate clang ominously shut. 'Time went on and we began to feel anxious and we watched the fort gate for any signs of our party returning,' wrote Gurdon. 'Still all remained quiet, and we could not tell what was going on.'[7] Sometime around midnight, while Chatterton and Gurdon waited anxiously, a voice yelled from the wall of the fort, 'The Chief Commissioner will not return.' Within seconds from the walls erupted a blazing line of fire from hundreds of rifles. Ducking and diving this line of flame, bullets zipping all around them, the British officers headed back to the residency building.

What had happened to the six men who entered the fort? It would take weeks for the full story to emerge. Many facts remain jumbled to this day. Let us try and unravel this mystery.

The west gate was commanded by Prince Angao Senna. The cease fire came as a relief, it seems, for this young man, happy that the British wanted to parley. One of those less pleased was the old Thangal General; in bad health and quite grumpy he arrived at the gate and made it plain that he did not think it fitting 'to hold a durbar at night and certainly not while hostilities were still going on.'[8] The prince and the Yenkoba Major, another high state official, reminded the general that Tikendrajit had invited the British inside the fort and no harm could come to them. The old man refused to change his opinion and advised Prince Angao Senna not to get involved. Clearly uneasy in the presence of one who had served his father and grandfather with distinction, the young prince melted away from the scene as the Ayapurel arrived with orders to conduct the British to the durbar hall.

Once the west gate had shut behind them the British briefly shook hands with the Thangal General and Colonel Maisnam Samu Singh, known as the Luwang Ningthou. The whole party then walked in the darkness, their path lit by burning torches, some 200 yards to the inner west gate and a further 500 yards to the great stone lions guarding the Lion Gate near the durbar hall. It was by the steps of this building that things began to go wrong; the Ayapurel found that the doors were locked and the Keeper of the Keys could not be found. The Ayapurel made some apologies and went to look for chairs. A few minutes later Prince Tikendrajit arrived to find the British officers and Thangal General seated by the steps. He joined them though his advisers including the

Above: Frank St Clair Grimwood, Ethel's husband and the British Resident in Manipur.

Right: Ethel St Clair Grimwood – a studio portrait taken after her return from India as she is wearing her Royal Red Cross medal.

Below: The British Residency at Imphal.

Above left: Major-General Sir James Johnstone – one of Grimwood's predecessors as Resident and Prince Tikendrajit's enemy.

Above right: Every inch a prince – Tikendrajit Bir Singh, Senapati and Jubraj of Manipur.

Johnstone seated with Tikendrajit and other Manipuri leaders at Kohima during the 1879 Naga campaign.

Right: Maharajah Kula Chandra.

Below: A rare photo of the Resident's Gurkha escort drawn up on the lawn during Johnstone's time (courtesy the Alkazi Collection of Photography).

Government House, Calcutta.

Above left: A true patrician – Henry Charles Keith Petty-Fitzmaurice, 5th Marquess of Lansdowne, Viceroy of India, 1888–1894.

Above right: Lansdowne as caricatured by 'Ape' aka C. Pellegrini in *Vanity Fair* magazine.

Below: Loathed by many but quite liked by Lord Lansdowne – Viceregal Lodge, Simla, the Viceroy's summer headquarters.

Right: Maud, Marchioness of Lansdowne, a great hostess and true blue blood, a daughter of the Duke of Hamilton.

Below: Lansdowne with his Council. Second from left is Sir Andrew Scoble, between him and the Viceroy sits General Sir Frederick Roberts, on Lansdowne's left sits General Chesney.

Left: A wood engraving of Ethel Grimwood.

Below: The Residency seen from across its lake or, as some officers called it, 'the duck pond'.

Above left: The ill-fated Chief Commissioner of Assam, James Wallace Quinton.

Above right: Colonel Charles McDowell Skene – an engraving based on a portrait of him as a younger man.

MAJOR C. W. GRANT, V.C.
(*Photo: C. G. Brown, Bangalore.*)

Above left: Lieutenant Walter Henry Simpson.

Above right: Lieutenant Charles Grant V.C.

Above: Lieutenant, later Major, Edward Lugard, a portrait from his old age.

Right: Sir Mortimer Durand, Foreign Secretary to the Government of India, 1885–1894.

Below: The Imphal Residency guarded by Gurkhas on 23 March 1891.

The west gate of the palace at Imphal.

Right: Fighting during the retreat from Manipur.

Below: The Residency on fire.

Above left: Ethel as portrayed in the *Illustrated London News*.

Above right: Major-General Sir Henry Collett, professional soldier and keen amateur botanist.

A sketch of the Kohima column.

A typical bridge of the kind that had to be traversed by the Grimwoods on their travels and also faced by the invading troops.

Above: A stockaded post in the Manipur hills – note the defence of sharp pointed stakes.

Right: An Angami Naga warrior.

A polo match in Manipur.

Fighting the Manipuris.

Above: The *nongsa* guarding the durbar hall within the palace compound.

Right: Richard, 1st Viscount Cross, Secretary-of-State for India, the wise old politician who had the difficult task of defending the actions of Lansdowne in the British Parliament as well as soothing the mood of his Sovereign.

Prince Tikendrajit looking haughty as usual, despite being under arrest. (Courtesy of the Alkazi Collection of Photography)

Kula Chandra and the Thangal General (seated) during a break in the trial proceedings. (Courtesy of the Alkazi Collection of Photography)

Above left: Intelligent and inscrutable, Colonel John Ardagh, military secretary to Lord Lansdowne as Viceroy, author of a shocking top secret report.

Above right: Alan Boisragon, Ethel Grimwood's step-brother and, according to gossip, her lover.

Right: Queen Victoria, Empress of India. She met Ethel Grimwood at Windsor Castle on 1 July 1891 and was impressed by her beauty and grace. In her journal she wrote, 'Poor thing. I pity her so much!'

Above left: The Queen with her munshi or Indian teacher, Abdul Karim, shown here talking with one of the royal household, Sir Arthur Bigge.

Above right: The new maharajah who was appointed after the rebellion: Chura Chand.

Below: The memorial at Imphal to Quinton, Grimwood and the others killed during the rebellion.

Angom Ninthou and Mia Major, an army commander, remained standing. One person conspicuous by his absence was Maharajah Kula Chandra who was to claim later that he had no idea that the British were inside his palace that night.

By the time everyone was seated a large crowd of Manipuri sepoys and citizens had gathered to watch events. Their prince was, as ever, plain-spoken; Tikendrajit said that he had been willing to surrender himself to Quinton but had been prevented due to illness. Now the actions of the British in attacking the palace in an unprovoked manner made him unable to trust their intentions. They might attack again. Under the circumstances he could only treat with them if they laid down their arms. The Chief Commissioner argued that 'what had happened had happened'. The soldiers with him were those of the Queen-Empress and he could not command them to disarm. He suggested that they all meet on the next morning and try and resolve the impasse. After some minor conversation the meeting broke up. It had lasted barely 20 minutes.

Clearly concerned at the size of the growing crowd who had watched apparently in silence, Frank Grimwood asked the Angom Ninthou, whose name was Giridhani Singh, to see them safely to the west gate. This officer asked Tikendrajit for confirmation and the prince replied, 'Certainly, see them out.' The five Europeans and the Nepalese bugler were now hemmed in on all sides by a crowd of several hundred. Slowly the group edged towards the Lion Gate. Then an inexplicable thing happened, an event destined to change everything; without any warning and just as the visitors reached the gate it was suddenly shut in their faces.

Cries of 'Kill them' were heard and within seconds the situation had turned ugly. Mob fury is highly combustible and can explode quickly and without warning. Many of the Manipuris inside the fort that night had fought the British troops earlier in the day, they had seen a temple polluted, their idols overthrown, houses burned and looted, women and children killed. The British, in their eyes, had insulted their god-king at the residency durbar before launching an unprovoked attack on the royal compound. Now these foreigners, the men who gave the orders, were within their grasp. So the flash-fury of the mob exploded into a cry for vengeance.

Jostled and punched, hemmed in on all sides so tightly that they could not raise their arms, the British were hit with rifle butts, sticks and flying stones. The Angom Ninthou and Mia Major led the party back towards the durbar building. At first the two Manipuri courtiers had tried to talk restraint to the mob but calming words had no effect. During this slow retreat the Chief Commissioner was struck heavily on the arm and Lieutenant Simpson received a severe sword cut to his head and another blow on an arm. Sticks and stones rained down from all sides amid the shouts and general babble.

Bringing up the rear in this violent melee was Frank Grimwood. Just as the Resident reached the bottom of the durbar steps he was pushed violently by a Manipuri and as he righted himself a second man, a sepoy named Kajao Pokramba Phingang, thrust a spear upwards through Grimwood's back towards his heart. With a cry he toppled over, then either crawled, or was helped by the Mia Major to the space underneath the steps. Here the Manipuri official gave Grimwood some water in his dying moments. The bloodied and dazed Simpson, loyal to the last, crawled in by his friend and lay gasping, his clothes soaked in blood.

Quinton, Cossins and Skene were at the top of the durbar steps facing a howling mob. They quickly found that the doors were still locked. Defending them at the base of the steps were two court officials, the Angom Ninthou and Lokendra Birgit Singh, known as the Wangkheirakpa, with a servant of the maharajah's, forty-nine-year-old Jatra Singh. The noise had by this time reached the Top Guard area of the palace and Tikendrajit now returned in some fury; using a stick he struck about at the rioters and told them to disperse. While this was happening Jatra Singh put his back to the durbar hall doors and managed to break into the building. The four dazed Britons and their bugler stumbled inside. Speaking briefly with Quinton, Tikendrajit realised that his two friends, Grimwood and Simpson, were underneath the steps of the building. With the Angom Ninthou following, he ran back to help them. What Tikendrajit must have thought when he saw the body of Frank Grimwood, unconscious or dead, one can only try and imagine; it must have been almost incomprehesnible to him. With the Angom's help he dragged out poor Simpson and they carried him into the durbar hall. Ordering the Angom Ninthou to guard the sahibs well, he strode off to the Top Guard post.

Safe at last, at least temporarily, the bloodied and shocked four Europeans and their Nepali bugler were able to try to take stock of their situation. They had in a few brief minutes become the prisoners of the Manipuris and potential bargaining chips in any negotiations. A bad situation had turned inexplicably worse while one of their number had been murdered. Quinton still managed to remain outwardly calm. He took out a notebook and wrote down the name of Jatra Singh, apparently the only Manipuri who understood Hindustani, and who had brought them all water and washed Simpson's wounds, even using his turban to bandage the British officer's sword-cut and staunch the flow of blood running down his boyish face. Outside the rioters began to disperse. The whole shocking incident had lasted just 20 minutes. Beneath the building, in the dirty crawl space below the steps, Frank Grimwood lay dead.

It appears that Tikendrajit quickly set off to tour some of the palace's defences fearing that at any minute the British might launch an attack once it was realised that the Chief Commissioner's party would not be returning that night. The Angom Ninthou also went to the Top Guard building and ordered additional sepoys to guard the durbar hall. After he had left, an officer called Usurba, a man in his mid-forties, was summoned by the Thangal General who was sitting in the Top Guard. Curtly the tough old warrior who had ordered many deaths in his long career, said, '*Sahibloki machil tupchillo,*' or 'Shut the mouths of the sahibs' – in other words, 'Kill them!' Usurba, to his credit, refused to follow out this order without confirmation that it stemmed from Prince Tikendrajit. After a rebuke and Usurba's persistence, the Thangal General told him to fetch the prince. On the way Usurba met Jatra Singh and told him that he was expected to kill the British. Jatra was deeply alarmed and joined Usurba in his hunt for Tikendrajit. He was discovered supervising a gun emplacement on the south wall. Told of the order to kill, the prince replied: 'Did the old man really give such a command? Do no such thing; they are not to be harmed in any way. Wait, I am coming.' Usurba returned to the Top Guard and told the general what Tikendrajit had said. His response was instant and dismissive, yet demonstrated a hard streak of cold reason too. Describing the prince as 'a fool', the Thangal General added: 'We can never remain friends with the sahibs after this.'[9]

Tikendrajit looked in on his captives before proceeding to the Top Guard. Here he confronted the Thangal General. 'Ipou (grandfather), why did you order the sahibs to be killed?' he asked. The old man repeated his opinion that it was too late to turn back and the events of the past 18 hours made it impossible for the British and the Manipuris to be friends any longer. It was the old argument of a soldier – too late to turn back so better to strike hard and to hell with the consequences. Contemptuously he told the young prince: 'You are only a boy. I have served here for many years. We shall drive the Sirkar's (Viceroy's) people into the sea'[10] (some accounts say 'to Cachar'). Tikendrajit was intelligent enough to know something of the might of the British Raj. He replied honestly, 'It cannot be done,' then added that the whole matter would have to discussed in the morning with the maharajah. Still suffering from sickness and probably as exhausted as his prisoners – he had, after all, had little rest for many hours – the prince lay down and fell asleep.

Back in the durbar room Quinton used his pocket-book again and pencilled a message – 'We are in a trap, they want us to make over our arms.'[11] He gave this note to a guard (one assumes with a bribe), but it never reached the residency. Ten more dramatic minutes ticked by. Then Abungchao Yenkoiba, an officer designated to watch over the prisoners, was ordered to attend on the Thangal General who was preparing to go to his house for the night. Angrily the frail old man asked why the sahibs had still not been executed and claimed the order came from Tikendrajit. Back in the durbar hall Jatra Singh heard Yenkoiba tell a guard that the Thangal General had commanded that the prisoners be handed over to the state executioners. A horrified Jatra went off to look for Usurba and report this latest development.

Yenkoiba found the officer in charge of the executioners and ordered him to bring along his men. The fellow turned up with just one man carrying his dao and was promptly sent away to find some more. In the meantime a blacksmith, Tangjaba Yaima, arrived and fixed iron fetters to the feet of the prisoners, though their hands were allowed to be free. Did Quinton and the others realise that they were about to die? Probably not. They knew that prisoners were usually kept in chains and were most likely expecting to be taken to a filthy prison cell.

What actually happened next must have come as a terrible shock to Quinton, Cossins, Skene, Simpson and Gunna Ram. Heavily fettered, one by one, they were led down the steps of the durbar hall, stumbling and shuffling in their clinking iron chains, some 20 yards to the Lion Gate, then on to the spot where the stone lions, or *nongsa*, crouched. Here the public executioner, Sagolsemba Dhono Singh was waiting with a massive *tendong-thang* (long-handled sword) gleaming in the moonlight. Simpson was so weak from loss of blood that he had to be supported by one of the sepoys. A small crowd stood watching and its members remained silent, awed by the spectacle of ritual execution. Sagolsemba faced north while the prisoners were made to stand looking west. One by one they were beheaded as the huge blade was swung with a swish and blood splattered over the hideous stone beasts. Two of the victims needed two strokes each to sever their heads. What each victim thought in his last few moments is too horrible to be imagined. Witnesses said all five men went to their deaths bravely – there were no pleas for mercy, no hysterical scenes. Possibly they were so exhausted that they barely had time to comprehend what was happening. Dimly they may have realised that their deaths would be avenged. The little Gurkha was killed last. Finally, as if part of some macabre show, Frank Grimwood's body was dragged out from underneath the durbar steps and placed with the others so that he too could be decapitated.

Two priests by tradition had to decide where enemies should be buried after beheading. They made incantations and the executioners quickly buried the heads. All the time the crowd had watched in silence. Some of them may have been aware of a superstition in ancient scriptures of 'Puyat' – that the country would attain peace and prosperity when a white man's head would fall in front of the twin lions. After an hour blood was scraped off the grass, and the headless trunks were taken away. To the Manipuris the dead men were unclean, impure and untouchable, so the corpses were dragged away by ropes tied on the legs. So as not to desecrate the west gate they were dragged over a rampart and taken to a ditch north of the bazaar near a Naga village. All six men were buried in their clothes but their feet had to be lopped off to remove the fetters. The night was now very dark, the moon obscured by a bank of clouds. Returning to the palace the burial party of executioners and slaves saw flames rising high into the air from the residency compound...

After Frank had left, Ethel sat mournfully in thought for a few minutes until roused into action by Surgeon Calvert. She began by dishing out some more of the soup she had made on the previous evening. Fresh milk there was none but she had plenty of tins of the condensed variety. The wounded were grateful for her ministrations, especially Lieutenant Brackenbury who was very thirsty and in great pain. He gulped the soup, his face bathed in sweat. Calvert worked quietly with forceps and scalpel using as little light as possible for fear that his ministrations might be noticed by the Manipuris. Mrs Grimwood managed to provide a dinner of sorts to all in the building. Afterwards she sat for a time in the residency drawing-room with Captain Boileau, mixing bottles of water with condensed milk for the wounded downstairs. By this time the moans had grown quieter, even Brackenbury was dozing, only one man was crying out and he was mortally wounded in the head.

Ethel tried to go to her bedroom for a doze but found that a shell had crashed through the roof and the room was a wreck. She stepped out onto the verandah:

I went down the steps and stood outside in the moonlight for a few minutes. It was a lovely night, clear and bright as day! One could scarcely imagine a more peaceful scene. The house had been greatly damaged, but this was not apparent in the moonlight and the front had escaped the shells which had gone through the roof and burst all round us at the back. The roses and the heliotrope smelt heavily in the night air, and a cricket or two chirped merrily as usual in the creepers on the walls. I thought of the night before, and of how my husband and I had walked together up and down in the moonlight talking of what the day was to bring ... and I remembered the poor lad lying wounded in the cellar below now, who only twenty-four hours earlier had been the life and soul of the party, singing comic songs with his banjo, and looking forward eagerly to the chances of fighting that might be his when the morning came. I wondered where my husband was, and why they had been away so long... Captain Boileau came out, and I asked him if he would mind going down to the gate and finding out whether he could hear or see anything of the Chief Commissioner's party, and if he came across any of them to say I wanted my husband. He went off at once, and I fell into a doze in the chair.[12]

Ethel did not recall how long she slept but about midnight her brief reverie was broken by the 'deafening boom' of the Manipuri big guns. Another furious fusillade followed, sweeping the compound. 'Nothing could live before that fire except under the cover of the low wall,'[13] recalled Captain Butcher. The cannon started knocking huge chunks out of some of the residency buildings. All around the noise seemed to shake the very ground. Incredibly, only one officer, Lieutenant Lugard, and a bearer, were hit in this uproar – and both men were wounded only slightly.

Later there would be some dispute among the Manipuris as to who had ordered the hostilities to re-commence. Prince Tikendrajit claimed that he had been fast asleep and was woken by the gunfire. Prince Angou Senna tried to get the gunners to stop but was told that the order came from Tikendrajit, so he stayed at his post to supervise the shelling.

Back at the residency all the officers guessed, as Gurdon later put it, that the Chief Commissioner and the rest of his party had been 'treacherously captured'. He claimed that 'We wished at all risks to attempt a rescue, but the Manipuris assumed the offensive so strongly that it was all we could do to hold our position.'[14] There were 17 injured soldiers, a large group of followers and a white woman to consider. Ammunition was also low and it was clear that they could not hold out much longer. Gurdon's words hint at the uncertainty and demoralisation in the British command. Nothing had been done during the ceasefire to muster the troops or divide the line of defence into sections commanded by British officers. Almost 24 hours of physical activity and mental strain were developing 'a sense of confusion among the troops and indecision among the officers'. Captain Boileau in particular, the senior captain, 'had neither the sense of authority nor the vigour to command the support of the other officers, nor the singleness of mind to make a clear decision himself.'[15]

Around 12.30am on the morning of the 25th Lieutenant Chatterton, Skene's staff officer, called Boileau to a huddled meeting of all the officers since most of them wanted to leave the residency and make a fighting retreat. Boileau refused to take charge and said he would abide by the decision of the majority. Lugard and Chatterton both felt that the residency could be defended but, after some discussion, only the former officer refused to alter this opinion. Taking up a position in the open, all agreed, was impracticable. Boileau asked for a vote to be taken; only Lugard voted to stay and all the rest favoured a forced march towards Cachar.

Apart from bringing up some heavy guns the Manipuris had also stealthily crept into the residency grounds at some places during the ceasefire. Now, from vantage points much closer to the main building than ever before, they kept up a steady and unrelenting fire. This latest development started to see cohesion and discipline wither in the ranks. Captain Butcher explained:

> The men were utterly demoralised after being subjected to such a heavy artillery and infantry fire at a close range for such a long time without the hope of being able to return it with any effect. Men fallen in would not remain in the ranks, but tried to seek shelter. Some were actually found outside the compound wall before the retreat and had to be ordered back... The men were so unnerved that they would not go up into the Residency verandah where the ammunition was stored, to bring it down. I had to ascend myself and drag the boxes down, open them and issue, which I did with the help of Lieutenant Woods, Assistant Commissioner.[16]

Woods himself later said that the attack could not be pressed because of 'paucity of men and the ammunition just running out.' He estimated the attackers at 6,000 men. When he left the residency at 2am the fire was so hot that it clearly unnerved him as he admitted later: 'My first baptism of fire has been a severe one, and I hope never to see another with such fearful results to our arms. Had we remained in the residency I do not think there would be a man alive now.'[17]

Since the Manipuris knew the sequence of British bugle calls, Boileau and Chatterton agreed to go around the residency compound walls in separate directions to collect all the

Gurkhas together. This plan soon fell apart; it was assumed that the troops would make their way to the Cachar road and assemble there in good order, but those on the south wall withdrew in such haste that the enemy entered the compound before the full evacuation had been complete. This led to complete disorder.

Matters were made worse by Chatterton who told some soldiers, 'We have no ammunition. Try to save your lives.' Boileau led the advance party, stumbling through a gap in the wall, across some rough ground and over the river, where Manipuris fired at them from a village on the opposite bank. Once past this spot Boileau halted his unit and counted 165 Gurkhas.

He later stated that 'As the men were in a very disorganised state, and as I hoped the remainder of the men were coming along, I went on slowly.'[18]

Within the residency, as outside along the compound perimeter, confusion took hold once the order to retreat became clear. Calvert started by trying to get his wounded out of the cellar and onto the back lawn. Brackenbury was the first of the wounded to be moved. 'Simply riddled with bullets', as Woods described him, the young officer screamed in agony and begged to be left where he was. The shock and exertion killed him within a few minutes and he was carried inside again. Ethel Grimwood wrote how 'it made one's heart ache to leave that young lad lying there dead, alone in the darkened cellar.'[19] She wrapped a sheet over his body and made ready to depart herself. At lunchtime she had changed out of her winter gown into a blue serge skirt and white blouse with stockings and thin patent-leather slippers. There was no time to change again and so she set off in these light clothes already covered in grime.

'Outside the noise was deafening,' wrote Ethel, shells 'kept striking the trees and knocking off the branches.' Bustle and confusion was everywhere, servants 'knocking each other over in their eagerness to make good their escape.'[20] For a moment Mrs Grimwood thought she had been forgotten, but an officer approached to lead her away. Six yards after walking onto the lawn a shell exploded knocking branches off a tree and wounding Ethel in the arm. She lost the officer and for a few moments was paralysed with fear. Then, sensing others around her heading for the river, she joined them in flight.

One of the last to leave the residency building was Captain Butcher in charge of some Gurkhas and a few doolies. He did not find Boileau and the main body of men until they were a quarter of a mile from the residency. It was a little after 2am as Calvert and the wounded escaped over the moat at the back of the compound. The survivors now set off in the dark towards the south-west with the hope that they might meet up along the Cachar road with the 200 men of Captain Cowley's contingent who were believed to be coming from that direction.

'It was no easy matter to get on the Cachar road,' wrote Ethel in her memoirs. The residency gardens had some high thorn hedges after which there was a mud wall, quite low, but with a 6-foot drop on the far side. She was debating how to deal with this last obstacle when someone gave her a gentle push, 'as a sort of warning that I was stopping the traffic,' and she slid down the muddy bank into the arms of a friendly native. Crossing the Manipur River at night was also daunting since no one was sure of its depth. Calvert caught up with Ethel about mid-stream as she battled across in her heavy skirts. With a gentlemanly gesture and a laugh he scooped her up in his arms and carried her to the far bank. Playing Sir Galahad was all to no avail because the doctor slipped as he tried to step out of the river and the pair fell back together into the chilly water. Ethel recalled:

> I was covered with mud and shivering with cold, for my skirts were dripping with water and very heavy. But there was no time to be lost, and I climbed up the bank and crossed the road, on the other side of which was a deep ditch into which I retreated and lay down for firing was going on... We waited in the ditch for some time until all the Sepoys had crossed the river, and then we started off again to find the way to Cachar.[21]

Boileau and Butcher should have had a force, excluding wounded men, of around 430 Gurkhas. Well over half this number were missing, notably 140 men of the 42nd G.R. under Butcher's command who were left at the residency. In his defence the captain later said that 'it would have been impossible' to get men to go back and find the missing troops. On reaching the banks of the river Chatterton told Boileau that between 150 and 200 men who had been manning the north and west walls were missing. The young staff officer repeatedly asked Boileau to wait for men but the captain refused to do so until they were further away from the city. These matters were to be raised at a Court of Enquiry after the war and seem inexcusable; a small group could have gone back to find more Gurkhas and Boileau and Butcher's main body were not under fire during their halt. 'They could almost certainly have been kept in position during the time required to bring the remainder of the soldiers back between the compound wall and the river,'[22] notes Caroline Keen in her study of the uprising.

The terrible predicament of the Gurkhas, seemingly deserted by their British officers, was made worse by the general confusion in the darkness around the residency perimeter. Quite a number of men later said that they received no orders to withdraw. A havildar, Ratan Singh Thapa, was one of these, but hearing sounds of the retreat he collected 15 men and went in search of a British officer. Havildar Dhap Chand claimed to have been in the fort, not having had any order to retire (a command supposedly sent to the men ten hours earlier); he led 40 men back to the residency, saw that it was deserted, then headed for the hills and met up with Cowley's troops at Kowpoon. Manning part of the residency wall, Jemadar Durga Singh refused to move until 4am, shortly before the main building was set on fire. Realising that he had been abandoned he led 102 Gurkhas in an orderly withdrawal towards Cachar. Naik Kabiraj Thapa of the 44th G.R., with 20 companions, became isolated and refused to retreat until the enemy closed in on them. Thapa could not find a British or a native officer so he fled with eight of his comrades towards Kohima. Havildar Sahadeo Thapa got to Sekmai hoping to link up with the Gurkhas there but found only a burnt encampment. Some soldiers fled towards Tammu in the east, others were less fortunate; 50 Gurkhas, believed to have been in the fort between the inner and outer walls, carried on fighting until their ammunition ran out. They were then rushed by the Manipuris and forced to surrender.

Boileau and Butcher decided to march on, leaving their missing men to whatever fate awaited them. The road ran along the top of an embankment between the paddy fields some 10 feet high and exposed the British troops to sniper fire. Warned by friendly natives that the *thana* near Bishenpur was full of armed Manipuri, the column turned some 13 miles outside Imphal and headed for the hills across 3 miles of rice fields.

Earlier on the march, about 4 miles from the residency, Ethel Grimwood turned and saw that her old home was burning, 'the whole sky for miles round lit with a red glow, whilst from amongst the trees surrounding our house flames were leaping up.' She wrote:

All we possessed was there – all our wedding presents, and everything that goes towards making a place homelike and comfortable. I thought of my husband who I believed to be a prisoner in the palace, surrounded by enemies, witnessing the demolition of the house, and not knowing where I was, or what had become of me. And yet I thought he was better off that we were ... and I myself, knowing the Jubraj [Tikendrajit] so well, thought that he would be clever enough to see his own advantage in keeping them as hostages, even if he was not influenced by feelings of friendship for my husband. But it was hard to march on in silence without giving way. I was glad when the dawn came.[23]

Lieutenant Gurdon also saw the burning residency. He later wrote: 'Whether the building was fired by a shell or by hand is uncertain.' One thing is sure, within minutes the whole place was looted. Soldiers from the west wall joined villagers in ransacking the place; off went Ethel's best china and her silver cutlery, away went her carpets and clocks. Prince Angao Senna was 'quite unable to control his men, and virtually abandoned his command and went to sleep in the inner west gate.'[24] He was quickly woken by bugle calls announcing the presence of Tikendrajit who, on hearing the news, rushed to the residency to try and control the looters. He was too late; gone were Ethel's jewels, Frank's fine guns and three lakhs of rupees from the treasury. The fire grew into an inferno incinerating the bodies of Brackenbury and the other dead British troops.

For those trying to escape from Imphal and its burning residency their great hope was that they would meet Cowley's contingent who were expected to reach Leimatak, 30 miles from Imphal, on the 25th. If Cowley had kept to his dates then he ought to be less than 20 miles away.

The rice fields were tough going for Ethel Grimwood; her feet were cut and sore from the rough walking, the rapidly rising sun gave her a headache and threatened sunstroke until one of the officers gave her his helmet. Once they began ascending into the hills all those in the column felt a little better; the air seemed cooler, streams of pure sparkling water were found and they could afford a little breathing space. Kuki tribesmen followed the British at a distance. At the top of the first ridge some Manipuris in a *thana* ordered the sahibs back to Manipur and said the maharajah would allow only the memsahib (Ethel) to go free. 'We however were not inclined to listen to any overtures of this sort after what had happened at Manipur,'[25] declared Gurdon. A halt was finally made at 2,000 feet above the valley floor – a height confirmed by an aneroid barometer that one of Butcher's men had looted from Tikendrajit's house! The Leimatak mountain was 6,700 feet. Towards the summit 'it was a case of using hands and knees,' wrote Ethel. It must have been a trying ascent for the wounded who were suffering terribly from lack of food and jolted every stage of the way on the backs of medical orderlies and volunteers. Lugard wrote:

Mrs Grimwood ... bore up throughout the desperately trying march, marching almost bare-footed (as she only wore thin house slippers with fancy netted stockings which were soon torn to shreds) and setting us all an example.[26]

A young Naga who had been a *sais* (groom) for a time at the residency showed up at great personal risk to his life and presented Ethel with three eggs, 'expressing at the same time his sorrow at not being able to do more for me,' she wrote, 'He stayed till sunset with us, and then crept back to his village. I was much touched by this single act of kindness.'[27]

Command for Captain Boileau was not going well; while crossing the valley shots had been fired at the British from both sides and he sent a detachment to drive away the Manipuris. The soldiers got lost in the dark. He later reported:

We pushed on till we got to a position commanding most of the surrounding country, and here about 6pm we halted for three hours; but as we saw fires all round us, and as the cold on this exposed position was so intense, we determined, about 9pm, to push on again, and at 10pm found a secluded bamboo clump, in which we took shelter and halted for the first time since leaving Manipur – having marched continuously for nineteen hours, no one having had food for twenty hours, and the men having been under arms for forty hours. A party of fifteen men, in their endeavour to find the party who had got detached from us, also lost their way, and in the morning we found ourselves with only 29 rifles. All night we saw fires and expected to be attacked, as at 1am we heard heavy firing, which told us that our detached party had evidently been attacked.[28]

Next morning, 26 March, the British set off at dawn and finally reached the Cachar road only to be disappointed; there were no signs of elephant tracks or the footprints of soldiers denoting Cowley's column and transport. 'We pushed on some distance with great difficulty,' noted Lugard, 'until we found it simply impossible to get the worst of the wounded forward ... it was decided that the best thing for all was to conceal in the jungle the three worst cases and push on as rapidly as possible to join Captain Cowley, get help from him, and return for the wounded.'[29]

Further along the track a Manipuri guard of soldiers were found eating their breakfast. They fled on sight of the British force. Lugard recalled how the rice was 'greedily seized from the boiling pot by British officers and sepoys alike; caste prejudice didn't stand against starvation.'[30] 'How good it seemed,' recalled Ethel, who got embarrassed when the officers saved a small basketful just for her.

Even better than the half-cooked rice was the news from one captured Manipuri that Cowley was at Leimatak, barely 8 miles away. The prisoner also warned that several of his associates were lying in wait about half a mile further, near a steep gorge. Here a stockade had been constructed across the road. Lugard led a charge with a few men killing and scattering the enemy. A few minutes later Captain Cowley with his detachment of the 43rd G.R. were seen advancing up the gorge. Boileau reported:

Bringing up their men at the double, they drove off the Nagas and took up a position on the most commanding hill, and then advancing drove back the Manipuris, and eventually brought up the sick and wounded ... one sick man in the rear was killed by Kukis stealing down the hill, he having left the place to go to the stream for water.[31]

It was about 10am. After the handshakes and greetings of the two British units they marched in the direction from which Cowley had just come. Then there was a four hours rest before a further march of 5 miles. 'We were saved! That was the only thought in my mind,' recalled Mrs Grimwood who had sprained her ankle badly, another injury to add to her list of bruises and a wounded arm. The rescuers had potted meats with them and Ethel admitted that a chota-peg (whisky and soda) worked wonders. Once they reached camp she was given several 'luxuries' including a brush, a sponge, some woollen stockings and a huge pair of sepoy's boots but, as she joked, 'beggars can't be choosers, and as my ankle was very much swollen the commodious boots did not come amiss.'[32]

Cowley's journey towards Imphal had not been without incident. He had set off on 19 March with 2 other British officers, 4 native officers, 4 buglers, 200 rifles, 28 followers and a transport of 67 ponies, 16 elephants, 61 transport followers and ten days rations for all, 'except the transport animals, for whom rations had been sent on.' Heavy rains slowed the march. Skirmishes with Manipuris on the 25th caused further delays as well as alerting Cowley to the fact that something had gone very wrong at Imphal. That day he had linked up with 100 men who had become detached from Boileau's force. The news of the disaster at Imphal horrified and galvanised the young officer. The meeting of the two British columns was indeed fortuitous. General Collett was later to conclude that 'It appears absolutely certain that if Captain Boileau's party had not met with Captain Cowley, none of the officers or men, or Mrs Grimwood, with him could possibly have ever reached Silchar'[33] (Cachar).

Boileau and his colleagues now had to decide on the best course of action. Should they all return to Imphal and try and make a concerted effort to free the captives? One of the main difficulties, all agreed, was lack of ammunition; Cowley could provide plenty of Martini-Henry rounds for men of the 43rd, but nothing for the Sniders of the 42nd and 44th G.R. There seemed to be an average of about 15 rounds per man in these regiments. Some troops were already out of ammunition altogether. The combined troops and followers of the two columns had also eaten most of Cowley's supply of food. Exhaustion showed on the faces of all in Boileau's little army. Pitted with Cowley's men the two forces numbered about 367 fighting men and 142 camp followers. Two hundred Gurkhas were missing and upwards of 40 men wounded.

So it was agreed to head towards Cachar. Each morning they all rose at 3am and marched until sunset, by which time they were 'dead tired'. Several enemy thanas were taken and burnt, each one having 'every appearance of having been only just vacated by the Manipuris,' wrote Boileau. His soldiers were delighted to find rice and cooking utensils at each one. Naga villages were also found to be deserted and the men helped themselves to pigs, goats and more rice.

Six days after leaving the Manipuri capital, Gurdon rode into Lakhipur, which lay about 14 miles from Cachar. Here at last he could communicate with Calcutta. He was able to give the authorities their first accurate reports of the past week; 73 Gurkhas, he also learned, had reached Kohima; 16 were known to have been killed including Brackenbury and a native officer; 21 were wounded; this left 106 native officers and men missing – one-fifth of the original force. Gurdon concluded that the five British officers and their bugler who had walked into the palace were safe and most likely intended as bargaining chips in any negotiations.

On 3 April Boileau and Cowley's little army limped (literally, in Ethel Grimwood's case), into Cachar. The whole body of men including Cowley's troops were all exhausted. Some ill-informed newspapers would write of the 'stampede to Cachar' but, in truth, the British had moved relatively slowly, fighting all along the way (and followed by a large Manipuri army). Every officer was aware of the loss to British prestige and the need to see it restored quickly on the north-east frontier of India before it sparked a dangerous chain reaction.

The situation at Cachar had been tense for the locals. For a time it seemed very likely that the hill tribes might rise in general rebellion or hordes of Manipuris might attack along the frontier. A tea planter, M.J. Wright, wrote: 'We went to bed at night, wondering if before morning the merciless hordes would be upon us, and set fire to our bungalow.'[34] It appears that there were panic attacks and paranoia across the whole Assam border region.

Unbeknown to them all, a few hundred miles away over several chains of hills and forests one lone Englishman had responded to the disaster at Imphal with alacrity and courage. While the officers and men at Cachar began to lick their wounds, exhausted and to some degree humiliated, this officer and 80 Gurkhas had already beaten, and now prepared to fight again, a force ten times their number armed with superior weapons. The soldier was Lieutenant Charles James William Grant and at Tammu he was about to show his country's enemies what a Briton was made of.

A Plucky Fellow

While the main British column made its brave but somewhat ignominious withdrawal to the borders of Assam, some lone individuals – both British and Gurkha – were showing their mettle in other parts of Manipur.

One of these was Signaller Williams in charge of the Chief Commissioner's telegraphs. He had been ordered to wait at Sengmai after Quinton's meeting with Tikendrajit. He was kept in the dark as to the reasons for his wait and given 20 sepoys as an escort. During the evening of 23rd March, tropical rain falling in a deluge, William Melville, the superintendent of the Assam Telegraph Department, with his Eurasian assistant, Signaller James O'Brien, plodded into the muddy camp. There was nothing for it but for the three men to share Williams's tent, where they spent a miserable night as the rain continued to fall in sheets while they huddled together with wet instruments and other equipment.

Next morning Melville and O'Brien set off towards Assam. A little later that day, Williams discovered that the telegraph line was cut. He was not unduly alarmed at first since the Kuki and Naga tribesmen had mischievously done this on a not infrequent basis. It was on the 25th that the sergeant of a nearby thana told him that Quinton and the British officers were killed, the Gurkhas had retreated towards Burma and the Maharajah wanted no British to remain in his country. Williams rushed to get some things together from his tent intending to make a fast exit from Sengmai. Just as he emerged a body of Manipuri soldiers was spotted heading towards the camp. His escort loaded their rifles and prepared for a fight. Hearing these sounds the Manipuris dived for cover and began firing. 'Bullets came like rain drops upon us and 100 Manipuris with rifles, spears and bows and arrows, made a rush at us,'[1] Williams later recalled. He and his escort all scattered (five of the Gurkhas later made it to Kohima, the others were found in various stages of exhaustion by the relief column).

Williams hid in the jungle and was fortunate not to get burned alive when the Manipuris set fire to the dry grass. Later, with a bright moon as a guide, he set off in the general direction of Kohima. After 8 miles of walking he was ambushed by 6 Manipuri sepoys. The soldiers fired a volley at the signaller who later recalled with delight how 'all six missed me, though I was only 10 to 12 yards away from them.' Once more he escaped and fled up a hill where he hid himself until late the next morning. Exhausted, hungry and thirsty, Williams blundered through the jungle for three hours until he ran into more Manipuri sepoys. Since he had no pass from Tikendrajit they prepared to shoot him. He was stripped down to his flannel drawers and ordered to sit on the ground. A sentry was just taking aim when a Manipuri major arrived on the scene and in the nick of time stopped the execution.

Williams was just thanking his lucky stars about 30 minutes later when natives brought some of Melville and O'Brien's belongings into camp. To his horror the signaller was told that the two sahibs had been killed. The pair had been at a resthouse bungalow at Nyangkhang around noon on 25 March when a body of Nagas, acting under orders from the Manipuri commander at Sekmai, attacked the place; Melville and O'Brien, caught unawares, along with their *chuprassi* (bearer or main servant), tried to shelter behind some wooden pillars as bullets zipped through the room. O'Brien was unarmed and Melville was had only with a hunting rifle and two cartridges. A Naga bullet quickly smashed into O'Brien's chest killing him instantly. Melville, despite a crippled leg and a gunshot wound to one thigh, escaped through the back of the bungalow with his servant. Howling with glee the Nagas, joined by some Manipuri sepoys, charged into the bungalow. O'Brien was decapitated by a Naga and his headless corpse dragged outside as the small bungalow was put to the torch.

Later that day Melville was found alone and asleep by a stream just 100 yards from the resthouse. His death was quick and instantaneous; a Naga lopped off his head with a dao. Wrapped in cloth, the head was brought back to the village in triumph after another Naga had chopped off his hands as a war trophy.

On the morning of 27 March, Signaller Williams, barefoot and still clad only in his underwear, was taken to the gaol in Imphal where an iron chain was secured to his feet. Placed in a section of the prison reserved for Moslems 'and other castes', Williams found himself in a small house, 70 feet by 14 feet. He was not alone; his cramped space had to be shared with 38 captured Gurkha soldiers, 8 pony drivers, 14 Moslem servants of the Chief Commissioner and British officers, 19 Cachari construction coolies with a sub-inspector, 4 *syces* (grooms) and 5 wounded sepoys – a total of 89 men excluding the one lone Briton. At the sight of the smelly and stomach-churning red rice and rotten dried fish which was the usual prison fare, Williams told the Manipuri in charge that he would not eat this muck. To his surprise next day, 'I got fine white rice, four large fresh fish, salt and some curry-stuff, which I took and the servants cooked for me separately.'[2] It transpired that the local governor wanted to know about the telegraphic apparatus taken from the looted residency. Williams was told by this official that he could be given 'a fine house, good eating, good living' and even a *laichabi* (a woman) if he agreed to enlist in the service of the Maharajah. This offer the signaller 'politely declined'.

The British signaller and his telegraphic department colleagues had suffered bad luck. Yet there was one bright spot in the sad saga of the British retreat – this was at Langthobal. Here, some 4 miles from the capital and close to the road leading eastwards to Burma, was stationed the barracks of the Political Agent's bodyguard, some 33 men of the 43rd G.R. under *Jemadar* (native lieutenant) Birbal Nagarkoti. Lanthobal was a simple cantonment, the roads around it little better than paths, the officers living in huts made of bamboo and mud, the whole place interspersed with vegetable plots and gardens. Colonel Skene had ordered the jemadar to guard a large quantity of Government supplies which had been left there since the previous December. He also had responsibility for the safety of 23 transport ponies and 70 camp followers. One of his 33 men was also quite sick. The 43rd were armed with Martinis, each with the regulation 40 rounds, though the detachment had a reserve of 2,400 cartridges.

Jemadar Nagarkoti was not a pure Gurkha; he had been born 'a line boy', conceived and raised in the regiment's lines to a Manipuri mother and a Nepali father. The regiment had nonetheless given him a good education so that he knew how to read and write English fairly well, though some in the 43rd said he was 'thick-headed and in fact he was looked upon as being rather a fool.'

Early on the 23rd the jemadar had visited Skene at the residency where he was given no specific instructions but told to keep his troops in readiness. Accordingly, once back at Langthobal, Nagarkoti ordered his men to remain under arms. Later that night he got a note from Simpson telling him to be ready to march on the morning of the 24th but no time was specified. At dawn that day the sounds of the British attack on the palace were heard at Langthobal. Soon crowds of refugees – women and children carrying bundles – passed along the road. Some Indian traders arrived, begging protection; they spoke of looting in the city and the telegraph having been cut. The jemadar tried to send a syce through to the residency on a pony but both man and beast returned wounded.

Wisely the young Gurkha officer had made his men erect a defensive stockade from boxes of stores, mule saddles, sepoys kit and boxes of horseshoes. Just in time, this construction helped the Gurkhas to repulse an attack by spear-wielding locals. At 3pm he got a letter from Skene at the residency ordering him to bring all his men and their reserve ammunition. Now encircled by a growing crowd of Manipuris armed with rifles, the jemadar was unable to comply and sent a note back that while he would try and break through he badly needed reinforcements. It seems likely that this note was never delivered. In horror that night Nagarkoti and his men saw the flames of the burning residency. Around 2am they were attacked by a body of several hundred well-armed Manipuris. It was a fierce fight but the Gurkhas managed to see off their attackers. Two wounded Gurkhas of the 43rd next arrived from Imphal with the dreadful news that 'all the European officers were dead and that there was no one left in the residency.'[3]

Having now to act on his own initiative, but with great reluctance, Jemadar Nagarkoti decided that he must lead a fighting retreat towards Tammu on the Burmese frontier. Dawn the next day saw the 43rd fighting off another attack though this one was thankfully brief. The jemadar distributed the ammunition to his men, made sure the most valuable stores were on the ponies and led his withdrawal in good order. He later wrote:

> I had half my sepoys in front and half behind. The sick were in the middle, with the transport and the coolies, and also a guard of three men with some Government money which I had. I told them all to be of good heart; and that I would take them all right, and I made the coolies slope their bamboo spears on their shoulders to make them look as much like soldiers as possible.[4]

The retreat had its hair-raising moments: at one spot they had to stop and repair a bridge; several stockades were encountered and each had to be rushed, taken at bayonet-point and burned; stretchers had to be made for the wounded from bamboo and the dead had to be buried while for some time Manipuris on horseback harassed the column.

On 27 March the Langthobal detachment marched proudly into Tammu where they met Lieutenant Charles Grant. The jemadar was able to give Grant the sad and horrifying news that the Chief Commissioner of Assam, the Political Agent for Manipur and several officers were most likely dead, while 500 Gurkha soldiers had either been killed, captured or fled through the jungles towards Assam. Grant wired this news all over Burma and asked for permission to go and try and help those fleeing the country. He was, he admitted, especially concerned about the fate of Mrs Grimwood. Orders came about 11pm that night and the energetic Grant set off just six-and-a-half hours later with Jemadar Nagarkoti and 30 men of his 43rd G.R. (with 60 rounds per man), and one subadar and 50 rifles of the 12th (Burma) Madras Infantry (with 160 Snider rounds per man). In support of these fighting men came one hospital assistant, 28 camp followers, 6 transport followers, 3 elephants and some country labourers. The men of the 12th were Punjabi Moslems and a few Pathans from the North-West Frontier hills; 20 were old soldiers, but the rest were mere recruits who had only done eight months drill and fired a few rounds at target practice.

Despite the fact that about one-third of his small force had never seen action, Grant was brimming with enthusiasm and had complete faith in his tiny army of 80 soldiers. He was a bright-eyed and trimly bewhiskered young officer, aged twenty-nine years, who had been born at Bourtie, Aberdeenshire. His ancestors had all been in the army from his great-grandfather downwards; Charles's father was a general and his maternal grandfather a colonel, so it seemed natural for him to enter the Royal Military College at Sandhurst. From here he was gazetted to the Suffolk Regiment on 10 May 1882. Two years later he joined the Madras Staff Corps and was lucky enough to see action in Burma 1885–87 where he gained a reputation for dash and pluck in guerrilla warfare. He was, of course, the same officer who had entertained the Grimwoods only a few weeks previously and been Ethel's partner in her unfortunate attempt at cake-making.

The country Grant's little army first had to negotiate was one of deep valleys, hills rising to 6,000 feet and dense teak forests interspersed with jungle. Grant set off at the head of his column on an old Burmese steeplechaser called 'Clinker'. It was slow progress as each elephant was carrying 600 pounds of supplies and refused to be hurried along. As the troops advanced an ambush set by Chin tribesmen was thwarted by a clever flanking movement from Grant's advance guard. The next day the column was fired upon from 30 to 40 yards by a Manipuri picquet, which was quickly dealt with. Under a bright moon the advance continued. 'After proceeding a short distance it was found that the telegraph wire had been cut, taken down from the poles, and twisted about the road. This obstacle caused great delay in the dark.'[5]

Near the town of Palel, on the edge of the Manipur central plain, the column's progress was blocked by a barricade of tree trunks at a bend in the road. While clearing this obstruction the soldiers came under a heavy fire from the hills above the road. Fixing bayonets, Grant's men soon ejected their enemies from what turned out to be a shelter trench 90 yards long that had been held by 150 men. In their flight, these Manipuris left some of their guns and accoutrements. Palel itself was taken after only a minor skirmish around dawn and its 200 defenders under Nilmani Singh, known as the Ayapurel, ran off westwards. The British caught two prisoners, one of whom was the Ayapurel's cook. Questioned by Grant the cook said that 9 sahibs and 30 sepoys had been killed at Imphal, many others captured, but that 'a memsahib and a few officers had escaped towards Assam.' Somewhat sceptical of this news, the lieutenant considered whether he ought to return to Tammu. Then, he reasoned, his superiors could always recall him, so better to press on in the hope of finding a fort in which he could entrench his men. The Ayapurel's cook was sent on his way towards Tammu bearing a letter from Grant to his superiors explaining his actions. This the cook promised to deliver under the oath of a drawn sword.

After halting during the day at Palel, the troops set off again at 11pm crossing some lower foothills and then swampy rice fields. At 5.30am, with dawn in the sky, the soldiers were approaching the large village of Thobal that lay mainly on the Imphal or far side of a river about 3 to 6 feet deep and some 150 feet wide. Grant noticed that the bridge was in flames and galloped off to have a look. Near the river he was greeted by a hot fire from mud-walled compounds to the left of the bridge and trenches on the right side just across the river. He emptied his revolver at his foes and galloped back to his men while a bullet zipped through his jacket. His swift reconnaissance had, however, shown him that the bridge was beyond repair.

Hastily the column was assembled into a fighting formation – 10 of the 12th M.I. and 10 of the 43rd G.R. in a firing line at 6 paces intervals between each man, 20 more of the 12th in support 100 yards to the rear in single rank, and 20 more with 20 Gurkhas in reserve. Some 300 yards back Grant assembled a baggage guard with his elephants and 30 camp followers specially drawn from the hardy Khasia natives of the Shillong Hills. Ordering his men to fire volleys by sections the young lieutenant began his advance, 'one section firing a volley while the other rushed forward thirty paces,' he wrote, 'threw themselves down on the ground, and fired a volley, on which the other section did likewise.' This manoeuvre got the British to within 100 yards of the enemy. For 5 minutes Grant watched the puffs of smoke from the Manipuri loopholes. One man was killed by his side and he felt 'a sharp flick' as a bullet passed under his arm. The men, he noted, 'were behaving splendidly, firing carefully and well-directed'. He now signalled his supports to come up wide on each flank. They did so at a 'splendid rush', in fact with almost too much enthusiasm, tearing past Grant right to the bank of the river. Here, within

180 feet of the enemy, the troops lay down and fired at the heads of the Manipuris as they bobbed up. Perhaps this was all too much for the main firing line who now passed their comrades and jumped into the water. Grant later said, 'I was first in, but not first out, as I got in up to my neck, and had to be helped out and got across, nearer to the bridge, the men fixing bayonets in the water.'[6]

This British rush was too much for the Manipuris who started to retreat. Grant recalled:

We bayoneted eight in the trenches on the right, found six shot through the head behind the compound wall. At the second line of walls they tried to rally, but our men on the right soon changed their minds, and on they went and never stopped till they got behind the hills on the top of the map; our advance and their retreat was just as if you rolled one ruler after another up the page on which the map is.[7]

In a separate account Grant recorded that in the enemy rifle pits, 'numbers were caught, like rats in a trap, and bayoneted.' Getting himself to a viewpoint Grant halted 'in sheer amazement'; he could now see that the enemy's line was more than a mile long. It was later agreed that his men had faced over 800 Manipuri soldiers excluding officers. Six hundred of them, dressed in white jackets with white turbans and dhotis had been armed with Tower muskets, Enfield and Snider rifles, while 200 more in red jackets and white turbans had used Martini-Henrys.

Lieutenant Grant was now in possession of Thobal but his situation was precarious; his men had used up half their ammunition and three out of six days rations. The lieutenant knew that he would now have to 'sit tight' until either reinforced from Burma or a relief column came from Assam. He sent out a message to Tammu:

We seem to have the whole Manipuri army against us, and only ten miles from the capital. Send with relieving force ammunition, both Snider for us, and Martini for Ghoorkhas. I give no details, as this may fall into the enemy hands, but give your imagination full play. By all accounts I am the sole representative of the paramount power in the country.[8]

Despite his problems Grant resolved to dig in; the evening of 31 March was spent in preparing a defensive position, clearing a field of fire and making abattis from cut trees. Over a ton of rice and earthenware jars full of *goor* (sugar cane juice), along with some dhal and peas, was collected as rations. The small band occupied three mud compounds near the river on the Imphal side, an area of about 200 yards by 150 yards. Houses close by were knocked down to give a better line of fire. A covered way was constructed to get water from the river. To the British right was an open plain and thus safe, but there was some cover for an enterprising enemy on the left. Grant's front 'was fairly secure, as he had two compounds partially cleared beyond his camp proper, leaving a wall well in advance, from behind which he could check any rush.'[9]

That night passed quietly (Grant even shot a duck for dinner), but about 6am on 1st April the Manipuris were seen on the move along a road some 800 yards away. The lieutenant raised his rifle and at 700 yards hit one man in a group of ten. 'The group bolted behind the walls,' he wrote, 'and the little Ghoorkhas screamed with delight at a white heap left on the road, which got up and fell down again once or twice, none of the others venturing out to help the poor wretch.'[10]

The enemy retired but returned to the fray at 3pm and this time in full force. Grant lined his advance wall with 50 men, the rest were placed as a reserve in a small mud fort he had occupied. Slowly the Manipuris came on. Grant waited patiently. Then, at about 66 yards distance, the Manipuris started firing wildly. They did so for 30 minutes before retreating again to 800 yards. What happened next left Grant in what he later called 'a horrid funk':

Suddenly from the hill a great 'boom'; a scream through the air; then, fifty feet over our heads, a large white cloud of smoke, a loud report, and fragments of a 9lb or 10lb elongated common shell from a rifle cannon fell between us and our fort; a second followed from another gun, and burst on our right; then another struck the ground and burst on impact to our front, firing a patch of grass.[11]

Luckily the Manipuris now decided to replace shells with shrapnel. The *Pioneer* correspondent reported:

Our sepoys had no affection for the common shell with its noisy flight and loud report, but shrapnel they laughed at. It seemed to them that the enemy was running short of powder, as they did not continue with the first kind. The practice was good, but a few volleys from the Martinis at 1,000 yards killed some of the gunners, and the guns were withdrawn to 1,500 yards, one only coming into action. The shelling lasted up to 5p.m., when the second attack was made on the left front. This was repulsed and at sunset the Manipuris drew off to their original position. They had absolutely failed to make any impression upon the little column.[12]

Grant admitted later that his compound walls, 'which seemed so strong in the morning ... were like paper against well-laid field guns.' His troops, however, filled him with pride and even some of the camp followers had been courageous. This was especially true of a Punjabi trader called Hafiz Futeh Khan who had helped guide the 43rd G.R. towards Tammu and now carried water and ammunition to the fighting line, 'showing as much bravery as any soldier.' In a manner that might seem condescending to a modern reader unacquainted with the Victorian Indian Army, Grant later wrote: 'I was proud of the result of my personal musketry-training of my *butchas* (children)... Our total day's loss – one pony killed, and one man slightly wounded.'

All that night the Manipuris kept up a desultory fire. Grant, by contrast, refused to allow his men to waste their ammunition with return fire. Instead, after only two hours sleep, he was up again before dawn and encouraging everyone to repair or strengthen the defences against shellfire and make more places for cover. Much of the compound had been recently ploughed and so it was easy to fill every available container – rice baskets, pails, sacks and even Grant's pillowcase – with earth. Five parapets on the front and the flanks were built, each giving cover for 8 to 10 men.

At 3pm a patrol reported seeing a man signalling so Grant went out under a white flag of truce. He met a Gurkha of the 44th G.R., a Manipuri prisoner, 'who brought a letter signed by six or eight Babu prisoners, clerks, writers, post and telegraph men, saying there were fifty Ghoorka prisoners and fifty-eight civil prisoners and imploring me to retire.'[13] If Grant advanced these prisoners might be killed, but if he retired the Durbar might release them. He offered to return to Tammu if prisoners were brought to him.

Over the next three days a succession of messages was relayed between the Manipuri princes and Grant in negotiations for the prisoners. Cunningly the lieutenant met the Manipuris some distance from his lines so as to hide the small size of his force. He also made out that he was 'Colonel A. Howlett, Com. 2nd B. Regt' (actually his real commanding officer) so as 'to impress them with my strength and importance.' He even sewed his subardar's badges of rank on to his lieutenant's uniform to make it look more impressive. The trick worked; Grant even managed to deceive Signaller Williams who had been released from the Imphal gaol on the orders of Tikendrajit, given a shabby coat and pants with boots several sizes too big for him and told to negotiate. The unfortunate and unhappy Williams set off 'on a fine horse with Manipuri ornamented saddle with fringe tassel and white thread balls,' a bugler and a flag signal man. Near Thobal, Williams was met by Prince Angao Senna who was commanding more than 2,000 troops with four 7-pounder guns. He was told by the prince that if an amicable settlement could be reached with Grant, then Williams would get a large reward. Williams told Grant the real fate of Quinton, Grimwood and the other murdered officers including Melville and O'Brien. Grant wrote to Prince Angao Senna and got a reply that the British prisoners had been released and were on their way to Assam. Naturally the British officer was sceptical and refused to retire without holding a hostage of high rank. 'Directly a wire comes to me from Assam that the prisoners have arrived safely I will send him back to Manipur territory,'[14] declared Grant, who added that if any of the prisoners were harmed then British officers would not be able to prevent Sikh and Punjabi soldiers from killing every male and setting fire to every house in Manipur.

This bargaining ended in stalemate. During all these negotiations Grant's troops had continued to strengthen their camp. *Panjis* – sharpened bamboo spikes – were placed around the perimeter and ladders constructed to help deal with any roof fires.

The Manipuri Court Chronicle scribe reported that the British had refused to negotiate. 'Thus the whole country took the decision to go to battle.'

A little before dawn on 6 April the Manipuris launched a major assault. Fifteen shells screeched through the air and struck the British lines, wounding two of the elephants. Less than an hour later, the guns fell silent as the Manipuri infantry in their white, black and red uniforms prepared to advance. The little British-led force of fewer than 80 Gurkha and Punjabi soldiers now faced off against some 2,000–3,000 enemy – probably thirty times their number! Once again Grant waited. When the attackers were just 200 yards away he finally gave the order to fire. The Manipuris scattered towards any trees or walls they could find as the small band of 43rd G.R. and 12th M.I. blasted them with steady volleys. Finding that the attack seemed to be strongest on his left front Grant sallied forth with 10 Gurkhas, crept out along the river, enfiladed the walls on his left and in a few minutes had cleared that side. The British troops were so well positioned that by 11am no impression had been made on the camp and Grant felt strong enough to try and clear his front a little. This time he went out with only one havildar and six Gurkhas. Grant himself was armed with a double-barrelled 16-bore breech-loader and his revolver. Stealthily these 8 soldiers crept up a ditch between the road and the compounds, got to a corner, and enfiladed a wall behind which were about 100 of the enemy. Grant described what happened next:

I had my D.B. sixteen bore shot-gun, and six buckshot and six ball cartridges, and as they showed their heads over the wall they got buckshot in their faces at twenty yards. When my twelve rounds were fired, and the Ghoorkas were also doing considerable damage, we rushed the wall, and I dropped one through the head with my revolver, and hit some more as they bolted. When we cleared them out we returned to the fort along the ditch having had the hottest three minutes on record, and only got the Ghoorka havildar shot through the hand and some of our clothes shot through; we had killed at least ten. Next day I visited the corner, and found blood, thirty Snider and fifteen Martini cartridges, and one four-inch long Express cartridge .500 which accounted for the unaccountable sounds I had heard. Next day I heard I had killed the 'Bhudda' (old)

Senaputti, or the commander-in-chief of the old Maharaj, father of the present lot of scoundrels, and also two generals; but that is not yet confirmed.[15]

Back in his fort, now called 'the 12th Burma Fort', Grant found that he had only 50 Snider rounds left per man and 25 for the Martinis. The men were ordered to lie down and rest behind the walls while one in six kept watch for half-an-hour at a time. The soldiers were also ordered not to fire until the enemy was almost upon them. This attack never came. The British officer picked off a few of the enemy who showed their heads from his position in the east corner of the fort, where he spent the rest of the day while his men smoked and chatted. He noticed how none of them seemed bothered by the bullets that regularly cut the trees a foot or 6 inches above their heads. British losses in the battle had been 2 sepoys and 1 muleteer wounded; 1 pony killed, 2 wounded; 2 elephants wounded, 1 of them severely. Grant's particular annoyance was that some shrapnel had destroyed his breakfast just before it reached him!

The column had been under arms for more than 15 hours and all deserved and now got a decent night's rest. It was later estimated that the Manipuris had fired 8,000 rounds at the camp that day alone. The Manipuri position was later examined and found to be carpeted with cartridge paper (most of it from the Indian Army arsenal at Dum Dum).

During 7 April the soldiers re-built or further improved their camp. More bamboo spikes were stuck into the ground. Dysentery had now started in the 12th M.I., but the men seemed cheerful and there was no grumbling in the ranks. At noon a Burmese postman appeared carrying a letter from the Maharajah to the Viceroy. He was able to tell Grant that less than 200 Manipuri soldiers now faced him out of the 2,000–3,000 who had attacked on the previous day. On opening the letters Grant was amused to see Kula Chandra complaining about the actions of a certain 'Colonel Howlett', though he thought the rest of the letter was 'a tissue of miserable lies and stupid excuses'. The lieutenant quickly wrote a letter to his superior officer at Tammu, Captain Edward Presgrave, explaining briefly all that had happened, how the Manipuris were 'terrible cowards' and concluding: 'Bring your haversacks full of ammunition. There's lots of food here, but my ammunition is running short. Bring medicine also.'[16] He wrote in French using Greek characters (Presgrave later complained that Grant's French was abominable).

Two days later a man with a white stick and a letter stuck in its cleft appeared. The missive was from Presgrave and dated 3 April. It advised Grant to retire. Presgrave had orders to assist Grant but not to reinforce him. 'I *was* sick,' noted a disgusted Grant, 'but the orders were most peremptorily worded. So at 7.30pm on a pitch-dark rainy night we started back – a splendid night for a retreat, but such a ghastly, awful job!'[17] The gallant defence of Thobal was over.

The rain fell as only tropical rain can fall. Two wounded elephants meant that the column did barely one mile per hour. Grant recalled:

> We were drenched to the skin, and were halting, taking ten paces forward, when the lightning flashed, and then halting the column half an hour at times, but the feeble Manipuri, of course, would not be out on such a night, and we passed through three or four villages full of troops without a man showing.[18]

Finally, around 2am, Grant, stumbling along through the mud, almost dead-beat and half asleep from fatigue, literally blundered right into Presgrave who suddenly stood before him, lit by a flash of lightning. It was an odd and very lucky meeting; the captain had heard rumours that Grant had been captured and most of his men killed or taken prisoner. For 36 hours Presgrave had marched with 180 men (including 40 mounted infantry) and 11 boxes of ammunition. No kit of any kind was taken and Presgrave's orders were explicit:

> Major-General considers it imperative to try and assist Grant. He therefore wishes that you to take as many men as possible, not less than 100, with all your mounted infantry, and advance rapidly, but cautiously to Thobal... Husband your rations and ammunition as much as you can, and tell Grant to hold out in extremity. Spread reports as widely as possible of the strength of the force advancing upon Manipur as it may help to cow

opposition ... the great object is to try and save Grant and bring off his force and not to stay out longer than necessary.[19]

The two small columns now joined up to return to Palel. Here they surprised 300–400 Manipuri soldiers who had not expected the sahibs to return. Grant charged with the mounted infantry, but 'Clinker' was shot high in the foreleg. As the animal fell Grant was thrown over its head. He picked himself up and covered in the horse's blood set off after the Manipuris for 3 miles. Later it was claimed that 40 of the enemy were shot during this rout. That night the Honourable Major Charles Leslie and 400 men of the 2nd/4th Gurkhas arrived with two mountain guns. Grant thought it all 'very nice and jolly; but to our disgust we have to halt here for rest of ours, rest of Ghoorkas, two more guns and General Graham.'[20]

The young officer's gallant defence of Thobal was to be immortalised as the late Victorian Indian Army's own Rorke's Drift. So proud of him was the C-in-C, Sir Frederick Roberts, that he wrote how a report of Grant's operations 'may be published as an example of what is possible for one British officer with a handful of devoted native soldiers to accomplish by prompt initiative, resolute courage and soldierlike skill.'[21] Roberts's delight was genuine and understandable; it was as if one cool and brave officer with just 80 troops had restored the national honour – and the honour of his beloved Indian Army. In his textbook on Indian frontier warfare Captain George Younghusband used Thobal as an example 'of a successful defence by a small body of troops against vastly superior numbers'. He went on to say:

It must be remembered that the Manipuris had an army, more or less regular, which had originally been trained by Europeans, that they were armed with modern breechloaders, with an unlimited supply of ammunition, and that they had just gained what would by them be considered a signal victory over a strong force of Gurkhas led by British officers.[22]

In his *Small Wars: Their Principles And Practice*, Major Charles Callwell thought Grant's defence was a perfect textbook illustration of dash and audacity by a small force facing a larger foe. The officer's use of bluff to mislead the enemy was also much admired.

Grant was high in his praise of the bravery and coolness of his men, Gurkha and Punjabi alike. He commended all of them for an Order of Merit (the Indian Army's equivalent of the Victoria Cross). There was talk that he might get brevet rank and D.S.O. or even a V.C., 'but when all is settled, if I get anything at all, I will be content,' he wrote, 'and it will be about as much as I deserve. I have asked leave if I might stick to my men as they had stuck so well to me at Thobal.'[23] This feeling of respect was mutual; a reporter asked the Indian soldiers about the victory: 'How could we be beaten under Grant Sahib,' they replied, 'He is a tiger in a fight.'[24]

10

The Empire Strikes Back

It was late on the evening of 28 March, while the Viceroy was camping at Nani Tal on a tour of the North-West Provinces, that the first of what was soon to become an avalanche of disturbing telegrams arrived. Lansdowne now prepared to cancel his trip and return to the imperial summer capital at Simla, high in the Himalayas. The news from the Foreign Department in Calcutta had come via Burma and spoke of a 'rumour ... very vague', that there was 'a serious outbreak in Manipur'. It continued:

> Disturbances said to have occurred at places so far apart as Kohima and Tammu. Chief Commissioner's tents said to have been burnt, and fighting to have lasted two days. Quinton ought to have 400 Gurkhas with him, so it seems unlikely he can be in serious danger. Wire to Manipur is reported cut.[1]

That same evening more alarming news arrived from the Deputy Commissioner at Kohima:

> Naga fugitives from Manipur report severe fighting and at least one British officer killed. Fighting took place in Manipur town. Eighty rifles under Grant left Tammu for Manipur to-day. If disaster really has happened in Manipur, reinforcements will be necessary here as we cannot spare more than 200 men from here, and if the Manipuris have been able to cope successfully with Chief's large force, it appears to me useless to send small force without guns against them.[2]

Next day came Lieutenant Grant's news from Tammu after meeting Jemadar Nagarkoti. He reported that the whole of Quinton's escort had been cut up, but was uncertain 'if the Europeans were killed or not.' Grant had concluded: 'The Chief Commissioner, Resident and wife, and officers may be holding out.'[3]

Later on the 29th Kaviraj Thapa, a *naik* (corporal) of the 44th G.R. and Bazbir Rana, a sepoy of the 42nd G.R. stumbled half-dead into Kohima. They had more details to relate including the death of Brackenbury, though they suggested that some Europeans might be prisoners. 'An expedition in force absolutely necessary to subdue Manipur' wired Mr A.W. Davis, the deputy commissioner. The General Officer Commanding Shillong Garrison wrote the same words to his military superiors and added ominously: 'We shall have much sickness.' Two days later 16 more Gurkhas arrived from Manipur; they reported that Quinton and his colleagues were 'probably wounded' prisoners of the Manipuri Durbar. That same day, 31st March, the Foreign Department in Calcutta asked the authorities in Assam and Burma to try simultaneously to get a message through to the Manipuri princes demanding the 'immediate release' of the Chief Commissioner and all British subjects.

Midnight oil had been burning in the stuffy rooms of Army Headquarters, India, at Simla and on 1 April the Viceroy was able to wire London that having conferred with the Commander-in-Chief, India, troops were being readied to advance on Imphal from three directions – Cachar, Kohima and Tammu. About 7pm on 31 March the Foreign Department had got a wire from Lieutenant Gurdon (as related in Chapter 8). Slowly the whole picture of the disaster was emerging, but it was inconceivable to all British officials that the Manipuris had not kept the Chief Commissioner of Assam and his associates alive as potential and valuable bargaining chips. 'I have no present apprehensions for Quinton's safety,' Lansdowne telegraphed London. General Roberts decided he had better write to the Duke of Cambridge, Commander-in-Chief of the British Army, (and cousin to the Queen). He began his letter of 3 April: 'I guess your Royal Highness has never heard of Manipur.'

Fighting had already begun again, though of a limited nature; early on 31 March the deputy commissioner at Kohima had attacked the enemy stockade at Mao, 40 miles away and just over the Manipur frontier. One hundred and fifty military police fell upon the thana firing rockets into the stockade and after putting up a short fight the defenders fled for their lives. The military police under Captain MacIntyre then burnt the place and two Naga villages, 'concerned in killing or attempting to kill fugitive sepoys.' Davis was delighted at his actions, which had 'arrested any possible danger of attack on Kohima', he told his superiors. Before leaving Mao the deputy commissioner sent on a message to Imphal demanding details of all that had transpired there.

In the palace ever since the executions the atmosphere was one of confusion; the general consensus was to try and militarily defend Manipur so long as sensibly possible, while diplomatically hoping to mitigate all that had taken place. It would not be an exaggeration to say that the court was in a state of shock. Thanas along the Cachar road had been instructed to arrest all European officers. Only Mrs Grimwood and Indian troops were to be permitted to flee the country. On the northern border the garrison at Mao had been defeated by Davis's men, while in the direction of Burma all the efforts to subdue a lone British officer called 'Colonel Howlett' (the cheeky Lieutenant Grant) had come to nought. It was a small relief to the princes when Grant slipped quietly away since it looked for a time as if the British had withdrawn altogether.

Davis's demand reached the palace and it needed a reply. This letter was not signed by Kula Chandra or Prince Tikendrajit, but it was most probably conceived by the latter; dated 4 April, it was sent in the name of the Manipuri Durbar. The document was largely factually correct at first and claimed that the British had attacked without warning so that Manipuri actions were in self-defence. The mutilation and burning to death of children had enraged the people with many killed and wounded on both sides. There was no mention of the truce, the night durbar or the grisly executions and 'the impression was given that the Chief Commissioner and his companions had perished in the general hostilities.' The letter concluded with the Maharajah stressing his personal innocence:

I regret very much the sad occurrence. All Her Majesty's employes (sic), troops and subjects surviving are well cared for. I took no aggressive part... The disaster has happened only on rash ill-advised acts on the part of the officers concerned. It is not known to my policy. Such barbarous acts have been committed, and I think my subjects were justified to fight for the cause of their religion, wives and children.[4]

Later Kula Chandra's insistence that he had not supported the violent outbreak looked lame when it became known that two days after the residency attack he had led a victory celebration and grand procession though the city.

On 5 April 46 Gurkhas had been set free and given a healthy five rupees each as a gift. Non-combatants including telegraph workers were also released and on the next day the residency's six political agency clerks were permitted to set off for Cachar. It is not certain whether the release of all these captives was a real gesture of reconciliation or a safety measure in response to Grant's threat from Thobal. A week of calm in the capital now followed. The Manipuri New Year was celebrated with a *sangkhranti* to Vishnu and it seemed as if the British 'had vacated the field'. News came on 16 April that a large army was approaching from Burma. This was followed by a disturbing portent in the sky – the chariot of the god, Pakhangba, was seen to float down decorated with a flag. Wise men were summoned but could not agree on the meaning. Next came news of skirmishes with British columns advancing from Cachar and Kohima. Their numbers were said to be in the thousands. The hastily re-assembled durbar called for volunteers and appointed new commanders to defend the homeland. Then, to the consternation of all Manipuris, came an eclipse of the sun.

It was on the 8th of April, after several days during which the British authorities hoped that the Chief Commissioner was a prisoner, that the Maharajah's letter reached Lansdowne. He was aghast on reading its contents. Now it was clear that Quinton, Skene, Grimwood, Cossins, Simpson and Melville were all dead. The shockwaves rippled across the whole British Empire to be reported in newspapers as far afield as Vancouver, Singapore and London. Old generals smoking their cheroots in the East India Club in St James's had to think back 34 years to the Great Mutiny to recall executions of so many civilians and officers. Pin-striped diplomats chatting under the glass roof of the India Office's ornate dubar courtyard in Whitehall had no precedent for such a disaster; potentates however wicked simply did not go around beheading Raj officials, especially men with the rank of Chief Commissioner, it simply was not done. Just a few old India hands could recall Captain Skene (oddly enough, a relative of the murdered colonel at Imphal), political superintendent, cut down by a mutineer's tulwar at Jhansi on 8 June 1857; another analogy was Major Charles Burton, Political Agent, hacked to death in a vain attempt to save his family in the Kotah Residency on 15 October 1857. These events, awful as they might be, were part of a larger canvas and long past. By 1891, almost at the turn of the century, it seemed incredible that the most senior British figure in Assam, his aides and officers, could be executed in some semi-ritualistic and barbaric fashion – and unarmed after a peaceful durbar. The sword of the British Empire's retribution would now fall swiftly upon Manipur and its inhabitants in a show of force quite disproportionate to political or miltary requirements.

In its infinite wisdom the Raj sent out bad news, such as the notice of an unexpected death, in garish yellow envelopes. So it was that the families of the murdered officials received notification about the fate of their loved ones. Ethel Grimwood was in Cachar when she got the news of Frank's murder. After reaching safety 'in my travel-stained and ragged garments', she had taken her first bath in ten days. After undressing Ethel noticed that she was covered in leech bites and one or two of the blood-suckers were still sticking to her body. Everywhere in Assam people of all classes showered her with kindness. She later admitted that 'I found myself made quite a heroine of.' She wrote two letters to Frank, assuming he was still a prisoner, and had them sent on to Manipur. Exactly one week after reaching Shillong the bright yellow telegram arrived. A lady friend gently broke the awful news to her. Next day came more details. Ethel could not comprehend it all at first, completely 'stunned' by the shocking events. Her 'one ray of comfort' was that Frank had died quickly and had been spared the fate of the other captives, he had not heard the big guns destroying his residency, nor seen his wife struggling through the jungle. She later wrote: 'Had I known, when we left the residency that night, that he and I were never to meet again on God's earth, I could never have faced that march.'[5]

The 'Manipur Field Force', as the British invasion army was so designated, intended to approach Imphal from the north, west and east, its three columns all under the overall command of a remarkable soldier, a small, white-haired brigadier-general who, besides having seen much frontier campaigning, was one of the greatest botanists in India. Henry Collett was the son of a clergyman from Thetford in Norfolk. Born in 1836, he had entered the Bengal Army in 1855. Within three years he was fighting ghazis on the North-West Frontier of India, then serving in Oudh for some of the final operations against mutineers in the closing stages of the great rebellion. Collett gained a healthy respect for the fighting abilities of tribesmen on India's north-east frontier on 2 February 1862 when he was severely wounded in the foot during an attack on a stockade during the Khasia and Jaintia Expedition. The injury left him with a limp for the rest of his life. Six years later, during the Abyssinian War, he met Frederick Roberts and the two became lifelong friends. A decade later 'Bobs' asked Collett to be his Assistant Quartermaster-General in the early stages of the 2nd Afghan War. It was Collett who suggested the enemy's left flank might be turned at Peiwar Kotal on 2nd December 1878 after spying out a route over a pass called the Springawi Kotal. He also accompanied Roberts on his famous march from Kabul to Kandahar and was rewarded with a C.B. The normally acerbic Charles MacGregor, Roberts's chief of staff, a man who rarely had a good word to say about anybody, called Collett, surprisingly, 'One of the best men in the service'.

It was during his time in the Kurram Valley in Afghanistan that Henry started studying plants. From 1886 to 1889 he commanded a brigade in Burma and between fighting dacoits, he found time to collect 725 species. In operations against the Chins and Lushais in 1889–90 he had commanded the eastern frontier district while still studying and collecting flora and fauna. In time he would become a world authority on orchids and know more about the plants of the Himalayas than any man alive.

General Collett personally led the column from Kohima in the north taking with him 3 guns of No 8 mountain battery, 100 rifles of the 13th Bengal Infantry, 200 of the 42nd G.R., 400 of the 43rd G.R. and 300 of the 44th G.R., with 200 Assam Military Police. The western column from Cachar was commanded by Lieutenant-Colonel R.H.F. Rennick, described by the C-in-C, India, as 'a plucky go-ahead fellow, and has got his wits about him'.[6] An old soldier who, like Collett, had seen action in Abyssinia, Afghanistan and Burma, Rennick led 2 guns of No 8 mountain battery, 364 rifles of the 18th Bengal Infantry, 99 more of the 42nd G.R., 275 of the 43rd G.R. and 112 of the 44th G.R., with 708 officers and men comprising the 1st battalion, 2nd Gurkhas supported by 202 men of the Surma Valley Light Horse and military police and 48 Calcutta volunteers and pioneers. From Tammu marched the third column. It was under an ex-gunner, Brigadier-General T. Graham, another seasoned veteran and friend of Roberts who had seen action in the Hazara campaign 1868, marched from Kabul to Kandahar in 1880, fought in Burma 1886–87 and personally had overall command in a campaign against the Himalayan Kingdom of Sikkim in 1888 for which he was promoted and given a C.B. With Graham were 4 guns of No 2 mountain battery, half a battalion of the King's Royal Rifle Corps (the only regular British line regiment who would serve in the Manipur campaign), 2/4th Gurkhas, 12th (2nd Burma) Madras Infantry (M.I.) and 32nd (4th Burma) M.I. – a total of 1,800 men. An additional 200 men of the 2nd battalion, Oxfordshire & Buckinghamshire Light Infantry, were ordered up but subsequently sent back due to transport difficulties.

Collett realised from the start that the chief problem facing the columns – especially his and Rennick's – was one of logistics. First the men had to be assembled; some troops had to come 117 miles from Negriting, the nearest landing stage on the Brahmaputra River, to meet others assembling in Kohima. Then the march to Imphal was 87 miles – but the Kohima column had to take with it the Field Force's supplies, which meant a mammoth job of collecting and managing 13,000 pack animals and 500 bullock-carts (the majority requisitioned from none-too-happy planters) as well as an army of porters. To add to Collett's difficulties, the monsoon season had also just started. Luckily the resourceful Davis co-opted 1,500 Nagas as porters. Eventually the column set off on 20 April and crossed the frontier four days later. Writing colourfully a correspondent described the column winding its way 'like a gigantic snake ... sinuous in the extreme.' He went on:

> It follows the contours of spurs which stretch down from a precipitous range, on our left, into a valley, where the terraced cultivation of rice abounds. Spear heads, shining in the sun, indicate where our Nagas are toiling along, and splashes of brown among the bright green of the jungle, show that our sturdy Gurkhas, in

khaki, have set their faces towards Manipur. 'Our kookries are thirsty for blood' is the significant phrase uttered by one of them. They are burning to wipe out the disgrace which attaches to the defeat of 500 Gurkhas by the despised Manipuris, and in their ranks are some who were actually in the fight of 24th March.[7]

A Gurkha of the 42nd, 'too weak to stand being terribly emaciated', was found lying in a narrow gully on a hillside. Nagas had taken his rifle but spared his life. He was a lucky man; seven dead bodies had been recovered from the jungle.

From Myaung Khang on 24 April Collett wrote to Kula Chandra ordering that all British subjects be released and that 'if any harm should befall them, your life will be forfeited.' Once at Manipur the maharajah was ordered to surrender and told he would be put on trial, 'but no promise can be given that your life will be spared,' wrote the general gravely.

From the lowliest Naga coolie up to his own staff officers Collett had nothing but praise for his army. He later reported:

The spirit and behaviour of the troops has been throughout excellent. Much rain fell during the March, and as we had no tents, the men suffered considerable discontent in bivouac, but it was cheerfully borne as becomes good soldiers. The only complaint I ever heard was that the enemy did not stay to fight.[8]

Colonel Rennick's column got off to a bad start; travelling with the body was supposed to be Mr R.B. McCabe, deputy commissioner of Assam, an 'excellent' political officer due to replace Frank Grimwood at Imphal who, it now transpired, was a drink-sodden wretch. Much to Lord Lansdowne's embarrassment, he was forced to explain matters in a letter to his superior, Viscount Cross, Secretary of State for India:

I have had a serious disappointment in the matter of Mr McCabe… His services had been so brilliant that I had before the Manipur trouble arose, recommended him to you for the grant of a C.S.I. [Companion of the Star of India]. To my horror I received a few days ago a telegram saying that the wretched man had of late been continually drinking, and that there could now be no question of employing him.[9]

McCabe did not get his C.S.I. and Major Horatio St John Maxwell, deputy commissioner of Cachar, went in his place.

The route from Cachar to Imphal was 126 miles and reckoned to be nine marches. Yet, while easier than the Kohima road it still traversed nine hill ranges with narrow valleys and several swift-flowing rivers, swollen by the monsoon rains. The bridge across the Barak River was destroyed and a temporary one had to be built. At the Irang River the column arrived just in time to prevent the Manipuris from destroying a second bridge. The continual rain made things unpleasant for the troops without tents and cases of cholera began to be reported. Rennick was feeling gloomy on 19th April when he wrote:

> Heavy storm and rain last night, continuation of which makes me more apprehensive as to the possibility of keeping up the lines of communication... Half the elephants are wild, unruly brutes, and I have already dropped over 120 bullocks as useless up to date; my Naga coolies from Lushai are broken down and unhealthy; and they with local coolies have cholera in their way which will cause numerous defections; the rivers might rise at any minute and utterly paralyse all attempts to supply the column; there is no grazing for bullocks, and bamboo leaves are distant from all stages; the ponies from Lushai have almost done their work. I have found it hitherto impossible to establish any heliographic or lamp signalling as the weather is so cloudy... I am prepared to carry out the orders I may receive after this warning, which I consider my duty to submit.[10]

No fighting took place until the advance party reached Laimatol where the track rose 5,000 feet before dropping through the final misty and rain-sodden hills to the Manipur valley. The soldiers came under a sharp fire from three strongly fortified stockades on a ridge overlooking the road. Rennick sent Captain Boileau forward as one of two officers to take charge of operations. One can imagine Boileau's delight of having a chance to redeem himself after the Manipur debacle, a feeling he no doubt shared with Butcher and Cowley who were in the same column. In his report Rennick stated:

At nine in the morning the guns were brought into action on the enemy, who opened fire from the first stockade, which they abandoned the moment Captain Cowley, with the 43rd Gurkhas, crowned the heights. The column was engaged from this point up to three o'clock, crowning the heights, turning positions, and clearing away barricades and obstacles formed of felled trees for over half a mile, and advanced cautiously through this defile, giving time to Captain Butcher and Lieutenants Williams and Cole with their Gurkhas to develop a turning movement by the left at Hangai, a precipitous and rocky stronghold, which thoroughly commanded the road and which was held by the enemy, estimated at about two hundred strong. This movement was so successfully and gallantly carried out by the above-named officers, over and around a very steep hill, that the enemy precipitately evacuated their position for fear of having their retreat entirely cut off. A few volleys brought down some of them, who were carried away, but their wounded commander is a prisoner. There were no casualties on our side.[11]

At Bishenpur, 17 miles from Imphal, cholera on the increase, Rennick concentrated his column ready for the assault on the Manipuri capital.

The only column to see any serious fighting was the one advancing from Tammu. It was originally thought that Graham, commanding the Myingyan district of Burma, would be the first general to reach Imphal where he was told not to offer false clemency to any person involved in the deaths of British officers, though the ladies of the court were to be treated 'with all respect'. The Manipuris, however, were determined to stop the advance of Graham and his men.

The British advanced guard consisted of 400 of the 2/4th Gurkhas under Major Charles Leslie with Captains Rundall, Drury and Carnegy and Lieutenants Grant, Ducat and Peterson with regimental surgeon, Dr Clarkson; 100 rifles of the 12th M.I. with Captain Presgrave and Lieutenant Charles Grant (of Thobal fame); 40 mounted infantry, also composed of men of the 12th under Lieutenant Cox; and 2 guns of No 2 mountain battery under Lieutenant Persse.

A scouting party of mounted infantry rode as far as Thobal and found Grant's old position now occupied by more than 500 Manipuri soldiers. They fired a volley at the British 'but no harm was done.' Five miles to the north-west of Palel was a large village called Kakesen, where the locals had brought rice and vegetables to the column. The villagers complained of being threatened by the Manipuri troops (hardly surprising as they were helping the invaders) after a body of native soldiers set up camp near the village. To oust them Major Leslie attacked at dawn on 23rd March with 150 Gurkhas and his mounted troops. The enemy fled in all directions and 17 of them were killed.

Next morning Cox was sent out with 34 of his mounted infantry on a reconnaissance. Six miles north of Palel, near the village of Langatel, he found that the enemy had thrown up a *morcha* (mud fort) on an open plain about 200 yards left of the main road. He estimated it was held by some 500 soldiers. They appeared to have two old jingal guns and a picquet on a neighbouring low hill. Cox was mystified; the Manipuri position to his British military mind seemed to be 'inexplicable' since it was surrounded by open country and 'the enemy had not the ghost of a chance of escaping' once surrounded. He rode back to report. Leslie now asked Graham for permission to attack. The general was expecting the King's Royal Rifle Corps (K.R.R.C.) to reach Palel by next day so he told Leslie to be patient. Later that day Graham reached Palel himself with the headquarters of the 12th M.I. and 2 more mountain guns. The K.R.R.C. were still delayed. The general thus agreed to a careful reconnaissance early on the 25th to decide where to site the mountain guns.

At dawn on the 25th a party of 50 rifles, 2nd/4th G.R. under Captain Drury and a Lieutenant Grant, plus 50 men of the 12th (Burma) M.I. under Lieutenant Charles Grant, assisted by Cox's mounted infantry, set off. The horsemen got to the left (or west) of the Manipuri position, while the infantry sneaked around some hills to the right (or east) of the mud fort. Drury told H.Q. that he felt the enemy were now hemmed in despite a few bullets being harmlessly fired at his men. He asked for reinforcements and extra guns so that he could launch an attack. General Graham ordered out another 150 rifles of the 2/4th Gurkhas under Captains Rundall and Carnegy and 2 guns of No. 2 mountain battery under Lieutenant Persse to reinforce Drury and attack the *morcha*.

The British were in for a surprise; the Manipuris had actually chosen their position with great care. Commanding at Thobal was the Wangkheirakpa, the same official who had tried to shield Quinton and the others from the rioters at the durbar. He now ordered two majors named Paona and Mia to blockade the road. The fort had been sited where the Khongjom River flowed in a wide arc completely hidden by high grass. The river flowing in a deep nullah protected the fort on three sides. Ditches full of sharp stakes had been dug on the orders of Paona. It had been intended originally to site some heavy guns here but the swift British advance had caught the Wangkheirakpa off-guard and he did not bring up his cannon despite three requests from the majors to do so. This was to be a fatal blunder. Paona realised that success was impossible (he had, in reality, about 200 men), but retreat was a matter of dishonour. It is said that he drew his two swords, one in each hand, and exhorted his soldiers:

Fellow citizens and countrymen, our bullets are not able to reach them. We cannot retreat and die – my brother-in-law Yenkhoiba would despise us, for he is even now, with drawn sword, marching in the midst of the army. We shall not survive, but we shall not turn back![12]

By 11.30am the British were ready to attack. Persse had placed his mountain guns on a mound some 1,000 yards to the east of the fort and he now opened fire, blasting the earthwork and its defenders with 47 rounds of shell and shrapnel. 'The first shell went plumb into the fort,' wrote Grant, 'soon they started shrapnel and made lovely practice, the enemy replying with two small guns and rifles.'[13] Earth and huge plumes of dust shot up into the sky, but the Manipuris, to their credit, refused to budge. Under the overall command of Captain Rundall, the senior officer present, the British infantry began to move forward; two lines of khaki troops marched up the road while other soldiers advanced on the enemy's right flank. It was a textbook manoeuvre and for a time the Manipuris halted their fire to watch as the silent British troops angled their two lines into a 'V' formation preparatory to storming the fort. Finally the order was given to fix bayonets. Two hundred and fifty of these slim instruments of steel death clinked in unison into their sockets. The Manipuris responded by pouring a volley at the British but their aim was too high. With a rush the British charged, 'shoulder to shoulder' into the long grass, their run stopped short when they saw ahead the nullah that protected the fort on its east, south and west sides. The nullah was quite deep and full of water. After a slight hesitation the soldiers scrambled down its sides and into the water 'in knots'. Now they could see the fort quite clearly, a circular construction with walls about 4 feet high, beyond which appeared the roofs of some grass and bamboo shelters. 'All round the fort outside were scattered a few trenches,' wrote *The Pioneer* correspondent, 'in which were sharp *pangis* covered over with grass, for our men to tumble into, no doubt. The fort was about 40 to 60 feet in diameter.'[14]

The British were now under a heavy fire and some men were hit or knocked over. According to the official history:

Both Gurkhas and Sikhs were magnificently led by their officers and native officers and advanced under heavy fire with the utmost steadiness and coolness. One of the enemy's men stood opposite to Captain Drury and held up a cleft stick with a piece of white paper inserted into it. Taking this for a flag of truce Capt. Drury held up his hand to stop his men, who began to cease firing. The man seeing this laughed and fired.[15]

A few moments later and Charles Grant, who was urging on his men, 'felt a tremendous blow on the neck, and staggered, and fell, luckily, on the edge of the ditch, rather under cover; but feeling the wound with my finger, and being able to speak, and feeling no violent flow of blood, I discovered I wasn't dead just yet. So I reloaded my revolver and got up.'[16]

The fighting was intense as each Manipuri soldier prepared to give his life. Captain Rundall reported:

Directly ... officers and men saw the treachery they rushed into the work ... even when our men got in the enemy would not give way, some firing out of the ditches and shelter trenches, others with clubbed muskets and swords furiously resisted, and both sides engaged in a desperate hand-to-hand fight which, however, did not last long, as the enemy could not withstand the determined onslaught of our officers and men who, with swords, bayonets and kukris cut them down in heaps.[17]

The Pioneer correspondent wrote that the 'whole of the trenches all round were full up to the top' with Manipuri dead. Seventy bodies were counted inside the fort and 52 outside. Several Manipuri soldiers fled northwards but they were pursued by the mounted infantry and killed. It was later said that only eight survivors of the *morcha's* garrison made it back to Imphal.

Thus ended what the Manipuris would later call the Battle of Khongjom. Lieutenant Carnegy got shot in the thigh, Captain Drury had his hand smashed by a rifle butt and, besides Grant's neck wound, Lieutenant Cox had chased a man up a knoll, fired his revolver at him once, then had two misfires before the Manipuri turned and at point-blank range shot his assailant severely in the shoulder. In total the British had lost 2 men killed and 13 officers and men wounded, most of them from sword cuts. Among the injured was brave Jemadar Nagarkoti who had been hit in the jaw, the bullet having entered his mouth, smashed a few teeth and exited through his cheek. Another wounded man was old *Subardar-Major* (senior native officer in an Indian regiment) Kulpatti Gurung of the 2nd/4th Gurkhas. Tragically one of those killed was his son, Jemadar-Adjutant Kiree Ram Gurung. The young officer had lost more than half of his face blasted away by a dum-dum bullet. In gory but honest terms a correspondent wrote:

> The battlefield was a bloody enough sight to suit even the taste of a Rider Haggard. In one or two places bunches of mangled bodies were seen, where the shells had done their deadly work. Two large standards – one white and the other red – that had floated gaily in the fort in the morning were now found torn to shreds, also the result of the shell fire. The slain were all placed in the trenches and the mud wall knocked down and thrown over them.[18]

Rundall concluded his report of the action by saying that 'many old soldiers who have seen much fighting in previous campaigns, tell me they have never either seen or taken part in a fight where such a determined or stubborn resistance was shown.'[19] This remark was a compliment to the courage of the Manipuris just as much as to the valour of his own troops.

Next day the column advanced to Thobal and found the place deserted by the enemy. All three columns – a little under 5,000 soldiers and a corresponding army of camp followers – were thus ready to fall on the Manipuri capital.

About dawn on 27 April 1891 a lone rider, Trooper Knowles of the Surma Valley Light Horse Volunteers, stealthily rode into Imphal to scout the city. Knowles, like all in his corps, was a tea planter. The Surma Valley Light Horse, a smart outfit, was considered to be numerically the strongest auxiliary cavalry corps in the Empire consisting of two squadrons divided into six troops. A heavy rain had fallen all night, not a soul was to be seen, all doors seemed shuttered and the city lay 'wrapped in silence'. Knowles guided his mount through the muddy streets and into the palace via the west gate. The whole compound was eerily deserted. Turning his horse around the trooper dug in his spurs and galloped back to re-join Rennick's column fast approaching the city.

Why had the Manipur princes fled the palace or failed to defend their capital? The answer lay in the battle at Khongjom where the Manipuri defeat, combined with a portent of disaster predicted by the court astrologer, had made the durbar believe that further resistance to the British was useless. Kula Chandra early on the 26th had sent away his advisors, priests and women of the royal household. All were given gifts. Images of the gods were taken from the temples and delivered into the safekeeping of a royal priest who got 1,000 rupees for his trouble. The Maharajah dictated a letter to General Collett saying that while he wished to come to terms he would not stay in the palace to surrender himself. Instead, with a bodyguard of 200 men, he and his royal brothers, including Tikendrajit, fled eastwards. Soldiers and many locals who had filled the palace since the revolt now dispersed to their villages. Just before leaving much of the royal arsenal was blown up in a tremendous explosion that could be heard 17 miles away at Bishenpir. The conflagration destroyed much of the palace and several houses nearby.

Rennick led his men into the city about 7am. Imphal had fallen without a single shot being fired (much to the chagrin of many British officers who were looking forward to a stiff fight).

Flames and smoke from the armoury filled the sky but, at least for a time, the rain had stopped falling. The Kohima column arrived one hour later and shortly after this Graham's troops also reached Imphal. Collett placed 500 soldiers in the palace compound, the rest of his army he wisely quartered several miles outside the city and on his lines of communication. The Queen-Empress had telegraphed the Viceroy that there must be no 'inordinate reprisals' or 'wholesale punishment of the innocent, or incitement to bloody revenge'. Perhaps recalling the events of the Great Mutiny, Queen Victoria wisely pointed out that vengeance 'only too easily encouraged, would not redound to our honour, or add to our power in the future.'[20] This order was passed to General Roberts who in turn told Collett that 'the Manipur disaster may cause our troops, particularly the Gurkhas, to wreak their vengeance in a cruel manner; please do all in your power to prevent them from resorting to unnecessary bloodshed, or taking the law into their own hands after the fighting is over. Remember that it is absolutely essential there should be no indiscriminate punishment.'[21] Replying to the Queen, the C-in-C, India, assured his monarch that Generals Collett and Graham were 'humane men of great experience, excellent judgment and proper feeling, and I am certain they will keep their troops well in hand.'[22] The Secretary of State for India passed the Queen's concerns on to the Viceroy and got a typically patrician reply back from Lansdowne: 'Please remember when you read of the destruction of villages, that a frontier village means a few trumpery mud walls and some grass mats, the whole of which can be replaced at very slight cost, and with little trouble.'[23] (Perhaps it was lucky for Lansdowne that Cross never showed this letter to the Queen. It would almost certainly have resulted in a stinging rebuke). By first nightfall Collett was making plans to send two-thirds of his soldiers back to India and Burma. The monsoon rain returned, a heavy tropical downfall, as the troops set up camp in the mud.

The Times correspondent wrote of the palace being 'in a heap of ruins. It has been gutted of everything and nothing remains but its crumbling walls.'[24] Dramatic stuff but not quite true; the British found 4 7-pounder muzzle loaders, 8 3-pounder smoothbore bronze guns, 1 2-pounder muzzle-loader, 1 mortar, 1,290 firearms of all kinds, 910,000 rounds of ammunition, 972,000 percussion caps,

180 barrels of gunpowder and elephant gear for the 7-pounders. It was clear that unknown to a succession of political agents the Manipur Durbar had been surreptitiously stockpiling ammunition (supposed to be just 60,000 rounds) and guns for years. Both gunpowder and caps had been manufactured locally and like the ingenious gunsmiths of Peshawar, their cousins on the other side of India, they had turned out several Martini and Snider imitations. A rifle was also found that had been presented to Maharajah Chandra Kirti in 1872 by the then Viceroy, Lord Northbrook. Lieutenant Simpson's 'double barrel express' also turned up.

That evening Captain James Willcocks, chief transport officer on Collett's staff, went for a walk through the ruins and in an outlying building stumbled upon what he called 'the photographic studio of the late maharajah'. Since we have no record of Kula Chandra having an interest in photography we can be pretty sure that what Willcocks had discovered was the remains of Frank Grimwood's studio. The officer picked up 'some good developed plates, which proved most interesting' and in one room found a number of cameras and fine lenses, 'but I was just too late as a British soldier had kicked most of them to pieces before I arrived.'[25] One wonders what stories those trampled glass plates could have revealed – of days on the lake, happy princesses, smiling Ethel, nautches and more. Willcocks indulged, like most officers and men, in some minor looting; he took a silver trumpet as a souvenir and went off on a wild goose chase for the Maharajah's jewels.

Some officers were billeted in remaining palace buildings while Collett blew up other parts of the place including the fearsome dragon *nongsa* whose graven images had been splattered with the blood of the British officers. There was little left of the residency; after its looting the Manipuris in a frenzy had torn the place down brick by brick. Scores of Ethel's beloved flowering plants had been uprooted and the nearby graves disturbed. Soldiers were shocked to see that the grave of one of Johnstone's infant sons had been vandalised. The bodies of two Gurkhas had been hastily thrown into Mr Heath's grave, the others were found on the polo ground. 'The heads of all of them had been severed and buried separately in a small, brick-lined hole.'[26]

Next came the grisly task of exhumation and identification. Unfortunately the corpses were so decomposed and mutilated that

Lt-Colonel Michell, Graham's adjutant-general, called it 'the most dreadful task I ever had to do'. Serving with the King's Royal Rifle Corps was Frank's brother, Major G.G. Grimwood, but even he could not positively identify the remains. Melville and O'Brien's bodies were discovered one week later by Mr Pinhey, the new superintendent of telegraphs, as he lay a line near Myangkhang. Some Gurkhas had found the skeletons in a ditch. Pinhey personally took charge of the burial and read the service.

The funeral of the five Imphal officers and their brave bugler took place on 30 April and Collett, son of a vicar, read the burial service. It was, according to Willcocks, one of those present, an 'impressive' ceremony. The coffins were draped in the Union Jack, troops lined the route, minute-guns were fired and a party of the K.R.R.C. let off three volleys over the graves. *The Pioneer* reported:

> Each of the regiments with the force furnished a company to take part in the procession, and the streets were lined by Gurkhas, and so, in the presence of their countrymen, and of a few Manipuris, the murdered officers were laid to rest.[27]

So, by the end of April 1891 the Manipur Uprising was over. It would only be a matter of time before the royal family were apprehended and those guilty of murder might face justice. Yet in Simla, London and other places the recriminations and mud-slinging had just started. The need to blame someone for the disaster – Quinton, Skene, Grimwood – was under way, the Indian Army high command, humiliated by the debacle, wanted to know why such a large escort had not better defended itself, or why the retreat had been botched. Newspapers were starting to ask if the war had been unjust, unnecessary and badly planned by the Viceroy and his advisors. The clamour around Lansdowne would see him having to work hard to defend himself while HM Govt. faced mounting criticism in Parliament. This dilemma of cover-ups and scapegoats would lead to a clash between the Viceroy and the Queen-Empress herself, an inglorious end to an ugly little war.

11

Cover-ups and Scapegoats

In the spring of 1891 the Indian Empire was administered from two remarkable buildings in London and Simla. The former of these was the India Office in Whitehall, whose Gilbert Scott-designed Italianate exterior was part of the same block that housed the Colonial Office in its north-west corner. This 'tremendous mediocrity, vast and uncompelling', in the words of one critic, had its colonial portion decorated with symbolic figures of Empire, while the India Office had a tower facing St James's Park and motifs of the Raj. It was the interiors that demonstrated best who was the poor and who was the rich cousin. It is true the Colonial Office 'was furnished in dark mahogany and deep leather with smoky coal fires', not a bad place from which to administer the affairs of St Helena or British East Africa, but it was drab compared to the India Office full of imperial busts, clocks, fine furniture and paintings inherited from the East India Company's old quarters in Leadenhall Street. The interiors had been designed by Matthew Digby Wyatt, the E.I.C.'s surveyor. With a budget boosted by private funds, he set out to create a Mughal palace in Whitehall – there were immense staircases, a riot of oriental artwork and Raj symbols, a library containing a stupendous collection of books and priceless Asian documents and a majolica-ornamented durbar hall or courtyard with a glass roof supported on cast-iron beams. Any visiting maharajah – and none ever dared to visit London without paying their respects to the Secretary for State – would be impressed by the grandeur of the place, decorative details picked out in blue and gold leaf. The twin doors of the Secretary of State's office were specially designed to be wide enough to allow two Indian princes to enter comfortably side by side so as to avoid embarrassment or upset protocol. It was, in fact, a modest sized office for such a powerful man, though a huge mirror hung over one of its two marble fireplaces.

All such buildings have their quirks; there was no central heating and civil servants in winter were allowed just one bucket of coal per day as they toiled over the affairs of such steamy places as Gujarat or Mysore. In chilly weather the London fog – those famous Sherlock Holmesian greasy-green pea-soupers – would enter the building from the nearby Thames and twist eerily along the gas-lit corridors and into the damp offices.

In India, by contrast, every spring the Viceroy, his family and staff left sweltering Calcutta for the fresh and pine-scented clime of Simla, to work, relax and play. Only the British, some foreign observer once said, were crazy enough to try to run their vast possessions in the East Indies from a place 750 miles from the nearest port, 80 miles from a railway line and 7,000 feet up on the top of a mountain! A former Viceroy, John Lawrence, had pushed hardest for this 'hill-station' near his beloved Punjab as the ideal place to rule the Raj in summer and avoid the debilitating heat of the plains. In 1864 Lawrence got his way and the move had been going on ever since.

Simla was entirely British in character, a small village that had grown in higgledy-piggledy fashion into a parody of 'Olde England' with its mall, ivy-clad villas with names such as 'Barnes Court' and 'Balmoral', each one a nostalgic and sentimentalised memory of an English cottage. there was a fake Tudor Gothic church (Christ Church) and amateur dramatics took place in the Gaiety Theatre. There was an anglicised post office, town hall and, of course, several tea-rooms. The place was decidedly eccentric; the buildings were largely roofed in corrugated galvanised iron sheets specially made in England and painted red and sometimes green. Kitchens were normally separate and several yards behind each house. Terraces of English flowers formed the gardens. Simla straddled a narrow ridge with the villas on top, while a dirty and unkempt native bazaar (the main native quarter) tumbled in layers down the steep hillside. Two of the ugliest buildings in the town were the Army Headquarters and Secretariat, opened in 1885; Jan Morris describes them as: 'Stark, square and enormous, these preposterous buildings stood about the ridge with an air of plated aloofness, like armadillos, facing this way and that, with roofs of corrugated iron and complicated external staircases.'[1] Little wonder that Simla had its critics; one artist called it 'so English and unpicturesque', while Sir Edwin Lutyens, the architect who was to design the new imperial capital at Delhi, took one look at the place and commented: 'If one was told the monkeys had built it all one could only say, "What wonderful monkeys – they must be shot in case they do it again."'[2]

The Viceroy at the end of the 19th century, the very superior Lord Curzon, loathed Simla and felt that it was out of place in India. Lord Lansdowne disagreed; he loved it and the differing views of the two pro-consuls tells us much about them. Clearly Lansdowne missed England and held no romantic notions, nor felt any special attraction, for the East and its peoples. He was fortunate perhaps to be the first Viceroy to enjoy Viceregal Lodge, the grand mansion planned by his predecessor, Lord Dufferin. The building was completed only weeks before the Dufferins left India so they had little time to appreciate the place. It had a staff of 300 including 40 gardeners and was, over the next 60 years, likened to 'a Scotch hydro, a lunatic asylum, Pentonville Prison, St Pancras Station' and a vulgar mix of Victorian Gothic house styles. It did come, however, with special luxuries such as electric lighting, an indoor tennis court and a large basement kitchen.

Lansdowne never forgot his first sight of Simla 16 or 17 miles away sitting on its mountaintop. 'Your first impulse is to ask yourself how it got there,' he told his mother:

> The road winds gradually up to the summit, through thickets of ilex and tree rhododendrons with a few pines and deodars, and you find yourself on the 'Mall', the famous promenade of this place... I have said nothing all this time as to the change of climate, but oh! the joy of feeling the cool air entering one's lungs again and the emancipation from the ceaseless perspiration and thirst.

He thought Viceregal Lodge was 'a fine building... a fine dining room, and Maud's sitting room is quite charming, with wonderful views towards three points of the compass,' but Lansdowne was critical of the furnishings:

Waste of space everywhere, absence of sufficient accommodation for guests in spite of the palatial dimensions, rooms in the wrong place considering the purpose for which they were built ... much of the furniture is quite deplorable, and that there are contrasts and combinations which would make you shudder. The carpets are mostly hideous ... from Maple's when such lovely ones are made here? This is quite incomprehensible to me. The dining-room which really is a fine apartment, is spoiled by a very second-rate Brussels carpet too light in tone for the walls, as all the carpets are shaped like oriental carpets ... one is reminded at any moment that they are only a counterfeit. I am sure that £1,000 could have been saved on the furnishings and a better job made. But, after all, it is an English house and not an Indian residence, and we shall feel more at home than we have yet felt.[3]

Lansdowne now had more to shudder about in that April of 1891 than bad Brussels carpets. His simple request that the Senapati at Imphal be arrested had somehow gone horribly wrong. It had turned into a war that no one had ever wanted, least of all the Viceroy, but for all that very much a war of his making since he had been so insistent that Tikendrajit had to be removed, militarily if necessary, from Manipur.

One can imagine how the Secretary of State for India must have felt on receiving a stream of bad news, most of it confused at first and inexplicable. Did he raise his eyes heavenwards to stare momentarily at the aquamarine sky of his domed office, seemingly sprinkled with gold stars, there hoping for inspiration? In April 1891 the holder of this august post was sixty-eight-year-old Richard Assheton Cross, first viscount of that name, a long-time friend of Prime Minister Lord Salisbury and, like him, a Conservative career-politician. Cross had already been in charge of Indian affairs for five years and watched over several crises large and small. He wore thick round glasses and had a full beard, once ginger, though now snow white. Until his elevation to the peerage in 1886 he had represented the good burghers and mill workers of Preston, Lancashire, for twenty-nine years. Richard Cross had been born at Red Scar just outside the town, educated at Trinity College, Cambridge, and been called to the Bar in 1849. Some fellow politicians thought him a 'fussy' man and it was true that Cross was a worrier. He liked to know exactly what was going on and expected honest and full disclosure at all times from his subordinates. This tough Lancastrian was not duped by Lansdowne's smooth excuses. The pair were set to clash over Manipur. As early as 1 April Viscount Cross told the Viceroy: 'I am still quite at a loss to understand how an escort of 450 Gurkhas should have been compelled to get away out of the country.'[4]

Equally confused was the Queen-Empress who was having her spring holiday in Grasse and busily learning Urdu from her Indian *munshi* (teacher), Abdul Karim. She was to take a special interest in Manipur affairs. She sent a secret cipher telegram to Cross on 6 April stating her opinion that 'Our Commissioners are not of the right kind: bumptious and not understanding how to deal with people.'[5] Her Majesty was angry that Lansdowne had not telegraphed her direct and an annoyed Cross put a flea in the Viceroy's ear giving him 'peremptory orders' to do so in future. Viscount Cross, like many others, had jumped to the early conclusion, though his opinion would later change, that the main blame rested with Quinton. He told Lansdowne on 9 April: 'I am not prepared to defend all he did; impossible to do so. There seems to me to have been a series of blunders both by the Civil and Military authorities.'[6]

The clamour and confusion was also being ratcheted up by the press. One of the first to rush into print and state his opinions was Major-General Sir James Johnstone, Tikendrajit's implacable foe. In his opinion Quinton should never have gone to Manipur in the first place. A good Political Agent could have arrested the Senapati. Sir James accused 'every one' of acting blindly and *The Times* noted:

> The neglect to seize the palace guns and magazine immediately on the first outbreak of the disturbance; the retreat to the Residency before native troops; the attempt to treat with their victorious leaders, in defiance of the rules of British diplomacy in India, are facts which need to be explained. The failure of ammunition at a later period in the fray is equally unintelligible.[7]

Four days later Johnstone wrote to the newspaper again, this time on the question of annexation, which he opposed in relation to Manipur. The people, he insisted, had simply obeyed their Rajah:

They feel their first allegiance due to him; and the Sepoys who fought against our people, did so knowing that a refusal to obey would mean death... Thus it would seem that we have a military outbreak, headed by two usurpers, to deal with, and not a rising of the legitimate ruler against the paramount Power.

Despite his blind hatred of Tikendrajit the ex-Political Agent had a deep love for Manipur and its people. He concluded his letter with a plea for tolerance:

Let us not destroy native life with its many charms; let the people be content with their picturesque surroundings, and ... leave the native Court to encourage all the various little arts and manufactures which are found here alone ... Let the people enjoy their stately little processions, their titles, their Royal festivals, their boat races, their dances, the thousand and one pretty ceremonies inseparable from a native Court which give a zest to native life; let them, in a word, retain their individuality as a people.[8]

Appoint a new and young rajah, advised Johnstone, educate him to be a wise and pro-British ruler, but not annex the state. Annexation, in any event, would create an annual deficit for many years and cause resentment among the people. The hill tribes might also become more aggressive.

This letter brought a flurry of replies from old soldiers and civil servants who favoured annexation. One of these was Sir George Campbell, an irascible former Lieutenant-Governor of Bengal, Liberal M.P. and holder of some unorthodox views. He declared Manipur to be 'wholly an enclave in British territory' and went on to say:

Sir James Johnstone is what is called in India a 'political' as distinguished from a civil officer. Such officers are always given to favour the system of a native State under the guidance of a Resident, and his native sympathies are natural and creditable. But, after all, there might be native colour, and regattas and polo under British rule. We must look to expediency in the matter.[9]

Sir A.C. Elliott, Lieutenant-Governor of Bengal, an I.C.S. man of great experience, also favoured annexation and wrote to Lansdowne urging this course. Even more extreme, since it demonstrated exactly the rush to revenge wisely deplored by Queen Victoria, was the view of Mr Ward, Judicial Commissioner at Rangoon, who wanted Imphal razed to the ground. He described the Manipuri army as 'an undisciplined rabble' and complained that 'Johnstone attached an importance to that miserable little State which does not belong to it, and rather encouraged the Maharajah in believing ... that Manipur was the centre of the world.'[10]

Pouring oil on the flames, Ethel Grimwood took up her pen to defend Frank's actions as well as her own. Her first letter was written while she was still resting at Cachar and unaware of her husband's death (though it did not appear in *The Times* until 29th April). She declared that her husband had been clearly informed on what was expected to happen at the durbar in the residency:

> That the Government of India had decided that the ex-Maharaja was not to be allowed to return, but that also the Jubraj [Tikendrajit], the Prince who turned him out in September, was to be banished for a term of years to India. This decision was to be announced in the durbar, and when the Princes got up to go the Jubraj was to be arrested then and there and conveyed out of the place that day by some of the 42nd (*sic*).[11]

This letter opened a can of worms; Lord Cross admitted to Lansdowne three days later that 'Mrs Grimwood's letter has caused us much agitation here' since it suggested that 'Mr Quinton inveigled the Senapati to the durbar for the purpose of treacherously arresting him there.'[12] Cross was surprised if this had really occurred and concluded: 'Mr Quinton must, I think, have lost his head.' (An unfortunate choice of words since this is exactly what did happen to the Chief Commissioner on the next day.) *The Times* supported Mrs Grimwood and in its editorial thundered:

> The whole expedition was planned in overweening confidence by a man who did not choose to listen to advice, and also took every precaution to conceal his intentions. Four hundred men with only forty rounds of ammunition were led into a town

defended by twelve thousand rifles and ten guns, to back up a cool request to the master of these forces that he would quietly surrender himself to exile. Unfortunately this even is not the worst. For as things stand at present it does not seem that we have much right to complain of the Senaputty's treachery, seeing that he was to be asked to a durbar and seized as he went away. It may be hoped that some better face may yet be put upon a transaction which at present seems to have been bad both in plan and in execution.[13]

The attack on Quinton, hardly surprisingly, caused his many friends in India to rally in defence of his memory. Sir William Wilson Hunter, an eminent I.C.S. man and author of a mammoth encyclopaedia, *The Imperial Gazetteer of India*, wrote to *The Times* on 5 May declaring that he had 'sat side by side' with the Chief Commissioner on the Viceroy's Legislative Council for four years and considered him to be 'an experienced, cautious, high-minded man ... apt to lean on the judgment of others rather than assert his own.' Hunter reminded readers that Quinton had gone to Imphal under orders from the Indian Government to carry out a specific policy and had 'sent a written ultimatum to the Regent warning him that unless the Senaputty was surrendered he would be arrested.'[14] In the House of Lords a former Viceroy, Lord Ripon, declared that 'it is impossible from my acquaintance with Mr Quinton's character that he should have had any hand in such an unworthy proceeding.'[15] Ripon's opinion was reinforced by Sir Andrew Scoble, one of the Viceroy's Council, who told Lansdowne: 'Knowing Quinton so well as I did, it is to my mind perfectly certain that he consulted them [Grimwood and Skene] both, and was guided by their advice. The blame, therefore, ought not to rest on him alone. Skene probably thought that a *coup-de-main* would succeed, as it has so often succeeded in Indian history, and Grimwood probably overrated his own influence with the Senapati and the Manipuris generally.'[16]

Viscount Cross was not happy: 'Great blame must rest somewhere,' he told Lansdowne on 24 April. One week later a member of the Viceroy's Council was in London and told the Secretary of State all about the plan to arrest Tikendrajit during the residency durbar. His lordship considered this to be a 'mistake in the first instance'. On 8 May Lord Cross told Lansdowne bluntly that 'The several persons in authority must have lost their heads – all of them,' a remark that ought to have bothered the principal person in authority, the Viceroy.

Yet the man in charge of things at Simla sat unmoved, certain in the knowledge that he was not to blame. The whole matter was quite simple, as he told Cross:

> That Quinton's actions should have been compared to that of one who asked a man to dinner and had a policeman in the house to arrest his guest, shows how completely the situation has been mis-understood. Quinton's proceedings were all above board... The Senapati was ordered to present himself, and as a subject of a subordinate State, it was his business to obey the summons. The Government of India had a perfect right to expel him as a rebel and conspirator... The moment that this is understood, it seems to me quite immaterial whether the arrest took place in the Durbar or not.[17]

Lansdowne refused to budge from this opinion; the villain in the piece was Prince Tikendrajit, 'a great scoundrel', he told his mother. Talk in some of the newspapers that a durbar was 'invested with the spirit of sanctuary' was 'pure moonshine'. Tikendrajit had been behind the uprising, though as he told Cross on 20 May, 'It is quite clear to me that Grimwood was on far too intimate terms with the Senapati.' While admitting that Ethel had shown 'great bravery and endurance', her husband began to feature increasingly in Lansdowne's correspondence as being 'in' with Tikendrajit, 'and would be a reluctant interpreter of the orders issued, that made him (Quinton) so reticent, and it was this reticence that frightened the Manipuris and paved the way for the disaster.'[18]

While all this debate, with some mud-slinging, occupied the newspapers and official correspondence, events had been moving in Manipur to apprehend and punish the guilty. On 7 May the Thangal General surrendered. *The Pioneer* correspondent cruelly described him as 'a decrepit old man, tired of being hunted from place to place...[19] That same day, some Manipuri police sent out by Major Maxwell, the new Political Agent, discovered the princes (without Tikendrajit). Two days later Kula Chandra was arrested and returned to the capital under a military guard.

Parties were out every morning searching for Tikendrajit. His eventual capture was on 23 May and reported by *The Pioneer*:

The actual capture was effected by one of Major Maxwell's constables, who was visiting a suspected house in a village about half a mile from the Pat, in fact, in the city of Manipur itself. It was intended to surround the house by night... The Senapati, however, saw the constable approaching and made a bolt for it. The constable overtook him, and the two men had a tussle, in which the Senapati got the best of it, and nearly strangled the other. At this juncture another of Major Maxwell's men came up, and threw a lump of earth at the Senapati, cutting his mouth badly; and the two men having over-powered him, impressed the services of a Manipuri, who carried him on his back to the fort ... the event seemed to excite but little interest, and small attention was paid by the passers-by while the late *de facto* ruler of Manipur was ignominiously carried along on a coolie's back.[20]

No time was wasted in bringing to trial Kanjao Pukhramba Phinsang, called Kanjao Singh, the man who had speared Frank Grimwood. He was identified by the Mia Major. It turned out that Kanjao was a ruffian with a history of violence. He gave no reasons for his action in spearing the defenceless Political Agent, though it was suggested that the crowd might have intimidated him. Maxwell, acting as judge, found Kanjao guilty of culpable homicide and condemned him to death by hanging. Also quickly executed was Niranjan, a Manipuri officer who had the bad luck to be a British subject and former soldier in the Indian Army. He was convicted of treason and, like Kanjao, publicly hanged.

The Times had already declared as early as 6 April that the Manipur disaster 'resulted from some serious blunder or series of blunders by the officers on the spot.' A Court of Inquiry sat through much of May charged with ascertaining exactly what had transpired 'from the time Mr Quinton arrived until the several fugitives reached Silchar, Kohima and Tammu.'[21] The Court was also required to investigate the suitability of Quinton's escort and the sufficiency of the available ammunition. President of this military inquiry was Colonel H.M. Evans assisted by Major Eaton Travers, a Gurkha officer on the Indian Staff Corps, and Captain

A. Birch, Royal Artillery. Once their names were announced *The Statesman* newspaper in Calcutta pointed out that the men were 'servants of the state, immediately subordinate to the Executive Government, and dependent upon it for their promotion',[22] so unlikely to be impartial, Colonel Evans commanded the 43rd G.R. and was, as historian Caroline Keen points out, 'hardly a neutral observer... It was later suggested that Evans chose to blame the European officers of the 42nd and 44th rather than to believe that his own men of the 43rd had deserted under fire.'[23]

The Court of Inquiry was to operate in the strictest secrecy; the Indian Army had no intention of washing its dirty linen in public. After listening to evidence from key witnesses, the Court concluded that the force of 400 men detailed by Collett ought to have been sufficient for the purpose of ensuring Quinton's safety and securing the objects of the mission. The ammunition problems were swept aside by a judgment that 'no man was out of ammunition, but that all were very short of it,' an observation that seemed to relieve Skene (and to a lesser extent, Quinton), of any negligence. Trying to arrest Tikendrajit at the residency durbar was termed 'infelicitous'. The officers, especially Skene, ought to have realised that if the Manipuris heard sounds of the British approaching the palace they would resist. There had been no well-considered plan of action, either offensively or defensively. The Court regretted that nothing was done all day on 24 March to rescue Lieutenant Brackenbury and his party. In summing up the proceedings the Adjutant-General pointed out that 'Colonel Skene with the Chief Commissioner and his companions could at any time have secured their personal safety by withdrawing beyond the range of the Manipuri guns and effecting a junction with the Langthobal party and Captain Cowley's detachment.'[24] Trusting Prince Tikendrajit was deemed 'fatuous'. Quinton and the others entering the palace at night unarmed and depending on Grimwood's 'naive' thinking in 'trusting to the forbearance of a semi-barbarous army, inflated with victory', effectively sealed their doom.

The C-in-C, India, General Roberts, tried to throw some good light in dark corners; he praised the men who had volunteered to rescue Brackenbury and other wounded; similarly the men who refused to retire, and the treasure-guard 'who defended their trust; he praised the sepoys and medical orderlies who for many weary hours assisted 'the devoted supervision of Surgeon Calvert'. 'No stigma can attach to troops for a failure ennobled by such instances of soldierly and gallant conduct,'[25] declared Roberts.

So much for the rank and file. What of the officers? Captains Boileau and Butcher faced grave charges of dereliction of duty. The former officer was called first and the Adjutant-General accused him of abandoning the residency – in the words of Major-General Galbraith:

> Without observing established rules for conducting a retreat, that he did not parade his men or detail advance and rear guards before retiring, that he personally left before the evacuation was complete, that on ascertaining that a large number of men had remained behind, he took no measures to communicate with them, but left them to their fate, that he failed to maintain discipline and order in retreat, and that he allowed the remaining party to straggle and separate in a perilous and unsoldierlike manner.[26]

The evidence of his junior officers did nothing to help Boileau's defence; Chatterton confessed that there 'had been no regular "fall in" and no muster, prior to the commencement of the retirement, because I knew there were men still posted at the North walls.'[27] Lugard's evidence was even more damning; he told the Court that when he had argued with Boileau over the hasty departure from the residency the captain had 'seemed to waver at my words, indeed, he certainly did waver, and said something to the effect that perhaps we had better not go.' Lugard continued:

> This startled me as it seemed to throw the responsibility of changing the decision to go on me, the junior officer of the garrison, and I said something to the effect that the decisions must rest with him and not with me. I also felt that it was too late to change as the movement had actually begun.[28]

Boileau was questioned for three days and seems to have made matters worse for himself by offering a statement that 'practically admits the truth of the charges against him', according to a despatch to the Viceroy's Council. The captain, however, did make an 'impassioned plea' that he had served almost 21 years in India (20 in the army) and during all that time had only been home on leave for 11 months. He was due shortly to receive his majority with an increase in pay and had a wife and three children to support. The Court recommended to the Viceroy that Boileau be suspended from active duty, but Lansdowne and his advisors (with probably Roberts being quite vociferous), felt there was no alternative but to request to the Secretary of State that the captain be compulsorily retired from the army – he was not cashiered or court-martialled – at that rank. As an act of compassion to his wife and children after such long service he was granted a pension of £200 per year (about £15,000 today).

Despite this humiliation for Boileau he got off comparatively lightly compared to Captain Butcher. This officer was charged with failing to recall Lieutenant Simpson's party on the afternoon of 24 March, or of ascertaining Calvert's whereabouts before he left Tikendrajit's temple; he had not collected his men together in a proper manner before quitting the residency and left before the evacuation was complete; he had given Boileau, his senior officer, 'no support or counsel' and 'took no measures' to communicate with a large number of his men left in the residency compound, but 'left them to their fate'; and during the retreat he allowed his men to straggle and separate without maintaining good discipline.

Butcher's defence was even more of a mess than Boileau's; talking of the attack on the Senapati's compound he declared categorically that 'no women or children were killed or injured by our troops,' a remarkable assertion that flew in the face of other evidence. He even went further, contradicting himself in the process: 'If any women or children were hit by our bullets, our troops were not to blame, and in fact the Manipuris must have hit some of their own people, as there was a cross-fire in every direction.'[29] In his own defence the captain admitted that he had been so exhausted by the evening of the 24th that he was taking a nap when the shelling of the residency started. He did not know how many men were with him when he left the residency because 'It was very difficult, or almost impossible, to fall in the men in such a place, owing to the heavy fire which was constantly kept up by the enemy.'[30] He had 'presumed' that his men along the residency perimeter walls would retire. Even in retrospect he 'failed to see what advice he could have given Boileau in the circumstances.' Lansdowne and his Council, after reading the Court's findings, were appalled by Butcher's 'unsoldierly disregard for the welfare of his men and such neglect of the duties manifestly imposed on him by the situation'[31] that his compulsory removal from the service was recommended to the Secretary of State. Since he had only served 12 years in the army Butcher was granted a compassionate allowance of just 5 shillings a day (about £9,500 per annum by today's standards). He appealed and submitted a second defence but this was rejected, as was his request for a court-martial.

Lieutenants Chatterton and Lugard were cleared by the Court of Inquiry of any unsoldierly conduct; the former officer was praised for his work as adjutant of his regiment, while the latter soldier had been wounded in the residency as he tried to move injured sepoys. Captain Cowley was less lucky; General Roberts expressed his 'severe' disapproval of this officer's 'want of enterprise and soldierly instinct' in retiring from Leimatak on 26 March without any attempt to rescue Quinton and the others at Imphal. The C-in-C, India, was forced to admit that Cowley's column had hardly been in a fit state to advance and it was suggested that he was 'doubtless influenced by the opinions of his seniors – Captains Boileau and Butcher'. Poor Cowley, very much a scapegoat, albeit a minor one, was left to stew in some military juice as General Roberts observed condescendingly that he had simply missed the kind of opportunity to show initiative that came but once in an officer's career, if it came at all. The behaviour of Lieutenant Grant at Thobal was much more to the C-in-C's liking. On a happier note the Court praised Jamadar Nagarkoti for his initiative and bravery while conducting the retreat from Langthobal.

The Court of Inquiry got very little press coverage, though Indian newspapers were critical of the way its 'revelations' were delivered in secret so as to ensure that the Indian Army did not lose prestige in the eyes of the people. The feelings of Indian Army officers were summed up by Captain L.W. Shakespear, Indian Staff Corps, who called the Manipur debacle 'the sorriest reading of all regrettable incidents in Indian Frontier history.' He was embarrassed and surprised:

Why a resolute attack of a place whose ditch and ramparts formed no insuperable obstacle was not made instead of frittering away the force in small isolated efforts will never be understood; or why the Chief Commissioner and party walked blindly into the trap... Some time afterwards Manipuri officers told ours that there had been no intention to put up a big fight, and that if a resolute attack by us had been made they were all prepared to evacuate the place by the north gate.[32]

The historian, Caroline Keen, castigates the military inquiry on several grounds and Butcher and Boileau are given no quarter:

> The speed with which the proceedings were conducted, the lack of a court-martial and the fact that the findings of the Court of Enquiry were never published pointed to an undeniable reluctance to reveal the full facts of the British role in the uprising. However, the accusations tabled against the Government of India of using middle-rank officers as scapegoats to draw attention away from the shortcomings of its own senior officials was less credible. Both Butcher and Boileau were undoubtedly guilty of wilful neglect in carrying out their duties at the time of the retreat, and the charges, substantiated by a number of witnesses, were hardly trumped up.[33]

In high and low places words were also being muttered about the recently deceased Political Agent, Frank Grimwood, and his lovely and very much alive wife, Ethel, now back in Britain. She was due to meet the Queen and there was talk of her writing a book, which was clearly going to be a bestseller. Unbeknown to Mrs Grimwood, her days in Manipur were about to be scrutinised by one of the sharpest brains in the Empire and his report – classified as 'Secret' – would rock to the core the myth of Ethel and Frank, the perfect young couple and their happy days in Manipur. If even half-true, this document showed that the Grimwood's marriage had been a sham, it suggested a reason why Frank had been killed first and ahead of the other officers, and it linked all of this with reports of adultery, sex orgies and even paedophilia.

Dark Side of the Raj

Today the treasure trove that is the India Office Records is housed in the fantastic British Library in the Euston Road. Back in the 1970s these priceless documents were stored in an ugly and unprepossessing office building, a stone's throw from the Old Vic Theatre in Lambeth, south of the Thames. It was on a gloomy Saturday in March 1977, exactly 40 years ago (I know the date not because I have a photo-retentive memory – I don't – but because my library slips are still with my notes), that while doing some personal research for an article on Manipur I came across a letter whose contents took my breath away. It had been written by Colonel J.C. Ardagh, personal secretary to Lord Lansdowne and sent to W.C. Maitland, Lord Cross's private secretary at the India Office in London. The passage that gripped my attention concerned Ethel Grimwood and it ran:

> Ladies do not speak kindly of her. They insinuate that she preferred the company of her step-brother to that of her husband, and no doubt she was away from Manipur for the greater part of the time that she was there. Grimwood consoled himself with Manipuri ladies in a flagrantly open manner. Puca Sena, one of the Maharajah's brothers, says that he remonstrated about it, and suggested his keeping a girl quietly, as others had done before him, but eventually they quarrelled over it and ceased to be friends, Grimwood taking up with the Senapati.
>
> Photographing naked women was one of the causes of offence. A daughter of the Tongal General seems to have lived

promiscuously with Grimwood and Simpson, and the old Tongal took it much to heart, and it was resented generally by the Manipuris. The Senapati thought Quinton was bringing the ex-Maharajah to re-instate him, and was determined to resist this by force if necessary. Grimwood's wiring to Calcutta to find out the truth prevented the Manipuris rising up, but neither Quinton or Gurdon were informed of these goings-on by Grimwood. Mrs Grimwood was not in the hospital at all, there was no firing after 8pm when she helped bring the wounded to the residency, no one was wounded by a fusillade after midnight.

Ardagh concluded sarcastically: 'Now this is the lady whom the British public worship as a heroine.'[1]

Further research revealed a report marked 'Secret' and now kept with other memoranda of Ardagh's in the National Archives at Kew. In this document he outlined in more detail his views on Ethel and Frank Grimwood suggesting impropriety on both their parts; Ethel as an adulteress and Frank as a womaniser, a photographer of obscene pictures and (by twenty-first century standards at least), an implied paedophile.

At the time of my original research no one was much interested in the Manipur Uprising of 1891; almost nothing had appeared in print, apart from the occasional rehash of events in a regimental history or two, since Ethel's book, the only major account of the war, appeared more than 80 years earlier. The one exception was a well-researched article by the Indian historian, R.C. Majumdar, that had appeared in *Bengal, Past & Present* in 1959. Mainly addressing the causes of the rebellion and the subsequent trials, Majumdar mentioned a pamphlet contemporary with the events by a Captain A.W. Hearsey that laid down in print charges against Frank Grimwood's conduct as Political Agent. Fifteen years after my researches, Saroj and John Parratt's book, *Queen Empress vs Tikendrajit, Prince of Manipur,* was published in India. This was the first full account of the war drawing on several unpublished sources. While the book concentrated on the trial of the princes it referred dismissively to Majumdar's article and simply called Hearsey's pamphlet (he was now 'Hearsay'), 'scurrilous unsubstantiated assertions', an odd remark since the officer was long dead and no one was alive who had seen events first hand in 1891. Fourteen years later Belinda Morse in her brief but entertaining biography of Ethel Grimwood referred to Ardagh's findings but so far as Frank was concerned she made no comments. The one other writer to study the war, Caroline Keen, an expert on the princely states, laid out the charges against the couple in even more detail yet did not debate whether the Grimwoods were guilty as charged.

The accusations against the pair are quite shocking. If true they also affected the course of the uprising. It is time these charges were given an airing, to see if they might be warranted.

Let us start with Captain Hearsey (or Hearsay). I was unable to locate his pamphlet at the British Library or in any institution outside India. He remains thus a mystery figure though the Hearsey family had a long association with the Indian Army and it was Major-General John Hearsey who, on the parade ground at Barrackpore in 1857, faced down the first mutineer, bhang-intoxicated and violent Mangal Pandey. Captain Hearsey opposed the Manipur war and wrote: 'The trial of the accused Princes has been one of the most outrageous farces and parodies of justice that has ever been exhibited to the Indian nation.'[2] Strong words. Oddly enough, while Saroj and John Parratt criticise Hearsey for repeating rumours about Grimwood, they are happy to quote him regarding the trial of Tikendrajit. On the first page of his pamphlet he wrote:

The popular press have been incessant throughout the whole course of the trials of uttering constant and reiterated shrieks for blood; it has, to say, been a cry of hang first and try afterwards ... if this is the modern Englishman's idea of fair play and justice, I shall be proud that I call myself an Anglo- Indian.[3]

If Hearsey was so incensed by the verdict against Tikendrajit one is left wondering if there might have been some truth in his comments on Frank Grimwood's lifestyle. After all, there is no smoke without fire. People in Cachar were gossiping about Ethel Grimwood, while at Imphal British soldiers and Manipuri natives alike were harbouring dark opinions on Frank Grimwood. All this gossip reached the ears of the Lansdowne and his Council and it was agreed that the Viceroy's private secretary should do a little secret investigation.

He was the perfect man for the job. While it is convenient perhaps to see a report on the Grimwoods as part of a muck-raking exercise initiated by and convenient to Lansdowne, this theory is not consistent with the man who was the muck-raker. John Charles Ardagh was the son of a pious Protestant parson from County Waterford and quite simply one of the sharpest brains in the British Army. Fifty years old, with hooded eyes, hair neatly partly and plastered down on his scalp and a prominent nose that jutted out from his long, lugubrious face, Ardagh had been involved in secret intelligence work since 1875 and latterly head of Section E (Ottoman Empire) of British Army Intelligence. He was supposed to take holy orders as a youth but in 1858 opted instead for a career as a military engineer. He was frightfully intelligent – a graduate of Trinity College, Dublin (like Quinton), with honours in mathematics and a prize in Hebrew. He passed in first and first out of the Royal Military Academy at Woolwich, a remarkable achievement. Those who worked under Ardagh found him to be 'a mystery to us', as one of them, Lord Edward Gleichen, explained:

> Ardagh, silent, monocled, skinny-necked (he always reminded me of a marabou-stork, I fear), the writer of beautifully expressed far-seeing memoranda on the most abstruse questions ... never spoke, and when he sent for us to give him information on certain subjects, there was a dead silence on his part whilst we talked. I once gave him a full account of Morocco matters during the space of something like half an hour. He leant back in his chair, never interrupted once nor took a note, and at the end he slowly screwed his eyeglass in, and said in a hollow, faded voice, 'Thank you.' Yet he had absorbed painlessly all that I had told him, and the issue was a masterpiece of writing.[4]

This reserved, super-bright, rather scary officer was working on a new mobilisation scheme for the army when, in October 1888, he was offered the post of private secretary to the new Viceroy by Lansdowne himself. Ardagh's immediate response was typical – 'I replied that I thought he had mistaken me for someone else' – but when the War Office gave its support he accepted his new role. He saw the job if done properly as 'the hardest of any in the world', as he prepared the workload for his master and 'Every moment comes in a telegram, a letter, or a pile of documents requiring attention.' Ardagh summed up his chief duty as protecting the Viceroy 'against everything from which he can be relieved'. Shortly before retiring from the post in 1894, he declared that he had been rather 'a general secretary, or *chef de cabinet*, than a private secretary'. Admitting that he knew no native languages nor had any special local knowledge, Ardagh concluded that he came to his post without liabilities or prejudices to warp his judgment. 'In purely personal matters,' he wrote, 'the impartiality and independence of a person unconnected with India have certain merits.'[5]

This, then, was the man delegated to find out the truth about Ethel and Frank Grimwood. There can be no question that he spoke with several army officers and private individuals as well as Durand at the Foreign Office. Kept with his report are his three main sources of information: a letter from Lt-Colonel St John Michell to Durand; another letter to him from the Pucca Sena and a third signed by the female members of Kula Chandra's and Tikendrajit's families.

Ardagh complained that Mrs Grimwood had been represented in the Press as a heroine whereas, in reality, 'some of her statements are ... absolutely untrue and the rest highly coloured.' In the years 1889 and 1890 she had been absent from Imphal for 19 months in total and 'occasioned some scandal' at Shillong by her relations with her half-brother. Ardagh added: 'It is said that her relations with her husband were very strained when she was at Manipur in 1891.' Frank Grimwood's behaviour while Ethel was away – amusing himself with native girls, taking obscene photographs and eventually acquiring the Thangal General's beautiful daughter as his mistress, whom he then shared in a *ménage* with Simpson – was conduct blamed on Ethel, 'because if Mrs Grimwood had lived with her husband at Manipur, he would not have desired to console himself with Manipuri girls.'[6]

Later, during the retreat, Ethel 'seriously embarrassed our officers by pressing them to retire and, but for her clamour, it is improbable that the officers would have ignominiously retreated.' Working himself up to a pitch Ardagh, who clearly disliked Ethel immensely, wrote:

She never showed any one the way, the road being perfectly straight, and well-known to all. She was never wounded. The story about Captain Butcher shooting five men over her prostrate body is pure fiction. The story of Captain Butcher reserving two cartridges, one for her, the other for himself, is pure fiction. She was on intimate terms with Captain Butcher and slept under the same blanket on the way down, to the scandal of the party, and she has effectively ruined his military career. And for all this she has received the Royal Red Cross and a large pension![7]

To understand Ardagh's apparent misogynistic prejudices, and those of others like Colonel Michell, who accused Mrs Grimwood of acting 'most injudiciously before the disaster, especially in writing to the Jubraj [Tikendrajit] (she carefully abstains from mentioning this fact),' it is first necessary to try and understand the late Victorian attitude to adultery. This is hard for us in the twenty-first century; our attitudes to extra-marital sex and homosexuality have softened and become liberal while, on the other hand, Victorian restraints on prostitution and early teen sex seem remarkably lax; it is a case of socio-sexual swings and roundabouts through the ages.

Firstly, one must understand that the Victorians had, in the words of social historian, Ronald Pearsall, 'an extravagant sense of sin, especially when it affected other people, and in few societies have people been more eager to throw the first stone.'[8] Adultery by a husband was of little consequence, but adultery by a woman was treated like an offence against property – the female belonging to the male – and for the female it carried a strong sense of guilt. The 1857 Matrimonial Causes Act declared that a husband could only be divorced if adultery was combined with something else (such as incest). 'Verily, sex, love and marriage are eternal' wrote one Victorian 'expert' and many agreed with him. They had the Bible on their side; churchmen and Victorian novelists portrayed the adulterous married woman as a sinner, 'irrevocably finished as a human being'. If a lady such as Ethel Grimwood had carried on a promiscuous affair under the noses of Assam society (as represented by the white planters, officers, civilians and their wives of Shillong) and shown no sense of guilt then society would have been incensed. To enjoy sex lubriciously was the behaviour of a whore.

Alan Boisragon, Ethel's half-brother, was just seven years older than her, tall and reasonably good-looking. They had been friends since childhood but separated during her years in England. It is not at all impossible for the pair to have had an affair or, at the very least, an infatuation. Many tongues must have whispered behind the potted palms in Shillong as Alan escorted his attractive relative to a ball, holding her tightly on the dance floor, or walking arm-in-arm along the esplanade. Gossips possibly did not know the pair were related. Others who did might have been even more offended by the apparent intimacy and the fact that Mrs Grimwood spent so much time away from her husband.

No letter has ever surfaced between Ethel and Alan that hints of an affair. The jury must still be out on this one. Yet it is curious that when Ethel took the long sea voyage back to England after the uprising she was accompanied all the way by Alan and not by any female relative or companion.

What seems undeniable is that something was amiss in the Grimwoods marriage, something hidden and certainly not mentioned in Ethel's best-selling memoirs, which paint a false picture of a romantic and idealised relationship. For her to be away from Manipur for over half the time of her husband's appointment as Political Agent suggests something was not quite right. Was it ill-health? Ethel hints as much in her memoirs without giving us concrete information. Was it sexual? There was a doctor attached to the residency, but if Ethel had been given gonorrhoea or something similar by Frank then she would have felt safer and happier consulting a white doctor in Assam than an Asian one at Imphal – Assam meant secrecy whereas any gossip in Manipur would have been totally unacceptable and might have affected Frank's career. Perhaps Ethel had a miscarriage or something similar? We will never know.

If adultery is discounted, as well as bad health, Ethel might have decided to stay away to avoid arguments with Frank. Drink was often a problem in the tropics but there is no indication that either Frank or Ethel were alcoholics. There is, however, a body of evidence that he liked Manipuri girls. So, we must ask ourselves, did Ethel get wind of Frank's illicit behaviour? Perhaps she saw a glass negative or print that disturbed her? Perhaps Frank, Tikendrajit or Walter Simpson said something that gave the game away? Was this why the Grimwoods argued? If she knew what Frank was up to, it would clearly have been upsetting for Ethel and good reason to stay away and try and cheer herself up in Alan's company at Shillong.

She may even have consoled herself, as did the Princess Alexandra of Wales, that despite her husband's sexual escapades, 'He always loved me the best of all.'

The reasons remain pure conjecture, and we will never know. After the Resident's death, his widow was determined to protect his memory from the slurs of officials and the press who suggested that he had somehow been partly responsible for the Manipur disaster. In Ethel's eyes this meant protecting his reputation at all costs. She was also well aware of the slurs on her own name, but after meeting the Queen and getting the Royal Red Cross medal (and a hefty sum in book royalties), she could afford to ignore these recriminations. Ardagh kept his report 'Secret' because apart from being political dynamite its contents could never be proved in a court of law.

It was from Michell that Ardagh had received the information regarding Ethel's behaviour on the night of the 24th and through the retreat. The colonel claimed that he made 'the fullest investigation' and interviewed every member of the party that reached Cachar including all officers, sepoys – and Ethel. His conclusion was: 'In no way did she act heroically.' Mrs Grimwood's biographer, Lady Belinda Morse, states that Michell was distantly related to Ethel through Boisragon's family. He was elderly, nearing retirement, 'possibly unbalanced' and 'seems to have had a personal grudge against the Moore family, as well as Ethel,'⁹ though she gives no evidence for this assertion. Yet Michell claimed to have 'endless evidence' to support his claims.

Almost as I completed this manuscript some other gossip regarding Ethel surfaced (and I must thank Professor Ian Beckett who sent me details); her name was being bandied about at the highest levels in the army. Colonel William Nicholson, military secretary to General Roberts, told another of 'Bob's' inner circle, Major Reginald Pole-Carew, that she did no more than any other woman would have done under the circumstances and that the walls she sheltered under at the residency were so thick as to prevent her being in any great danger. Another officer recently returned from India, Major Neville Lyttelton, wrote to his wife that no soldiers in the country had subscribed to a fund set up to help Mrs Grimwood, even though it was being promoted by the Prince of Wales. 'I don't know whether everything will be made public that is known about,' he wrote, 'but she will get a bad exposé if it is.'¹⁰

Several of the 'lies' referred to by Michell and Ardagh were actually the result of bad newspaper reporting – *The Englishman* newspaper in Calcutta, for instance, had published on 4 May the stories of Butcher firing with 'unswerving aim' over Ethel's body during the retreat as well as the two cartridges tale. Mrs Grimwood was able rather effectively to correct some of these misrepresentations in her book. She wrote:

> It has been said lately by some that this retreat to Cachar was in a great measure due to my presence in Manipur at the time, and that my helplessness has been the means of dragging the good name of the army, and the Gurkha corps in particular, through the mire, by strongly influencing the officers in their decision to effect 'the stampede to Cachar'. But I scarcely think that they would have allowed the presence of and danger to one woman to deter them from whatever they considered their duty; and had they decided to remain in the Residency that night, I should never have questioned their right to do so... I think that the honour of England is as dear to us women as it is to the men... But such an insinuation as I have quoted is not, I am happy to think, the outspoken opinion of the many to whom the story of Manipur is familiar. It is but the uncharitable verdict of a few.[11]

Ardagh's insistence that Ethel bedded down with Butcher on the retreat and had sex with him sounds shocking. The reality, one suspects, may have been quite different; it is possible that on a chilly or wet night during the retreat the captain had tried to console a dispirited (and fully dressed) Ethel by offering her his blanket. She may even have gallantly suggested with a laugh that they share it. Such a happening would have been enough to start tongues wagging and the story might have been embellished by gossip-mongers. To suggest that she was having an affair with Alan Boisragon is one thing. The idea that she slept around with Captain Butcher is entirely something else. The real Ethel Grimwood was more complex than her book suggests but a slut she was not.

Charges of sexual misconduct are easier to level at Frank Grimwood. The first of these is that he took obscene photographs of Manipuri girls. Here again we must tread carefully; the idea of Frank setting up his tripod and camera, then dropping his trousers to appear *in flagrante delicto* with some Manipuri maidens seems ridiculous. So too is any accusation that he got Manipuri girls to strike lewd solo poses. What is possible, however, is that he may have taken perfectly innocent nude or semi-nude photo-studies in his studio. A keen photographer such as Frank would have known something about nude photo-art which had a history dating back to the 1840s and was taken seriously on the Continent, especially in France, from 1850 onwards. Posing young women in the nude, or semi-nude, sometimes with flowers, or in semi-classical art poses was perfected by several early masters of photography including Charles Puyo and Marie-Alexander Adophe in Paris and Frank Eugene in New York. Their work was exhibited and discussed by other keen photographers.

One can almost see an excited and breathless Frank at work. Before him stands a shy but smiling Manipuri princess or court girl encouraged by the strange Englishman's charm and power. Perhaps he has put an exotic orchid in her lustrous long brown hair or one of the roses from Ethel's tea-garden? He suggests after a few pictures that she might consider unfastening her gown, a hint of breast perhaps, a semi-nude side view, each pose taking Frank closer to his goal. These sessions done in private between Grimwood and well-bred Manipuri girls aged between about 13 and 16 years (at which age most girls got married), must have been gossiped about by princes in the palace and fishwives in the bazaar. Only Prince Tikendrajit seemed to approve. Even the mildest of semi-nude images would probably have been labelled as 'obscene' by a man as strait-laced as Ardagh.

Sadly, one cannot dismiss the possibility that Grimwood took nude photographs of children. He and Ethel had become favourites with the younger members of the royal family. These kinds of pictures were immensely popular in Victorian times. They were not considered pornographic because the children looked innocent and the Victorians worshipped childish innocence. Clearly there was a sublimation of paedophile urges in many of the admirers of this kind of photography, displayed quite openly for sale in a way that nude images of adult women were not. 'The obsessive preoccupation with pre-pubescent girls seems to have been a predominantly

Anglo-Saxon affair,' notes Jorge Lewinski in his history of nude photography. During the 1880s and 1890s postcards of nude nymphets were extremely popular and sent through the post. Collectors may have had sinister motives, yet no stigma attached to them. This seems odd to us in the twenty-first century but it was a more innocent age. The most famous child photographer was the Reverend Charles Dodgson, better known to the world as 'Lewis Carroll'. The author of *Alice's Adventures In Wonderland* told a friend, 'Naked children are perfectly pure and lovely.' No one has ever accused Carroll of being an overt paedophile and it is to be hoped that Grimwood, if he took any nude photo studies, saw this just as an art form. Yet the 'Cult of the Little Girl', as Pearsall called it, 'included the influential art critic, John Ruskin, who waxed lyrical over artist Kate Greenaway's drawings of little girls as well as the diarist, the Reverend Francis Kilvert, who said of a youngster on a swing, 'Her flesh was plump and smooth and in excellent whipping condition.' Judge this as you will.

The other major charge was that Grimwood kept the Thangal General's daughter as his mistress and shared her with Simpson. The Pucca Senna had told Durand that previous Political Agents – Dr Brown, Major Trotter, Mr Primrose – all kept 'Manipuri girls for amusement's sake' and Grimwood had been told that this was okay provided he did it discreetly. But according to the women of Kula Chandra and Tikendrajit's households the Resident was smitten by the Thangal General's daughter whom they described as twenty years old, a girl who could read and write Bengali, Hindi and a few words in English. 'At first she had illicit intercourse with Bengalese, and then Englishmen' is how the women described the girl who they seemed to view as a slut. Availing himself of Ethel's long absences, Frank Grimwood, so it was said, invited *laisebis* (beautiful girls) onto the residency lake, as well as *tanks* (pools) and streams, 'sporting with the girls', apparently in company sometimes with Tikendrajit or Simpson. Then it was back to the residency for photo-sessions, more partying or a nautch. The Thangal General's daughter, knowing no shame or fear, began to visit the residency in daylight. Simpson was allowed to have sex with her either separately or in a *ménage a trois* with Grimwood.

Is it likely that there was substance to these allegations? In view of the fact that they were reported by officers such as Hearsey and

Michell, princes like the Pucca Senna and ladies of the court the answer has to be: 'Yes'. Everyone seemed to have heard the gossip that Frank Grimwood had maintained the Thangal General's daughter as his mistress as well as possibly dallying with other girls. We know from another I.C.S. official, Henry Cotton, that at least one Manipuri Political Agent had fathered children from two native women. Add to this the fact that military and civil officers in nearby Burma were known frequently to keep native mistresses, factor into the picture Ethel's long absences, and it seems highly likely that Frank did indeed have extra-marital sex with Manipuri girls.

In the days of the East India Company many British officials had taken native wives. Colonel Skinner, founder of the yellow-coated cavalry known as Skinner's Horse, had 14 wives and 80 children. Sir David Ochterlony, British Resident to the Mughal Emperor at Delhi, had 13 wives; his favourite was a former Brahmin dancing girl who called herself 'Lady Ochterlony' and was the mother of his youngest children. Times change. By the 1890s miscegenation was frowned upon by the British Establishment. A Eurasian or Anglo-Indian sub-class that had developed in India as a result of mixed race marriages was now viewed with disfavour by successive Viceroys. English gentlemen, it was felt, needed to keep themselves aloof from hi-jinks with women of other races. The British concluded that Indians were more lascivious than themselves. The *Kama Sutra* seemed to prove it, as did child marriages and polygamy. More and more white women were encouraged to join the 'fishing fleet' and look for husbands in the East. The memsahibs helped to maintain a rigid social hierarchy by the 1890s. This was intended to 'correspond to the political hierarchy and that sexual behaviour should be subordinated to the need of both.'[12]

The white officer class and the rank and file white soldiers led entirely different lives. It was accepted that the animal sexual instincts of non-commissioned ranks had to be catered for in some way. These men could not be expected to show the same moral restraint as a gentleman. Most regiments maintained a local brothel or had access to Indian prostitutes. The problem was starting to get out of hand; rates of venereal disease infections had risen by 1890–93 to 438 per thousand soldiers (compared to just 203 per thousand in the army in Great Britain).

British officers in late-Victorian India might carry on affairs with single or married white women in places such as Simla, the big cities, or even out of boredom at a lonely cantonment on the dusty plains, but they did not keep native mistresses. Missionaries and memsahibs had put paid to that kind of thing. As one officer told his brother: 'My dread of furnishing you with "whitey-brown" nephews, as you call them, is a sufficient argument to deter me from keeping a Sable Venus to tuck my clothes in at night etc.'[13] The days of every officer habitually keeping 'a native dictionary' fell away fast after the Mutiny. Back then Captain Garnet Wolseley had told his brother, Dick, in a letter how his native mistress 'answers all the purposes of a wife without giving any of the bother.'[14] The mood of the times is apparent even in the only work of Victorian pornography to deal with the Raj. In 1889 appeared *Venus In India*, a two-decker novel first published in Brussels and supposedly written by an officer of the General Staff, Charles Devereaux. It is most likely that the name of the author was a pseudonym (Ronald Pearsall suggests that the author might have been the Honourable George Talbot Devereux, a son of Viscount Hertford, but the evidence for this is sketchy), but whoever he was he certainly had travelled in India and had excellent knowledge of the 2nd Afghan War. The 'hero' of the tale has various sexual couplings all over India but, curiously enough, miscegenation never rears its head; every one of the white officer's 'encounters' involves a memsahib. It seems odd but there are no British-Asian adventures in its two volumes of lustful fantasy.

The exception that broke the rule was Burma (and, so it appears, the north-eastern frontier of India). These areas had relatively few British missionaries or white women. Successive Bishops of Calcutta and Viceroys might fulminate across the decades against what seemed to be accepted behaviour in Burma but little seemed to change in this torpid backwater of the Raj. Even Kipling wrote of his Burmese girl 'a sitting and I know she waits for me'. He fell in love with the free spirit of Burmese women and wrote:

When I die I will be a Burman ... and I will always walk about with a pretty almond-coloured girl who shall laugh and jest too... She shall not put a sari over her head when a man looks at her nor shall she tramp behind me when I walk: she shall look all the world between the eyes, in honesty and good fellowship.[15]

He claimed that his *Mandalay* poem was inspired by a beautiful Burmese girl he had seen sitting on the steps of the Moulmein pagoda when he visited the place in 1890. The first British ruler of Burma, Lord Dufferin, also extolled 'the grace, charm and freedom of Burmese women' who had no caste, no purdah, married whom they wanted and divorced when they chose.

In 1882 Colonel W. Munro, Deputy Commissioner at Bassein, complained that his superior officer refused to promote him because he had a native mistress. The I.C.S. was loath to do anything and admitted that Munro 'has got a large family about him by a Native woman.' The official British attitude towards miscegenation rumbled on; a Chief Commissioner three years after the Manipur debacle declared that an officer with a Burmese mistress 'degrades himself as an English gentleman.'[16] One year later, two I.C.S. men married their native mistresses. An investigation showed this to be quite a common practice. The I.C.S. was unmoved. Even when Lord Curzon complained in 1900 that a Mr Walter Minns was living with not one but two Burmese women in a *ménage* the I.C.S., who judged the culprit as 'an excellent Burmese scholar', simply waited for the matter to blow over and later appointed their man as Deputy Commissioner of Rangoon.

In one respect Frank Grimwood was on safe ground; his employer, the Indian Civil Service, almost never allowed a sexual scandal to damage a career. Blind eyes were usually turned on those guilty of sexual misconduct since the I.C.S. did not ordinarily concern itself with the private morals or behaviour of its officers. One had to do something wholly outrageous to merit punishment. The anger of a Viceroy was simply not enough to warrant dismissal.

This attitude is nicely illustrated by the shocking tale of Howard and Clarke. In 1902 a Mrs Howard, a chaplain's wife no less, complained to the Viceroy that a young I.C.S. man named Robert Clarke had seduced a girl of 12 in her care. It happened that the seducer was Mrs Howard's lover and the young victim her daughter, Dorothy. Clarke claimed at first that he had never touched a woman and that Mrs Howard was a 'nymphomaniac' who had pursued him to Kashmir. An investigation revealed that the woman had lived 'more or less openly' with Clarke as his mistress at Ladakh. Even worse, young Dorothy, 'decidedly big for her age and very good-looking,' according to the Bishop of Lahore, had come into Robert's tent early one morning 'and a great deal of kissing and cuddling occurred.' On another occasion she persuaded Clarke to get into bed with her, though 'he did not stay there more than two minutes,' just time enough for her to touch his body with her hand. Mrs Howard wanted to marry Clarke, or get a lot of money from him. Failing these two propositions she wanted him 'punished'. It was all an ugly and rather extraordinary business made more so when it was revealed that young Dorothy was not a virgin. Curzon was appalled by this 'extreme and revolting immorality', but Denzil Ibbertson, one of the I.C.S men on his Council, thought that Clarke did not warrant dismissal from the service because there had been no public scandal. Curzon soon found that his entire Council were not so hot and bothered as him; Sir Edward Law, the Finance Member, refused to 'attach any importance to any statement made by a woman who accuses a man of seducing her daughter and demands as repatriation that the man shall *marry herself*, or give her money.'[17] Next the Viceroy asked the Secretary of State to step in but he declined to do so. Six years later Clarke quietly became a Deputy Commissioner.

Back in Manipur in 1887, Captain James Willcocks, a young officer serving on the Burmese frontier, tried to see the Thangal General to organise a supply of rice. The old man suavely asked after Willcocks's health before saying, 'I am just going into the courtyard to see the contractor and I will return in a few moments.' The minutes ticked by. He did not return. Then appeared 'a very smartly dressed young lady in the national dress, viz. a sack of rich material, fastened under the arms and reaching a little below the knees; her hair was cut straight across her forehead in a fringe, showing that she was unmarried, and she was not in the least abashed.' This was the old general's lovely daughter and Willcocks was describing the girl who within a year or so, if the rumours were true, became Grimwood's mistress. The girl told Willcocks that her father had been summoned away to the palace on urgent business. Some time later he ran into the Thangal General again and the old fellow asked whether he thought his daughter 'was a nice-looking girl?' Willcocks replied: 'Yes, but she is far too good-looking to be your daughter.'[18]

We will never know for sure if Grimwood had sex with Manipuri girls or whether he shared the Thangal General's daughter with Simpson. Curiously enough, in Colonel Alban Wilson's biography the author wrote an odd line regarding the caste prejudice in Manipur. 'This always struck me as an excess of zeal,' recorded this old Gurkha officer, 'seeing the alliances the women contracted with all sorts of people.'[19] Major W. Hill, 2nd Gurkhas, also wrote in 1891 of the 'friendliness' of Manipuri women towards his troops, a suggestion that the easy-going nature of Burmese women was to some extent repeated in Manipur.

For such a proud man as the old Thangal General the knowledge that his daughter was debasing herself as a plaything for British officers must have seemed terrible. He must also have been aware that 'vile things' were being spoken about his child and himself behind his back by others at court and even the common people in the bazaars. In the words of the royal ladies: 'Thangal, who was proud of his fame, took this to heart and therefore, on the breaking up of the Durbar, on the night of 24th March, and after the Jubraj [Tikendrajit] had left the Top Guard, he remained behind, and with a view to avenge himself, instigated the murder of Mr Grimwood first.' Lieutenant Simpson had also carried on with the Thangal General's daughter. 'This is the reason why Mr Simson (*sic*) was struck with a view to despatch him also, just after Mr Grimwood was struck.'[20]

Simpson had, in fact, been struck first in the melee but no matter. Here at last we have a logical reason why Grimwood and Simpson were specifically targeted after the durbar broke up. The Thangal General, one suspects, had by that evening, after a whole day of bloodshed and fighting, decided that things in Manipur would never be the same again. When the night durbar was mooted he was not happy, but once it became obvious that it was going to take place (because Tikendrajit had willed it so), he decided quickly to make the most of the opportunity and revenge himself on the hated Englishmen who had defiled his daughter and, more importantly, his honour. This theory is in keeping with what we know of the old man as a ruthless realist. Even the court ladies called him 'cruel-hearted', adding rather interestingly how he was 'the richest man in Manipur, and so most of the people were in his hands.'

We will never know for sure if Frank Grimwood was murdered by accident, the good Resident speared as he stood standing in the wrong spot at the wrong time. It is as likely that his immorality – sexual behaviour for which he had been criticised by Manipuris – led to the implacable hatred of a ruthless old man who felt that he had nothing to lose in taking a life, a man who took his chance and avenged a dark stain on his family honour.

13

Viceroy versus Victoria

Early on the dust-laden sunny afternoon of 1 January 1877 the citizens of Delhi stopped their work to hear a cannonade the like of which made many shiver with memories of the terrible days of the Great Mutiny 20 years earlier. Sherbert sellers and shopkeepers, gardeners and grooms, washerwomen and wives listened to the regular booming of the great guns sounding out a salute 101 times. This was the climax of the Delhi Assemblage, a display of British pomp and might dreamed up by a new and romantic Viceroy, Robert, 1st Earl Lytton, intended to overawe the Indian princes and demonstrate the power of the Raj as well as test their loyalty to the British throne on the day that Queen Victoria was proclaimed 'Kaisar-i-Hind' – Empress of India. This political *coup-de-théâtre* was really the brainchild of the British Prime Minister, Benjamin Disraeli, who felt that a display of loyalty to the Crown on such an auspicious day would reinforce the image of the British as heirs to the Mughal emperors.

The festivities had started at Christmas. The assemblage was vast: sixty-three rulers of native states with their retinues; about 800 titular princes and nobles; ambassadors from exotic lands such as Burma, Siam and Nepal; deputations from far-off Yarkand, Chitral, Yasin and Kashgar; the Governor-Generals of Portuguese Goa and French Pondicherry; all the foreign consuls; senior British officials; 15,000 soldiers; editors and correspondents from 14 foreign newspapers and all the main Indian ones – 100,000 people camped on a grassy plain just outside the city. Here 2,000 labourers had erected three iron pavilions to seat the Viceroy, princes and other dignitaries. These structures resembled Victorian piers in circus colours. Commissioned at £5,000 to do a painting of the ceremony the artist, Val Prinsep, was appalled by it all. 'A kind of thing that outdoes the Crystal Palace in "hideousity",' he wrote, 'Never was there such Brummagem ornament or such atrocious taste.'[1]

Beyond the pavilions stretched a vast tented plain, lit at night by gas made from castor oil supplied at his own expense by the Maharajah of Jaipur. The sight was one of gorgeous colours, most notably the camp of the native princes, a mass of blue, yellow and scarlet with gold knobs on the tent poles. All the arrangements, which could have been a disaster, worked out fairly well. Only the Khan of Khelat begged poverty and asked Government for help; he came with 100 armed retainers in a train that was kept locked as he was terrified of this new mode of travel. When the Khelatis arrived at Delhi, a British aide sent them a ready-cooked meal. They 'appropriated all the cutlery, ate the cakes of Pear's soap provided for them, threw out the beds and used the washing basins and jugs for the purpose of eating and drinking.'[2]

To celebrate the Queen's new title as Empress of India nearly 16,000 prisoners were released and an amnesty extended to all those who had rebelled two decades earlier (save Feroz Shah, a relative of the King of Delhi, and Nana Sahib, the butcher of Cawnpore).

On the great day Lady Lytton wore a gown by the designer Worth of Paris, a creation of purple silk and velvet, adorned with her best pearl and diamond necklace. 'It was handsome and picturesque without being too gaudy,' she thought. The Lytton's two daughters wore dresses and hats in matching blue-green velvet. The Viceroy himself, something of a dandy, wore the robe of Grand Master of the Star of India in blue velvet with a long ermine cape. The princes sat in their semi-circular stand, some 800 feet long, facing the Viceroy on his throne. After the band had played the Grand March from Wagner's *Tannhäuser,* a herald, Major Barnes, an enormous soldier 7 feet tall in his leather boots, read out a proclamation from the Queen. This was repeated in Urdu by Mr Thornton, the officiating Foreign Secretary. Then came the cannonade – three salutes of 31 guns with a *feu-de-joie* between each one, making a total of 101 guns. The Indian princes visibly jumped in their seats when the cannonade began and the *feu-de-joie* caused several elephants to stampede and trample a few unfortunate natives.

Lytton stood up and read out a telegram received from Her Majesty. Afterwards the whole assembly rose spontaneously and cheered. Several of the princes tried to shout out but their words were drowned in the uproar. The first of them had been Maharajah Scindia of Gwalior who had said, '*Shah-in-Shah Padashah* (Monarch of Monarchs), may God bless you! The Princes of India bless you and pray that your sovereignty and power may remain steadfast for ever.' Writing to the Queen, Lytton told her that Scindia's words held 'a special significance ... not apparent in the translation ... it permanently and publicly fixes your Majesty's suzerain, and more than suzerain, power in India beyond all possibility of future question.'[3]

The Queen was delighted. The Royal Titles Bill had suffered a shaky passage through Parliament in the previous summer. Disraeli had tried to explain to Her Majesty that she was only Imperial in connection with India. She refused to listen. Before the end of 1876 the Queen told her private secretary that she wanted to have a troop of Sikh cavalry as a permanent escort. That New Year she signed cards as 'V.R. & I.' – *Victoria Regina et Imperatrix*. At dinner on 1 January 1877, while guns were booming out her new status in India, one of the Queen's sons, Prince Arthur of Connaught, toasted the health of 'the Empress of India'. After dinner Disraeli asked 'Her Imperial Majesty' if she was wearing all her Indian jewels. 'Oh no,' replied the Queen, 'I'll send for the rest.' The Prime Minister had to wait patiently until three large portmanteaux were dragged in.

The years rolled by but the Queen remained ever entranced by those words, 'V.R. & I.' Deeply romantic by nature, the lure of the East and its mysteries held an endless fascination for the aging sovereign. She truly felt she was the ruler of India and would listen for hours to stories of this exotic land from visitors. Its peoples, their lives and vicissitudes concerned and deeply moved her. She also took great care reading her despatch boxes on Indian affairs. Ten years after the Delhi Assemblage, the Queen-Empress celebrated her Golden Jubilee. From Agra came a proposal; John Tyler, superintendent of the central gaol, wrote suggesting that the Queen might like to have some Indian servants during her Jubilee. Victoria liked the idea, especially since she was expecting several Indian princes to attend. With the help of the local Political Agent at Agra, two Moslems were selected – portly, jovial Mohammed Buksh and tall, good-looking Abdul Karim. It was not long before Karim, son of an Indian Army medical orderly, had established himself as the Queen's favourite. His popularity grew so fast that it horrified royal courtiers. Queen Victoria was never colour-conscious and ignored all who complained about Karim. It was not long before he stopped serving at table and became her *munshi* (Indian clerk and teacher). She asked him if he would teach her an Indian language. He suggested Urdu, the language of the Mughal nobility. The result was that for the next 13 years, until her death, Queen Victoria filled a page of her Urdu language journals every day of her life. In time she would learn to write it and speak it very well for a white woman, a remarkable achievement since the Queen was already well into her seventies when she had her first lesson. Indian visitors to Windsor were usually astonished to be greeted by the Queen in Urdu. Due to Abdul Karim, Queen Victoria was introduced to curry. She liked it so much that curry was on the royal menu for luncheon for the remainder of her reign.

Rapidly Abdul Karim stepped into the shoes of John Brown, the Queen's loyal Highland servant who had died in 1883. In time Abdul, who had many good qualities and was loyally devoted to the Queen, became universally loathed by most of the royal household largely due to his self-important airs and manners. He also had a bad tendency of asking the Queen for gifts, ranging from medals to property. She was besotted with him and told her doctor (who hated Abdul Karim), that he was 'excellent, so superior in every sense of the word'. In February 1890 when the munshi was ill, Dr Reid noted on 1 March: 'Queen visiting Abdul Karim twice daily, in his room taking Hindustani lessons, signing her boxes, examining his neck, smoothing his pillows, etc.'[4]

Although not as antagonistic towards the munshi as some others at Court, the Queen's private secretary, Sir Henry Ponsonby, realised that she discussed Indian affairs with Abdul and tended to accept his version of things. Gradually his views of the Raj, seen through Moslem-tinted spectacles, became hers. In particular, Abdul Karim seemed to suggest to the Queen that while her humble subjects across India revered her, this rule was threatened by the unthinking behaviour of British officials who often rode roughshod over Indian feelings and prejudices. Often very critical of her Viceroys, Queen Victoria was at first very pleased with Lord

Lansdowne because he assisted in her request to get a grant of land at Agra for the munshi. When Abdul Karim went home on holiday he was allowed an audience with the Viceroy (who thought him a 'smart' young man), an honour the Queen much appreciated.

News of the Manipur Uprising was followed very closely by the Queen who, on 6 April, told Lord Cross that she had reservations about the suitability of some Political Agents and members of the I.C.S. Two days later she laid the blame at 'some great ignorance and imprudence'. She had by this time made clear her annoyance with Lansdowne, who was not keeping her informed well enough. Cross told the Viceroy that the Queen 'will want a letter from yourself. I think she has an idea that, however good our Commissioners may be in ordinary times, they are not much of the right kind of stuff for serious troubles.'[5] As newspaper reports became more critical of the Indian Government, so too did the Queen get more angry; on 20 April she telegraphed the Prime Minister, Lord Salisbury, that 'the Manipur disaster is a very sad thing. Fear bad advice was given from Calcutta.' This was a direct accusation of mis-handling either by Lansdowne, Durand at the Indian Foreign Office, or both. 'If former Maharajah had been reinstated, nothing of all this would have happened,' continued the Queen, who had clearly heard or read Johnstone's comments, as she concluded, '*This* is opinion of well-informed people who have lived in the country.' The Prime Minister replied that it was too early to have a clear opinion, 'But it seems at present as if Quinton himself was greatly at fault.'[6]

On 2 May the Queen-Empress, now obsessed by Manipur, dictated a memo from Windsor that laid down her views. She wrote:

> The disaster at Manipur is a dreadful thing... Our dealings in India should be dictated by straightforwardness, kindness and firmness, or we cannot succeed. This disaster is most unfortunate, and the effect may be very serious in other parts of India. Our system of sending out ... people who merely get appointed from passing an examination must be altered, or we shall have some much more serious trouble in India. There is no doubt, from what the Queen hears from many sides, that the natives (though they are very loyal to the Queen-Empress and the Royal Family), have

no affection for the English rule, which is one of fear, not of love, and this will *not* answer for a conquered nation.[7]

Eight days later the Queen telegraphed Cross to ask if the Cabinet had decided on a new policy for Manipur. Her Majesty did not mince her words and declared: 'There seems to me to be a wish on the Indian Government's part to blame Mr Quinton exclusively, whereas people here think blame attaches to the former. Just hear Maharajah Manipur taken. Think it will never do to hang him.'[8] Viscount Cross sensed quite rightly that Abdul Karim was dropping his opinions into the Queen's ears. The Secretary of State wrote to his sovereign saying that Lansdowne was not trying to make Quinton a scapegoat. It had also been made clear to the Viceroy that 'H.M. Govt. expected to be consulted on any punishment of the Maharajah'.

Writing directly to Lansdowne, the Queen told him that 'our Commissioners and Political Agents in India are very inferior to what they used to be.' She suggested employing 'people of higher calibre socially, and more conciliatory as well as firm.'[9] Lansdowne was forced to reply defending his actions and those of his administration. He reminded the Queen that 'there is a tendency to remember the successes and forget the failures of bygone generations.' He defended Quinton as 'a gentleman much respected by all who knew him ... a man who was certainly incapable of acting, as some people apparently believe he intended to act, in a treacherous manner towards the Manipur Princes.' The Viceroy went on to defend the need to arrest Tikendrajit by saying, 'Considering the conduct of the Senapati and his antecedents, Mr Quinton was, the Viceroy thinks, fully justified in arresting him at once if he refused to surrender,' though Lansdowne qualified his praise of the Chief Commissioner with the words, 'Had he [Tikendrajit] been arrested on the first day, Mr Quinton would probably be now alive.'[10]

If Lansdowne thought his letter might soothe the Queen he was in for a surprise. On 27 May Her Majesty wrote to him a letter that began politely enough, but it had a nasty sting in the tail:

What strikes the Queen-Empress, after perusing the various reports which were forwarded, is the action taken apparently suddenly by the Government of India against the Senapati so long after the revolt which disposed the original Maharajah (now in Calcutta), during which time all seems to have been going on quietly? Why was the time allowed to elapse if the Jubraj (as the Senapati was called) was so bad a man as to necessitate his expulsion from Manipur? The Queen-Empress wishes to add that she is not aware of any precedent for an arrest in Durbar, and fears it may have a bad effect in other Native States.[11]

One can only guess how Lansdowne felt when he had absorbed this figurative smack in the face. While he was master of affairs in India, the one woman he had to bow to had spelled out clearly, and precisely, some of his mistakes. How his neat, lordly moustache must have bristled.

On 30 May the Queen's concerns were discussed within the Cabinet. It was decided, as Lord Cross told her, 'that the Viceroy must either be recalled or supported, and that he could not be recalled and must therefore be supported.'[12] This was an honest but an astonishing admission by the hamstrung Secretary-of-State that he was far from happy with Lansdowne's explanations. After a tough time with the Queen a tetchy Cross wrote to the Viceroy from Balmoral: 'I quite put aside any question of treachery, and I fully admit all about the Durbar being a Court, but I can find no precedent for an arrest there. I still think, therefore, that the conclusion arrived at on the 21st at a meeting between Quinton, Skene and Grimwood (Grimwood dissenting), was a ruinous one, and most injudicious.'[13]

With newspapers in India and Britain publishing condemnatory articles, unsupportive letters arriving on his desk from the Secretary-of-State and accusations of improper conduct from the Queen, it was clear to Lansdowne that he was under attack. In his opinion it was all frightfully humiliating, disgraceful and unfair. Despite his smooth words to Her Majesty about the Chief Commissioner, he personally blamed the whole affair on Grimwood for being too 'intimate' with the Senapati and Quinton for being too 'reticent' to arrest him. On 30 May the Viceroy and his staff came under a physical attack at Simla from a huge swarm of locusts, 'as thick as sardines in a box'. Lansdowne hurried away to his office in Viceregal Lodge where he immured himself in his correspondence and wrote to Cross defending the right of the Government of India to decide on its own death sentences for murder without having to refer to H.M. Govt.

On 5 June Lansdowne sent a long and detailed memorandum to Lord Cross that set out his policy on Manipur. In a summing-up, he admitted requesting that the Senapati be deported after the palace coup, but: 'We did not prescribe method of his deportation; and we did not know Quinton intended to arrest him in Darbar.' He defended Quinton's actions, which were not treacherous and which Tikendrajit, as 'a subject of a subordinate Native State he was bound to obey.'[14]

More trials had been proceeding at Imphal overseen by Major Maxwell, the new Political Agent. Mia Major, who had fought gallantly at Thobal against Grant, was convicted of rebellion against the Queen-Empress and condemned to death. Two courtiers, Nilamani Singh, known as the Ayapurel, and his associate, Samoo Singh, the Luwang Ningthou, were charged with waging war against the Queen, abetting the murder of Grimwood and also the murders of the other British officers. The courtiers argued that they had taken no part in the fighting and had tried to prevent the mob attacking the captives. Maxwell's contention was that the pair had done little to prevent the violence or ensure the safety of Quinton and the other captives. He condemned both men to death. The Wangkheirakpa, Lokendra Singh, had been in command at Thobal, but there was little evidence to link him with the murders at Imphal. He was sentenced to transportation for life.

The death sentences were duly commuted to transportation. General Collett in particular was not happy about handing down death sentences since he felt strongly that court officials and soldiers had simply been acting under the orders of the princes. When commuting the death sentences passed on the nine sentries who had guarded the British captives, he noted:

I do not confirm the sentences passed on them because it seems to me that in the matter of the Manipur murders capital punishment should be reserved for those who form the main possession of rank and power in the state ... and should not be inflicted on persons such as the accused who are merely servants and subordinates ... being subordinates they had, I conceive, no practical alternatives but to obey.[15]

The wily old warrior known as the Thangal General, a figure at the very centre of the storm, was put on trial between 22 May and 1 June, a protracted affair due to his continuing ill-health. In a somewhat curious manner, as in the earlier trials, Maxwell heard the prosecution witnesses first before specifying a charge, then listened to the accused's statement and finally the defence presented its witnesses. No legal counsel represented the accused. Five prosecution witnesses were called but not one of them directly implicated Thangal in the order to execute the British prisoners. His defence witnesses made clear that the old man was away from the Top Guard well before and long after the executions. He had also, as several men attested, warned Quinton at the west gate not to enter the palace and had voiced his disapproval of a night durbar. From a legal standpoint the prosecution case was a weak one. Historians Saroj and John Parratt have concluded that '*on the basis of the evidence produced before Maxwell* there is no conclusive, or indeed presumptive, proof that the killing of Quinton and his companions was the result of anything Thangal General said or did.'[16] Listening impassively to all that was said, the old warrior refused to cross-examine witnesses and, one suspects, waited with equanimity for his inevitable death sentence handed down by Maxwell.

In August Major Maxwell was to conclude the trials by sentencing the seven Manipuris and one Naga accused of killing Melville and O'Brien. Again, the Manipuris were sentenced to transportation for life while the Naga, a man called Churai, who had actually beheaded Melville, was publicly hanged.

While reading all the trial reports and having talked with several officers, General Collett was forming his own opinions on the disaster. He wrote privately to General Roberts on 9 June, explaining that he felt the Chief Commissioner had mishandled a delicate situation:

If Quinton had not been in such a hurry, the Jubraj [Tikendrajit] would, in a few days, have given himself up, and marched quietly with Quinton back to India... But poor Quinton was in a great hurry to get away and back to Assam: the season was advancing; he always considered himself as peculiarly liable to malarial influences, and he was eager to get out of these hills before the really unhealthy season commenced. No one can doubt that Quinton mis-managed the business all through, and that he went to work in the very way calculated to bring on a disturbance and resistance. And yet he no doubt thought that a sudden arrest of the Jubraj when at Durbar was the safest way to do the business.[17]

Back in Britain matters were coming to a head with a debate in Parliament. In the Commons a former Indian Foreign Secretary, Sir Richard Temple, declared that an arrest in durbar 'was not properly justifiable, and it will do no good, either for the honour of England, or its influence in British India.' Muddying his own waters, Temple went on to defend the Indian Government for trying to arrest Tikendrajit and added that 'from the many possible modes of interference [it] chose the best.'[18]

MPs could have been forgiven for wondering on whose side Temple actually was. Then, to make matters worse, the Under-Secretary-of-State, Sir John Eldon Gorst, Lord Cross's deputy and main Government speaker on Indian affairs in the House of Commons, delivered an extraordinarily cynical speech in which he referred to Tikendrajit as 'an able man intriguing against the Paramount Power' who was struck down in accordance with the Indian Government's 'customary policy of cutting down the tall poppies, setting aside the man of ability and strong character in native States, in favour of the mediocre or incapable.'[19] This speech caused outrage when it was reported to Lansdowne and his Council. A disgusted Sir George Chesney said it would have a 'mischievous effect' as it implied the Indian Government was bent on some 'Machiavellian' course, whereas it had in actuality always tried to 'secure the services of the ablest men that can be found.' (Sure enough, Indian nationalists have trotted out Gorst's infamous remark ever since.)

Lord Cross now found himself stuck between three fires: an angry Viceroy, a confused Cabinet and a suspicious Queen. He told all who would listen that Gorst had been suffering 'from the effects of influenza and gout', rather lame excuses. The unrepentant Under-Secretary was given a severe ticking-off for his most injudicious speech. Why Gorst spoke in the way he did has never been fully explained, but an anonymous correspondent quoted by Lansdowne's biographer suggested that the Under-Secretary had been behaving erratically because of his annoyance of being left out of the Cabinet and so decided to 'kick over the traces'. In the House of Lords on 22 June, 'in language very rarely used by a Cabinet Minister in speaking of his Under-Secretary,'[20] Cross said Gorst's speech had been 'utterly opposed to all common sense.' Other speakers made clear that the annexation of Manipur was no longer a favoured option. The *Times* told its readers:

> The native Princes dislike annexation because it reminds them unpleasantly of their own tenure of power. Probably the inhabitants of Manipur would rather jog on in their old slipshod way than be squeezed into uniformity by British tax collectors. Indian finance is not so flourishing that any new burden need be assumed except under the pressure of overmastering expediency.[21]

At Imphal a special court was convened in June to hear the cases against the Manipur princes. President of the court was Lt-Colonel St John Michell who had two other judges, Major Richard Kirby Ridgway V.C., 44th Gurkhas, and Mr A.W. Davis, Deputy Commissioner of the Naga Hills. The prosecutor was Major Maxwell. Michell had wanted to conduct the trials in court martial form but, as he told Mortimer Durand in a letter, Davis would have been 'useless' as a prosecutor, 'a careless young gentleman, not given to study', so Maxwell had to take on this role as he was the only one who knew much about the law. Michell found the 'abominable' trials 'a perpetual anxiety' and the situation on the Bench was not improved by Ridgway, who spent much of his time in a bad temper because several of the press correspondents, such as Captain du Moulin (who represented *The Times of India, The Englishman* of Calcutta and the *Civil and Military Gazette* at Lahore), were picking up fees far in excess of the judges.

For thirty-two 'suffocating days' the court sat in stuffy, sweltering heat – not helped when two men dropped dead from cholera. Tikendrajit was tried first; there is a photograph of him at this time, hands free though his ankles were roped to guards on either side. Dressed all in white (if the black and white photograph speaks truly), including his turban, he stares out at us with the cool hauteur of a royal princeling. Initially he faced two charges: waging war upon the Queen-Empress and, secondly, abetment in the murders of Quinton, Cossins, Skene and Simpson. A third charge of actual murder was added to the indictment. The prince pleaded not guilty to all charges. Twelve Manipuris and three Indian Army soldiers were called as prosecution witnesses. After the evidence had been presented Tikendrajit answered more than an hour's worth of questions declaring that he had told Grimwood that he would surrender himself when he felt better, 'But I was never told that I would be arrested.' He reiterated the story about the Thangal General demanding the deaths of the white men, and that he had told Usurba and Jatra Singh that 'on no account were the orders of Thangal General to be obeyed.'[22]

The defence called six witnesses; they were all unanimous that Tikendrajit had been ill on the morning of the 23rd and that the British troops had attacked on the 24th without any warning. They also told how after the night durbar, the prince had driven away the mob with his stick and personally got Lieutenant Simpson to safety. All agreed that he had told the Thangal General clearly not to harm the sahibs. Without any legal help, Tikendrajit was given two days to prepare a detailed statement of some 3,000 words. Towards the end of this document he claimed to have learned of the deaths of the British on the next day and how during his sleep Thangal General had ordered the *lami* (executioner) to kill the captives. He claimed to have promptly reported this matter to the Maharajah and declared that the perpetrator was Thangal General. The court ruled, 'with the strange logic of wounded imperial pride,' that in *resisting* the attack on his own enclosure the prince had somehow committed an act of war! Tikendrajit's statement and the words of his defence witnesses were pronounced 'unreliable'. The judges concluded that he must have 'acquiesced' in Thangal General's plan to have the captives executed. On 10 June the president declared that 'the court directs that you, Tikendrajit Singh, alias Jubraj, alias Senapati, be hanged by the neck until you are dead.'[23]

The case against Maharajah Kula Chandra revolved mainly around the charge of waging war. Defence witnesses made clear that little was done at court without Tikendrajit's agreement. In his own statement Kula Chandra called himself 'a lethargic and indolent' person 'of whom nobody took much notice and he therefore could not be held responsible for what his younger brothers had done.'[24] He was, in his own words, simply 'installed as a puppet on the *gadi'* (throne), without 'power or influence as a sovereign'. Kula Chandra claimed to have tried to stop the fighting and to have rebuked both Tikendrajit and Thangal General for the murders. Eventually he was sentenced to death (commuted to transportation for life). The trial had not been without occasional moments of humour according to Colonel Alban Wilson; at one point Michell had asked an official of the royal household, 'What are your duties of your office?' The man replied that he had to clean the Maharajah's teeth and also his bottom. At this point Major Ridgway interjected, to the laughter of the court, 'Not with the same brush, I hope?'[25]

A death sentence was also handed down to young Prince Angao Senna. He had not been present at the executions so the judges assumed that he had issued the orders. Eventually the twenty-year-old prince was also to have his sentence changed to transportation for life. *The Times* in its editorial opinioned that it had been wrong to try the princes under British law and that the Indian penal code ought to have been used. A debate swirled around the princes; were they 'feudatories' accused of rebellion (and liable to martial law), or 'independent belligerents' who had connived in 'the murder of an ambassador under a flag of truce'. None of the princes had been represented by legal counsel and there are grounds for believing that they may have misunderstood some of the questions put to them. Finally they were made to sign statements in English and only an English transcript was kept, though parts of the trial had been conducted in Urdu and Methei.

In Great Britain the woman in whose name the princes had been accused of waging war was watching the case with ever greater interest – and far from happy with what she read in the newspapers. On 16 June the Queen told Lord Cross that in her opinion the Government of India ought to have consulted the Secretary-of-State before interfering in Manipur, and that the correct time to arrest the Senapati would have been when the former Maharajah was sent away. It was plainly wrong to have tried to arrest Tikendrajit at a durbar. She lambasted the Government for presenting a defence of Indian affairs that was 'weak, and goes too far, even trying to palliate the arrest in Durbar, which I understood you to say you would not defend. Think hanging Senapati would never do; it would create very bad feeling in Manipur and in all India. But shut him up for life in some distant part. Think no prince was ever hung. The Tongal deserves to be hung.'[26]

Similar epistles were fired off to Lansdowne who gamely tried to defend himself in a letter on 22 June in which he rejected any charge of 'dilatoriness' and explained that consulting with Grimwood and Quinton over what actions to take in Manipur had taken up several weeks. Delicately, the Viceroy tried to lay all the blame at Quinton's feet. He explained how an arrest in durbar was not wrong in principle:

It seems, on the contrary, natural that the representative of the paramount Power should command the rebellious subjects of a Native State to appear before him in open court, and should, if they refuse to accept his decision, then and there proceed to enforce it.[27]

On 30 June Lansdowne went on the attack again and in a letter to Cross more or less blamed everybody (but himself) for the disasters. In addition to slinging mud at Frank and Ethel Grimwood, the Viceroy also blamed everyone in the residency for not putting up a stiffer resistance; the casualties in the attack on the palace, he declared, had been 'quite insignificant' and the troops were 'practically intact' at the residency before the retreat. He laid blame on Skene this time because he 'did not think the situation was serious.' Lansdowne's generalisations were, it must be said, total nonsense,

After luncheon on 1 July 1891 the Queen met Ethel Grimwood at Windsor Castle, an event that had a lasting effect on both of them. Ethel looked 'a mixture of beauty, sadness, sweetness and grace' (as someone once said of the Princess of Wales), and just like the Queen's daughter-in-law she knew how to look stunning in a dress of severe simplicity, the perfection of the line enhancing her fine figure. The Queen wrote later in her journal of Ethel:

Lady Cross brought her in and presented her, leaving her with me afterwards. She is striking-looking, with a fine figure and a pretty, sad face, but looks much worn and weather-beaten. She was a little shy at first, but got over it by degrees, and answered all I asked her, telling me a great deal of what she went through, which is really more than any woman, and above all, a lady, has ever done! She was nine days on the horrible march, and almost all the time followed and pursued. She was lame from having fallen, when she ran the last stockade on leaving Manipur. There were 9 officers and 200 men, who however were reduced to 40 at the last. She was continually aimed at and had to lie down and hide in the long grass. She had no clothes but those she was wearing. Once she saw herself being aimed at, and the man close behind her, who was already wounded, was killed, knocking her over and covering her with blood. In this condition she had to go on her way. She was thankful that her poor husband was killed on the spot, speared she thinks by someone who might have owed him a grudge, and this she thinks may have led to the murder of the others. She knew the Senapati well and liked him very much, as she did all the Princes, with whom she used to ride about a great deal. She said she could not, and would not, believe he intended to kill the prisoners. But the Tongal, who commanded the troops, was a horrible blood-thirsty old man of eighty-six, who had killed no end of men, women and children when he went out to punish the tribes. Poor Mrs Grimwood ... still cannot sleep or bear to be alone. She was a good deal overcome once or twice in speaking. I gave her the Royal Red Cross, which pleased her very much, and pressed her hand and kissed her when she left. Poor thing. I pity her so much![28]

This remarkable interview demonstrated once again Queen Victoria's remarkable knack of putting ordinary people at ease (if not her own ministers), and her genuine humanity. The account also reveals that Ethel had her own opinions as to why Frank had been killed, secrets she took with her to the grave.

The Royal Red Cross had been instituted eight years earlier as a military reward for exceptional women. Its first recipient had been Florence Nightingale, nursing heroine of the Crimean War. Ethel Grimwood got it 'in recognition of her devotion to the wounded under most trying circumstances, during the attack on the Residency at Manipur'.[29] She was later photographed and painted wearing the red enamelled cross, edged in gold, with the words, 'Faith, Hope, Charity' on its upper limb and '1883' on its lower limbs, the silk ribbon with a thick deep blue stripe edged either side in crimson. Queen Victoria recommended a doctor to examine Ethel's swollen ankle. One week later Mrs Grimwood wrote to the Queen's lady-in-waiting to say that Her Majesty's kindness 'was far more than I expected or deserved – & it will always be a Red letter day to be remembered as long as I live.'[30]

Back at Simla the special court's sentences required the Viceroy's confirmation and he knew that his every move was being watched and criticised by H.M. Government and the Queen. At Imphal, his prisoners were also having a rough time. 'I am a prisoner in my own palace,' wrote a miserable Kula Chandra on 13 July, 'with heavy irons on my legs, living in jail with other common Manipuri prisoners ... under such circumstances death is rather preferable for me than to suffer all these privations.'[31] Alban Wilson recalled later in his memoirs that Kula Chandra was constantly complaining while under arrest. One day he asked to see a doctor about a pain in his toe. An Irish medico prescribed a good dose of Epsom salts or a 'Number 9' pill, which the ex-Maharajah refused to take, saying it was 'poison'. The irritated doctor then gave his patient a cuff around the head before stalking away. 'It is not often a King gets his ears boxed for refusing to take a purgative,'[32] noted Wilson gleefully.

The old Thangal General remained dangerously ill in prison. Calmly he took the news that his property had been looted by angry Manipuris and his wives and children claimed to be destitute. Did these relatives include Frank Grimwood's ex-mistress or had she by now found another lover?

The Indian Government could not prevent the princes from having access to a real lawyer to frame their appeals. The man who agreed to act for them was Mano Mohun Ghose, an advocate of the Calcutta High Court and also a barrister-at-law of Lincoln's Inn. Highly intelligent and an indefatigable worker, Ghose set out to show that a great injustice had been done. 'From the beginning several handicaps were placed upon his freedom to plead,'[33] note historians Saroj and John Parratt. The appellants were not permitted to have their appeals heard in an open court – 'a matter of right by every subject of Her Majesty throughout her dominions' wrote Ghose – whose representations could only be made in writing. Hamstrung, a disappointed Ghose pointed out that there was a vast difference between arguing a case *viva voce*, or in writing, since 'no one could possibly anticipate all the arguments that could be raised by the prosecution, nor could one single appeal be expected to convince judges in the way the spoken word could.' Ghose attacked the legitimacy of a court whose officers had no legal training and the fact that the princes had not been defended by professional lawyers, but left 'practically undefended, and the evidence against them was left almost where the prosecution chose to leave it.'[34]

In the first place Ghose argued quite brilliantly that the princes were not British subjects – neither British Law nor the Indian penal code related to them. International law required 'an express declaration of allegiance on the part of a ruler or subjects of a foreign territory', but no such declaration existed in the treaties between India and Manipur. The barrister concluded that the British Crown had simply allied itself with the sovereign state of Manipur. Behind closed doors in the Foreign Department the status of Manipur had been under debate; George Forrest, principal secretary, pointed out to Durand that I.C.S. historians such as Sir William Wilson Hunter and Sir Charles Aitchison (who had compiled a monumental *Treaties and Engagements*) both described Manipur as 'independent'. Durand wrote dismissively:

Hunter never wrote an accurate sentence in his life. I think we have made the position of Manipur pretty clear now... They have repeatedly professed their readiness to obey our orders etc., etc. We have upheld their Chiefs by force or arms and given away their territory, and asserted supremacy in a number of ways. But I knew that the remark by Hunter, coupled with the fact that Manipur has no Adoption Sanad, would do harm.[35]

The British case was presented by Sir A.E. Miller, Law member of the Viceroy's Council, who argued that the status of Manipur, though never defined in clear terms, provided several historical precedents that showed the rulers were dependent on the Raj. He also added that the murder of British subjects was a serious crime, 'even in states as independent as Afghanistan or Nepal.'

There was such interest in the case that Ghose's memorandum, together with a transcript of the trials, was rushed into print in

India and also published later that summer as a 121-page pamphlet by William Hutchinson in London. Prince Tikendrajit, probably on Ghose's advice, wrote directly to Ethel Grimwood begging her to intercede on his behalf. This letter greatly distressed her. At the same time the Queen, perhaps influenced by all that she had heard from Mrs Grimwood's own lips, redoubled her efforts to have the prince spared. She telegraphed Cross on 1 August: 'Trust Senapati will not be executed. He was not found guilty of murder and the effect is sure to be bad in India! That harsh crushing policy will not do now. He should be shut up for life.' Then, turning attention to the findings of the court, she wrote: 'There was too much not explained to make the case a clear one.'[36]

On 8 August the Secretary-of-State told Queen Victoria that the Viceroy had commuted the sentences on Kula Chandra and Angao Senna, but that Tikendrajit must hang. Immediately Her Majesty wired angrily to Cross and literally spelled out her views:

> I can only say I regret the decision as to the Senapati and trust my approval is not asked for, for I wish to give no opinion. We shall see whether it will be of use as deterring others. I cannot consider that the Senapati was not aware of our *intention to seize him* and thus HAD CAUSE for resistance. The Queen ... thinks we seem not quite clear in this deplorable affair and ought *not* to hang the Senapati, though certainly Tongal.[37]

Next day Viscount Cross defended Lansdowne's actions in a letter to the Queen. He pointed out that Tikendrajit's death sentence had been discussed within the Cabinet as well as at separate meetings with the Prime Minister and the Lord Chancellor. Personally, he felt clemency was right for the deposed Maharajah and Prince Angao Senna. He defended Lansdowne's 'imperative sense of duty' in demanding Tikendrajit's execution.

Obstinate as always when she felt that she was right about something, Queen Victoria refused to give up seeking clemency for Prince Tikendrajit. All her life she had a special respect, amounting almost to veneration, for persons of royal blood. It explained her kindly and forgiving manner to such exasperating royals as Prince Dhuleep Singh, Maharajah of the Punjab, who had tried to get the Russians to foment rebellion in India, not to mention some of her own family such as her hysterical, narcissistic grandson, the German Kaiser. These men were, she told other people, 'royal' and so deserving of patience and respect. Her Majesty was genuinely unhappy about executing a royal prince and on 11 August she wrote to Cross again:

The reason why she regrets the Jubraj's (for he and the Senapati are the same person) sentence of death being carried out are threefold. First, because she will not be convinced that the seizure in Durbar was wrong [right?] and gave the Jubraj an excuse for resistance, besides having been on such good terms with him for so long. Secondly, because *he* was not convicted of wilful murder, and thirdly, because she has a great and strong feeling that the principle of governing India by fear and *crushing* them, instead of by firmness and conciliation is one which never will answer in the end and which the Queen-Empress would wish to see more and more altered. To these reasons the Queen would add that hanging a person (and he a Prince) so long after he has been kept a prisoner has something cruel and cold-blooded about it. These are the Queen-Empress's feelings, which, however, she will not write to the Viceroy. She intends neither writing nor saying anything to him about it as he is evidently very sore about it.[38]

Despite telling Lord Cross that she would not write to the Viceroy the Queen changed her mind that same day after she was approached by Ghose. From Osborne House she sent a secret cypher telegram to Lansdowne at Simla. It read: '*Baboo* (a native clerk or educated Bengali) who defended Senapati appeals to me for commutation. Is it possible to do this?' The wily barrister, perhaps aware of the Queen's concerns, had indeed tried to get her to stay the execution at the last minute. Lord Lansdowne was unmoved by all this agitation. He swiftly sent a reply on the same day saying that a 'commutation of sentence would be a grave public misfortune and I regard as now absolutely impossible.'[39]

So much for the Queen's tremendous display of common sense, humanity and basic human decency. So much too for the wide concerns of the British Government. Lansdowne had decided months earlier that Tikendrajit must die. His death sentence was palpably unfair based on the evidence, even if one accepts the jurisdiction of the tribunal, though it also displayed a clear bias against him and the other prisoners. Tikendrajit's act of rebellion, noted the historian, R.J. Majumdar, 'was an act of self-defence against an unprovoked, one might say, treacherous attack.' The charge of murder, as the Queen had noticed, 'was certainly not proved ... the least that one can say is that Tikendrajit was certainly entitled to the benefit of the doubt.'[40] Majumdar and other historians have noted how the Indian Government seemed to have a 'special grudge' against the prince. Since Tikendrajit had played a minor role in the palace coup that started the troubles, one has to conclude that Johnstone, his implacable enemy (assisted by the ex-Maharajah in exile), had done a good job in poisoning the minds of those in official circles at Calcutta. Lansdowne came to the conclusion that the prince was the root of the uprising and was determined to have his pound of flesh. The Viceroy was a proud man and he suffered much humiliation during the Manipur debacle. It was his wish that the chief culprit, in his eyes, should die and so he insisted upon the execution against the wishes of his Secretary-of-State and his Sovereign.

Mud from the affair stuck, 'as it usually does when it has been thrown with good reason.'[41] The general feeling among many British army officers who served in Manipur was later summed up by one of them who wrote of Tikendrajit: 'Because the man was a useless rogue is no reason why we should have resorted to underhand trickery; it never pays.'[42]

In all, 22 Manipuris – including Kula Chandra and Angao Senna – were transported to the Andaman Islands. Their goods and properties were confiscated. Prince Zillah Singh was the only one of the princes to fare a little better; he was sent away to Sylhet along with the wives and children of the deposed princes.

Two gallows had been erected at Feida Mound in the royal market. Around noon on 13 August more than 8,000 Manipuris watched in awe as the Thangal General and Prince Tikendrajit mounted the scaffolds. Instantly the women in the crowd began wailing. Four hundred Gurkhas guarded the execution site to prevent any attempt at a rescue. One of the British officers described what happened next:

The Tongal pretended to be too ill to walk up to the gallows, and was carried up in a chair and placed beneath the noose, but the Senapati walked up and stood upright like a man. A sergeant of gunners, who was executioner, adjusted the rope round the Senapati's neck, tapped the Tongal General on the shoulder and said, 'Now then, old man, stand up or I can't hang you.' The Tongal gazed at him blankly, and then at the interpreter who translated the remark, on which the old fellow shook his head and roared with laughter. The interpreter said, 'Sir, the general states he will not rise.' The sergeant said, most persuasively, 'Just tell the old gentleman I'm not going to hurt him.' This, too, was translated, but the Tongal would not budge. Then ensued a most ghastly pause, whilst a man climbed up to the top of the gallows to lengthen the rope, and when it was adjusted both criminals were loosed off. The moment the drop fell, all the women in the crowd set up the most desolate wailing, which showed that the Senapati was a great favourite with the fair sex, but no regret was expressed for the Tongal, who was notorious for his cruelty.

The same officer added, 'No one who had seen the mutilated bodies of his countrymen, or the desecrated graves in the little cemetery, felt much sympathy for any of these people, though, as is customary, there was plenty of it expressed in England by those who sat at home in comfort.'[43]

Captains and Kings Depart

With British troops rapidly leaving the state and the chief conspirators either exiled or hanged, it was time for the British to restore order in Manipur as swiftly as possible. A war, such as the long campaign against 'dacoits' that had dragged on for years in Burma, was something too horrible to contemplate. After much discussion H.M. Govt. decided to follow the advice of Sir James Johnstone and others and not annex Manipur. Instead it was agreed that the state should pay an indemnity of 250,000 rupees over five years and the Manipur durbar was stripped of its political authority. One thing was clear – 'henceforth the kings of Manipur would be selected by and accountable to the imperial power alone.'[1]

Tasked with finding a new ruler was Horatio St John Maxwell, the new Political Agent. His eye fell on Chura Chand, a five-year-old boy, youngest of five brothers, from a distant collateral branch of the royal family (though he was a great grandson of an earlier Methei king called Nara Singh). Under Manipuri custom the child had no claim to the throne, but Maxwell knew he would make perfect raw material to be schooled in British ways and elevated to rajah (no longer maharajah), with a reduced salute of eleven guns. The fact that Chura Chand was intended as a pliant puppet on the throne was not lost upon British officers stationed at Imphal. In a letter Major W. Hill, commanding 1st/2nd Gurkhas, wrote on 17 September:

Yesterday Maxwell, the Political Officer, went to the village where dwelt the great grand-children of a one-time Rajah of Manipur.

He was shown a very poor tumbledown hut, in which dwelt in poverty, bordering on starvation, the family he sought. Paraded for his inspection were four very dirty villagers, and they were described as the great grandchildren of the late Rajah, Mir Singh. Is there not one other, the Benjamin, the child who was born at the time of his father's death? A small urchin, beastly dirty, and as naked as truth, was produced, and Maxwell informed the five year old brat that Her Gracious Majesty the Queen-Empress had been pleased to command that he be made a King, and then, turning to the proud mother, presented her with a cake of Pear's Soap (this is not a joke, but a solid fact), and bid her wash the King.[2]

Even Maxwell admitted that the boy's family were thunderstruck when he announced the purpose of his visit, lifted up the child and called him 'rajah'. The very young ruler was moved to a block of houses near the palace and his family were given 500 rupees a month to make sure he was brought up 'healthy and strong'. To reduce any discontent or feelings of nationalism, the Manipuris were told that the rajahship would be hereditary provided each successive ruler 'recognises the paramount authority of the Government of India.'

On 29 April 1892, before a huge crowd of 8,000 Manipuris, Chura Chand was installed by Major Maxwell. The Methei people seemed to accept their new king not out of pleasure but out of resignation. They were well aware he had been imposed on them by the British yet their culture and society demanded some kind of god-king figurehead. The old ambiguities that had bedevilled the Anglo-Manipuri balance of power were at an end when Maxwell made clear that Chura Chand was recognised as a tributary prince of the British Raj. The Political Agent also announced that the *lalup* system of forced labour was now at an end. It was replaced by those symbols of the British Empire in its dominions – a house tax and a uniform rate of land revenue. Several days of festivities followed and it all ended with a slap-bang firework display.

One person definitely not celebrating was the ex-maharajah, Sura Chandra, who had continued throughout 1891 to push forward his claim to the throne. When he got the news about Chura Chand it was, as Maxwell called it, 'like a bombshell'. Six months later his young son died of smallpox and a few weeks after that, the fat, incompetent Sura Chandra also passed away. There is a little gleam of happiness in his tale; the ex-maharajah's beautiful and youngest daughter, Princess Sanatombi, was wooed by Maxwell and romantically involved with him, causing something of a local scandal, until her death in 1906 (there is something ironic in the fact that Grimwood and his immediate successor as Political Agent both had trysts with Manipuri women).

Horatio St John Maxwell rose to become a colonel and served as Political Agent in Manipur on four occasions between 1891 and 1905. He conducted the affairs of the state as 'superintendent' during the rajah's minority. The first year of British rule saw an outbreak of smallpox decimate the population while misuse of rice stores led to a famine in late 1891 that lasted four months. As the decade progressed so things improved; a new treasury post and telegraph office were built in the citadel and a medical dispensary erected north of the polo field along with a new schoolhouse and a re-built bazaar. Men of the 42nd G.R. occupied new barracks in the citadel while the 43rd G.R. had quarters just beyond the moat. In 1892 the bridges and roads leading out of the country had been repaired and new rest houses built in the jungle. By March of that year, when the expeditionary arrangements ceased in Manipur, a new police force of 400 men had been raised, though the British thought it prudent to arm them only with muzzle-loaders.

Young Chura Chand was duly sent to Mayo College, Ajmer, the Raj's Eton for the sons of the Indian nobility. In 1907 he was formerly declared king and ruled until the year of his death in 1941. For most of his reign, Manipur slipped back once again into being a quiet backwater of the Raj. Lord Curzon, that most imperial of Viceroys, visited the place in 1901, a full decade after the uprising, and set his seal on all that had happened by declaring that the Manipuris were 'the most good-natured, harmless, though excitable, people in creation, who were only driven into a revolt against us by a series of blunders almost unparalled in history.'[3]

While kings depart slowly, captains move on much faster. Charles Grant, hero of Thobal, a favourite of schoolboys throughout the Empire who saw in him the living embodiment of the jolly, plucky heroes in their favourite G.W. Henty or Rider Haggard novels, duly got his Victoria Cross, promotion to the rank of captain and an immediate jump up the ladder to the brevet rank of major. His citation ran:

> Charles James William Grant, Lieut., Indian Staff Corps. For the conspicuous bravery and devotion to his country displayed by him upon hearing, on the 27th March, 1891, of the disaster at Manipur at once volunteered to attempt the relief of the British captives, with eighty native soldiers, and having advanced with the greatest intrepidity, captured Thobal, near Manipur, and held it against a large force of the enemy. Lieut. Grant inspired his men with equal heroism and ever present example of personal daring and resource.[4]

On the blistering hot afternoon of 6 July 1891 Grant had the coveted bronze medal pinned upon his chest by the Governor of Madras, Lord Wenlock, at Government House, Ootacamund. The band of the 1st battalion the Suffolk Regiment, Grant's first regiment on joining the army, were on hand to play, rather aptly, *See The Conquering Hero Comes*, before the officers and men shouted themselves hoarse. Grant stayed on in Madras as an A.D.C. to the C-in-C, Madras Presidency. By Christmas he had also found himself a wife and, over the next few years, he rose to a brevet colonelcy but he never saw any fighting again. He retired from the army in 1913 to enjoy his favourite pastimes of hunting and fishing, but on the outbreak of the Great War he re-enlisted and became a district conducting officer for the 3rd Royal Scots. Grant, ever cheerful, died at his home at Sidmouth, Devon, aged 71, on 23 November 1932. His medals were sold at a Spink auction in 2011 for £230,000 and are on loan to the National Army Museum. When his tombstone and burial plot at Sidmouth fell into disrepair the Royal British Legion replaced his crumbling headstone at a special ceremony in January 2015. The local chairman of the Legion, Dave O'Connor, was reported as saying, 'We are honoured that he chose to live in Sidmouth and we couldn't let his grave just fall apart and crumble.'[5] Mary, Grant's wife, lived on until 1959 and lies beside him.

Lansdowne and Roberts both championed a clasp or new medal for the Manipur Expedition. H.M. Govt. were not so keen.

Correspondence on the matter was 'spirited'; it was pointed out by the Indian Government that in addition to casualties in action some 42 British and 122 native officers and men had died of sickness, mostly cholera cases, on the campaign. Finally it was agreed that a clasp, 'N.E. Frontier 1891' be added to what was known as the 1854 Indian General Service Medal.

The Indian Army, full of pride, did not forget Grant's soldiers who had been with him at Thobal; their bravery was recognised by the presentation of the Indian Order of Merit – the Indian Army's own V.C. – to every one of them, along with six months' pay. Several men were quickly promoted. Never before or since has a collective award for bravery been given to so many Indian troops.

Henry Collett, the kindly rector's son who refused to smite the Manipuris with the sword of vengeance, died just ten years after the war. He had been knighted on his return from India and retired himself due to increasing deafness. His botanical magnum opus, *Flora Simtensis,* listing 1,326 species of the Simla region, was published after his death. One friend wrote at the time that Collett had all the Christian virtues of the greatest of late Victorian heroes – General Gordon – who had died a martyr's death at Khartoum.

Living for more than sixty years after those dark days in Manipur was Edward Lugard. His adventures during the fighting at Imphal and subsequent retreat had terrified his brother, Frederick, then deeply involved in carving out a new addition to the British Empire in East and Central Africa. Dealing with wily African kings along the shores of Lake Victoria, the elder Lugard brother did not hear how 'Ned' had been wounded at Imphal and 'nearly murdered' until it was all over. He wrote: 'Thank God for his escape, the boy is about the dearest thing in the world to me.'[6] Edward was fine; in 1893 he married his cousin, Charlotte Howard, and Fred was there to be his best man. In due course Edward Lugard got involved in his brother's empire-building; the fiercely moustachioed Frederick became Lord Lugard of Abinger and his younger brother helped in the creation of Nigeria, rose to the rank of major and was awarded the O.B.E.. He lived on until his ninety-first year, passing away on 3 January 1957, almost certainly the last participant in the defence of the Manipur residency.

Wars have winners and losers and the latter are not always on the losing side. Manipur effectively destroyed the careers of Captains Boileau and Butcher. The former officer became an army tutor preparing young men for entrance into Sandhurst and Woolwich. On the outbreak of war in 1914, notes historian Caroline Keen, 'he was employed as a recruiting officer in Kent for five months, and on the grounds that he had received no pay or gratuity for this work Boileau applied for an addition to his compassionate allowance following the war. The case was referred to the War Office, which promptly refused the application.'[7] As late as the 1960s his son, Colonel Digby Boileau, was trying to prove that his father had been made a scapegoat, 'sacrificed to public opinion chagrined at the loss of British prestige, and quite possibly wounded pride at a very high level. That a cloak of secrecy was cast over the whole business was not, I believe, out of consideration for my father, but to hush it up as quickly as possible.'[8]

Boileau fared slightly better than his subordinate, Captain Butcher; he appealed to the Under-Secretary of State for India in 1892 pleading that he had a right for his case to be heard in an open court. His appeal was refused. Four months later he tried again and was similarly unsuccessful. The final humiliation came when he was refused the Manipur medal clasp. Butcher appealed this time to the Queen and was told that he could not wear the clasp, despite all the fighting he had seen in Manipur, because of 'his unsoldierlike behaviour'. In retrospect it is hard not to see both Boileau and Butcher as scapegoats. Both men made mistakes, both might have acted differently with hindsight, or somehow saved the situation at Imphal just as Grant did at Thobal. But these errors of judgment did not make them cowards. Historians Saroj and John Parratt conclude that 'neither their errors nor the consequences which resulted from them were in any way comparable in magnitude to those of Chief Commissioner Quinton and of their own commanding officer, Col. Skene.'[9] Withholding the campaign clasp from Butcher seems particularly cruel and petty.

The murdered officers at Imphal left wives, children and other loved ones. Mrs Skene was given a £200 a year pension for herself and £25 for each of her children. Mrs Quinton, as the widow of a Chief Commissioner, fared somewhat better and got a £300 pension for life. When the India Office was informed that Quinton had maintained his mother and sisters for 30 years, 'whose means were very scanty', a special pension of £100 was granted also to his mother, and after her death, £50 to his sisters provided they remained spinsters. Less successful was Mrs Melville, who was originally offered a meagre pension of £100 a year and £18 for her sons. After a heated correspondence she was allowed an additional £50 a year provided that she remain a widow. Lieutenant Brackenbury's mother also tried to claim a pension but as she was already a War Office widow, no extra payment was permitted. The parents of Lieutenant Simpson, admittedly quite wealthy, received no compensation for the loss of their son. Perhaps saddest of all was Signaller Williams who had been taken prisoner by the Manipuris and made to negotiate at Thobal with Lieutenant Grant. Writing an account of his misfortunes for the Indian Government poor Williams admitted: 'I am at present without anything, and my loss is over Rs. 400, besides the few things that were left behind at Golaghat were sold off, my family believing I was really dead.'[10] Sadly the India Office files do not reveal if he ever got any compensation for his sufferings.

Ex-maharajah Kula Chandra, Prince Angao Senna and the others shipped off to the Andaman Islands penal colony endured a hard time before their circumstances improved. In 1896 they formed some of the first prisoners in the newly built – and soon to be notorious – Cellular Jail at Port Blair. It is unclear what happened to all of these Manipuris, but it seems that some were released in 1897 at the time of the Queen-Empress's Diamond Jubilee celebrations. The Ayapurel died that year in the holy city of Brindaban. Kula Chandra lived on four more decades and did not pass away until 26 January 1934. By this time he was living modestly in the small village of Radha-kund in what is today Uttar Pradesh state. Radha-kund is one of the most holy places for Hindus. It is to be hoped that this sad and simple, yet religious little man, was at peace close to where the Lord Krishna had once bathed. The very thought probably made him happy.

The principal political players in our drama were far less affected by the events of 1891 in Manipur. Viscount Cross's parliamentary career continued in style; he was later Chancellor of the Duchy of

Lancaster and Lord Privy Seal, fitting appointments for an elder Tory statesman. He retired in 1900, saw his son enter Parliament and died at the ripe age of 90 in January 1914. Monty Durand, Lansdowne's smooth Foreign Secretary in Calcutta continued his remarkable career in the I.C.S.; in the mid-1890s he was responsible for drafting a border between Afghanistan and British India that has lasted to this day, derided by many over the years, but a singular and lasting achievement, called the Durand Line. His later years as an ambassador in Tehran and Washington were not so successful; an argument with President Theodore Roosevelt saw him recalled from the USA. He died in 1924 and lies buried in Boldon churchyard, Minehead, Somerset.

Three years later Durand's Indian master, Lord Lansdowne, also passed away. He stayed in India as Viceroy until 1894. His biographer described him as a man who avoided blunders, was considerate, kind of heart and exceptionally courteous. The latter attribute may be true, the penultimate one partly so, but it is hard to agree with the others. His obstinacy and total belief in his judgments never left him. He remained to his dying day a patrician politician. His son once described him as 'aloof, severe, unbending'. His forward policy along the Indian frontiers was to have severe repercussions in the late 1890s. Lansdowne never accepted that anything he had done or said had caused the Manipur Expedition, nor did he lose a minute's sleep over the thousands of Manipuris and British soldiers who suffered or died in the war. The Viceroy's superior in Whitehall, Lord Cross, thought it best not to chide Lansdowne once the executions were over, but he told the Viceroy, rather pointedly in fact, that arrests during a durbar were never to be permitted again. The dapper, slightly built marquess was soon seen at Westminster on his return from India. A Liberal Unionist he aligned himself with Salisbury's Conservatives and was rewarded in 1895 with the post of Minister of War. In this role he got a lot of abuse when the South African War broke out in 1899. In a notorious parliamentary debate he blamed the failures of the army largely on the Commander-in-Chief, Lord Wolseley, who was made to resign and swiftly replaced by Lansdowne's Indian protégé, Frederick Roberts. Wolseley, a fine soldier who was just starting to suffer from memory loss, thereafter referred to

Lansdowne as 'the little reptile' and 'that contemptible creature'. In 1900 Lansdowne could not take the brickbats any longer and also resigned. He was a successful and vigorous Foreign Secretary 1900–1905, perhaps his finest hour, before incurring the wrath of the Liberals at the time of the famous 'People's Budget' in 1909 as leader of the Conservative and Unionist peers in the House of Lords. Recognised as an elder statesman, Lansdowne was given a Cabinet position in Asquith's 1914 coalition Cabinet. Lloyd George, however, had no time for the little marquess, now white-haired, and kicked him out a year later. In 1917 Lansdowne issued a letter calling for a statement of post-war intentions from the Entente Powers. This 'Lansdowne Letter' was seen as an unwise indiscretion and contrary to Cabinet policy. Today he is remembered, if at all, by several streets, schools and a park in Canada. Lansdowne Market, Kolkata, is one of his few memorials in India.

That Manipur was not annexed owed something to Sir James Johnstone's pleas that the state be allowed a measure of independence. He died two years after the uprising, but in 1896 his memoirs were published posthumously. In these pages he took several swipes from beyond the grave at Frank Grimwood and Prince Tikendrajit. Johnstone made clear that he disapproved of the new rajah, Chura Chandra, feeling that the throne could have been passed successfully to the family of ex-maharajah, Sura Chandra. The war, declared the old general, had been totally unnecessary, caused by 'an unseemly want of nerve when the news of the disaster arrived ... brought about by want of courage, nerve, forethought and common-sense.' He dismissed the attack on the residency, declaring that British troops 'might easily have held their own till daybreak,' when he optimistically predicted 'all opposition would have collapsed, and the rebels would have fled, leaving our people masters of the situation.'[11]

Johnstone was unfair all along in his assessment of Frank Grimwood. The younger man definitely had some failings, as this book has delineated but, personal behaviour aside, he strived honourably and worked hard to be a good conduit of communication between Manipuris of all classes and the Raj. A memorial to Frank can be seen in his old school cloisters at Winchester, a second in the ante-chapel of Merton College, Oxford. The former monument tells how he was 'treacherously murdered', the latter words it differently:

Frank St Clair Grimwood
Sometime Postmaster of Merton College
Born 18 January 1854
died a soldier's death
at the Manipur Residency
24 March 1891
Whilst doing high political duty
Righteously and fearlessly
on the frontier of the Indian Empire
Remembered with love and admiration
by his Oxford friends

One suspects that Frank would have been well pleased with both these memorials.

A new palace was later built in Manipur, much smaller than its predecessor which over the years was allowed to fall further into ruin. The moat today is wider than Ethel's 'wet ditch' but the Lion Gate seems identical to the 1891 one. Imphal, of course, became famous in World War II for a battle far more terrible than the one related in this book. The grounds of the old residency now form part of the governor's palace. Beneath a tall marble obelisk in the grassy lawns is a plaque which reads:

The Government of India
have caused this monument to be erected
to mark the spot where rest the remains of
THE BRITISH OFFICERS
who were murdered at Manipur
24th March 1891

———

JAMES WALLACE QUINTON, CSI ICS
COLONEL CHARLES McDOWELL SKENE DSO ICS
FRANK ST. CLAIR GRIMWOOD ICS
WILLIAM HENRY COSSINS ICS
LIEUTENANT WALTER HENRY SIMPSON ISC

———

IN THE SAME GRAVE ARE DEPOSITED THE REMAINS OF
LIEUTENANT LIONEL WILHELM BRACKENBURY ISC
AND OF SEVERAL SOLDIERS OF THE 44TH
GURKHA RIFLES
WHO FELL IN ACTION IN MANIPUR
ON THE SAME DAY

The present ruler of Manipur is King Leishemba Sanajaoba, great-grandson of Rajah Chura Chandra. Polo is still the national game and played with the same abandon that made it so spectacular for Ethel Grimwood to watch. It is still played on sturdy mountain ponies with heavy saddles and still without goal posts. One of the three patrons of the All Manipur Polo Association is Prince Charles! The 1891 uprising took on a special national significance after Indian independence. Today the Battle of Khongjom is observed as a holiday with laying of wreaths to the Manipuri heroes who died in the battle and lots of festivities.

Ethel never returned to Manipur or saw Frank's grave. When Tikendrajit was executed she was staying in Hove with the family of her husband's elder brother, Jeffrey, a magistrate. Soon after her return to England she started work on her memoirs. She worked hard on the book, which was published that November. *The Times* said it was 'a simple and thrilling narrative of deplorable disaster and heroic endurance,' praising Ethel's 'modesty' in relating her tale. *My Three Years In Manipur* was unquestionably an entertaining read, ran through three editions and made Mrs Grimwood well in excess of £800 (more than £60,000 today).

In 1892, still very much a celebrity, Ethel Grimwood's portrait by the artist John Hanson Walker was exhibited at the Royal Academy. After four years of widowhood she re-married. One might have expected this man to have been her step-brother, Alan Boisragon, but he was away in Africa and soon to have his own Manipur moment. Whatever her feelings for Alan while in India, things clearly cooled somewhat back in the damper climes of England. Boisragon also had his army career to consider, especially his role as Commandant of the Niger Coast Protectorate Force. In 1897 he was one of the few survivors of what became known as 'the Benin Massacre'. Newspapers in Britain later hinted that he deserved a court martial as senior officer for not having taken precautions against an attack. Benin destroyed his career as surely as Manipur ruined Boileau and Butcher's chances of success. Boisragon wrote a book about his experiences but some said it was a whitewash. For a time he served as Superintendent of Police at Shanghai before returning to London and dying in near-poverty in a humble Earl's Court flat in 1922.

Ethel's second husband was Andrew Miller, proprietor of a small paper mill in Surrey. It appears that her family and her Grimwood relatives disapproved of the match and felt she had married beneath herself; only two of her sisters attended the ceremony, a simple one, at the registry office, St George's, Hanover Square, on 30 May 1895. The mill closed in 1906. By this time Ethel and Andrew were living in Oregon, USA, where he had become a naturalised American citizen. She refused to give up her British nationality and remained an 'alien'. At some point the marriage broke down and the Millers separated. By 1920 Ethel was living in Newport, Oregon, a small fishing community on the rocky Pacific shore. Here she gave music lessons and took in boarders to supplement her meagre earnings. She now called herself 'Evelyn' Miller.

After the Manipur disaster Mrs Grimwood had told her sister, Mabel, 'I think the horrors of those hours will last to the end of my life.'[12] Who knows what her lonely existence was like, but as the years passed so Ethel began to suffer from hallucinations and general mental confusion. Placed in a sanatorium for a time, she died in Portland on 11 August 1928. She was just fifty-eight years old. Her worldly possessions were few; besides her two pianos (a baby grand and an upright), she owned few clothes, ornaments or sticks of furniture. Her estate was valued at just $300. Ethel had pawned her best ruby ring for $150 to pay her medical bills. Popular in the local community, where the quiet, modest music teacher with the refined English accent was well liked, several Newport friends attended her funeral. Andrew Miller, her estranged husband, re-appeared via his London lawyers to pay the funeral costs and any outstanding medical bills. A local newspaper made some references to 'distinctive service to her country', but got the facts wrong. Manipur seemed a long time ago and a world away.

Yet one wonders if Ethel, so distant from the steamy jungles in her quiet seaport in Oregon, ever pondered about those long-ago and heady days in India. Did they still fill her with terrors, as her health suggests, or did she sometimes smile, reminded of the handsome Senapati dashing past on the polo field, of the cheerful Nagas in the hill villages, her beautiful garden and menagerie of animals at Imphal, of colourful boat parties on the lake with excited Manipuri children, and of happier times with Frank before it all turned sour? Buried in her memoirs Mrs Grimwood wrote of Manipur, then and now, words that seem a fitting epitaph to all her adventures and this story of the Raj in the 1890s:

Things have changed there now, that is, as far as the comings and goings of men change, but the hills remain the same, and the face of Nature will not alter. Her streams will whisper to the rocks and flowers of all that has been and that is to be. So runs the world. Where others lived and loved, sorrowed and died, two hundred years ago, we are living now, and when our day is done there will be others to take our place, until a time comes when there shall be no more change, neither sorrow nor death, and the former things shall have passed away for ever.[13]

Appendix A

COMPOSITION OF THE MANIPUR FIELD FORCE
OFFICER COMMANDING: Major-General H. Collett, C.B.

CACHAR COLUMN – Commanding: Colonel R.H.F. Rennick

No 8 Mountain Battery	2 guns
18th Bengal Infantry	364 men
42nd Gurkha Rifles	99 men
43rd Gurkha Rifles	275 men
44th Gurkha Rifles	112 men
1st–2nd Gurkha Regiment	708 men
Calcutta Volunteers, Pioneers	48 men
Surma Valley Horse, Military Police	202 men

KOHIMA COLUMN – Commanding: Major-General H. Collett, C.B.

No 8 Mountain Battery	3 guns
13th Bengal Infantry	100 men
42nd Gurkha Rifles	200 men
43rd Gurkha Rifles	400 men
44th Gurkha Rifles	300 men
Assam Military Police	200 men

TAMU COLUMN – Commanding: Brig.-General T. Graham, C.B.
No 2 Mountain Battery   4 guns
4th Battalion, King's Royal Rifles
2–4th Gurkha Regiment
12th (Burma) Madras Infantry
32nd (Burma) Madras Infantry   1,800 men

Lines of Communication: 5th Madras Infantry

Source – *Frontier & Overseas Expeditions From India*, Vol IV.

Appendix B

'SECRET'

Draft Note Written by Colonel John Ardagh

(National Archives – Ardagh Papers PRO/30/40/12/3)

MRS GRIMWOOD AND MANIPUR

The letter written by Mrs Grimwood to a relative and published in *The Times* very shortly after the catastrophe at Manipur and subsequent letter published in *The Englishman* by Mr M.J. Apcar, with whom Mrs Grimwood stayed at Calcutta previous to her departure for England, with her half-brother, Captain Boisragon, late Royal Irish, represented her as a heroine who had displayed remarkable courage and devotion during the events of the 24th March at Manipur.

Further information placed her conduct in an entirely different light and showed that some of her statements were absolutely untrue, and the rest highly coloured.

When interviewed by a newspaper correspondent in London and asked how long she had been at Manipur she adroitly answered that she had been married 4 years. As a matter of fact, she was in 1889–90 absent from Manipur for 19 months out of two years, during which time she stayed at Shillong, and occasioned some scandal by her relations with her half-brother. It is said that her relations with her husband were very strained when she was at Manipur in 1891.

During her absence Grimwood seems to have amused himself with native girls, sporting with them in tanks and streams and

248

taking obscene photographs. Eventually the Thangal General's beautiful and gay daughter became Mr Grimwood's sweetheart, and Thangal who was proud of his fame took this to heart and therefore on the breaking-up of the Durbar on the night of the 24th March, with a view to assuage himself, instigated the murder of Mr Grimwood first.

Mr Simpson had also been a lover of the girl and he too had his life attempted. This is the story of the womenfolk belonging to Kula Chandra (the Regt.) and Tikendrajit (the Senapati).

The story in its main points is confirmed by Pucca Senna who during Grimwood's earlier stay at Manipur was on very friendly terms with him. Pucca Senna having remonstrated with him about his constantly having girls up at the Residency, gave offence and fell into disfavour, and Grimwood then became intimate with Tikendrajit who abetted him in his parties and their conduct became a public scandal. Sura Chandra (the Maharajah) remonstrated with Tikendrajit and incurred the animosity of Grimwood. This is the explanation which Pucca Senna gives of the [two words indecipherable] of himself and the Maharajah from Mr Grimwood and the friendship between the latter and Tikendrajit which undoubtedly existed.

Pucca Senna asserts that the revolution took place because Tikendrajit relied on the friendship and support of Grimwood, and he declares that Grimwood was the real cause of it. It is quite certain that Grimwood gave no support to the rightful Maharajah, though he was offered troops from Kohima, and also that he maintained his intimacy with Tikendrajit to the point of going out on a shooting party with him after he knew that he was to be deported.

The moral to be drawn from this part of the story is – that if Mrs Grimwood had lived with her husband at Manipur, he would not have desired to console himself with Manipuri girls and this occasion or scandal which resulted in a quarrel between him and the ruling party viz the Maharajah and Pucca Senna: – that if he had not taken Tikendrajit into his friendship, as the companion in his orgies, the latter would never have dared to oust his brother, nor would he have relied on Grimwood's support for the revolution.

The answer to the question, 'Cherchez la femme?' is therefore that Mrs Grimwood's conduct led to the revolution of September.

Now, as to the stories of Mrs Grimwood's heroism and her other statements. She says that her husband 'was studiously kept in ignorance of what was the object of the Chief Commissioner's coming ... so marked was this that further, the telegrams which passed between Mr Gurdon and the Chief Commissioner (Quinton) were communicated in the Italian language.'

Lieut. Gurdon, we know, was specially sent up to explain fully to Grimwood what was intended, and his statement shows the complete untruth of Mrs Grimwood's statement. He and Grimwood worked together at the composition of the Italian telegrams. Her relations with her husband were so strained that it is probable that he never spoke to her.

The she says that 'four sepoys were posted in her bedroom' before the Durbar. Chatterton, who posted all the men, says – 'there were no sepoys in Mrs Grimwood's bed-room, nor in any room inside the house.'

Again she says 'a sepoy was so near her when he was struck that his brains bespattered the body of her dress.' As a matter of fact no one was killed or in the Residency building from first to last. During the day the wounded who had been brought in were in the hospital, which she never was in at all. It was not until they were brought to the Residency during the cessation of fire that she ever saw the wounded and then she attended to Brackenbury and no one else. She was never under fire at all, as the lower building was shot-proof and quite secure.

She seriously embarrassed our officers by pressing them to retire, and but for the clamour, it is improbable that the officers would have ignominiously retreated leaving two-thirds of their men behind.

She never showed any one the way, the road being perfectly straight, and well-known to all. She was never wounded. The story about Captain Butcher shooting five men over her prostrate body is a pure fiction.

The story of Captain Butcher reserving two cartridges, one for her, the other for himself, is pure fiction. She was on intimate terms with Captain Butcher and slept under the same blanket on the way down, to the scandal of the party, and she has effectively ruined his military career.

And for all this she has received the Royal Red Cross and a large pension!

Notes

Chapter 1

1. La Terriere, *Days That Are Gone*, pp 63
2. Gilmour, *The Ruling Caste*, pp 59
3. La Terriere, pp 94
4. Gilmour, pp 73
5. Bence-Jones, *The Viceroys Of India*, pp 132
6. Grimwood, *My Three Years In Manipur*, pp 3
7. Ibid pp 4

Chapter 2

1. Grimwood, pp 7
2. Ibid pp 10
3. Wilson, *Sport & Service In Assam*, pp 235
4. Grimwood, pp 15–16
5. Ibid pp 16
6. Johnstone, *My Experiences In Manipur*, pp 63
7. Grimwood, pp 18–21
8. Ibid pp 21
9. Ibid pp 24–25
10. Morse, Calamity & Courage, pp 4
11. Johnstone, pp 97–98
12. Heath, *Armies Of The Nineteenth Century*, pp 100
13. Roy, *History Of Manipur*, pp 82
14. Johnstone, pp 71
15. Roy, pp 119 quoting Clark (J.). Review Of Correspondence Regarding Manipur Affairs, pp 23
16. Cotton, pp 114
17. Johnstone, pp 110
18. Ibid pp 106–107
19. Willcocks, *From Kabul To Kumassi*, pp 94

20. Grimwood, pp 26
21. Ibid pp 27
22. Ibid pp 30–31

Chapter 3

1. Grimwood, pp 95
2. Various, *The British Empire*, Vol II pp 220
3. Grimwood, pp 50
4. Johnstone, pp 110–111
5. Ibid pp 136
6. Coen, *Indian Political Service*, pp 14
7. Gilmour, pp 178–179
8. Ibid pp 182
9. Grimwood, pp 33
10. Ibid pp 32
11. Johnstone, pp 71
12. Singh, Documents, pp 13
13. Grimwood, pp 58
14. Ibid pp 56–57
15. Keen, *An Imperial Crisis*, pp 29
16. Ibid pp 81
17. Ibid pp 82–83
18. Wilson, pp 128–129
19. Khan, *From Kashmir To Kabul*, pp 15
20. IOL – LMIL/17/18/22
21. Ibid – Senior Papers D507
22. Johnstone, pp 205
23. Grimwood, pp 34
24. P.P. c.6353
25. Ibid
26. Grimwood, pp 39–40
27. Anon, *The Pioneer*, pp 80
28. Keen, pp 26
29. Grimwood, pp 74
30. Ibid pp 40
31. Johnstone, pp 75–76
32. Grimwood, pp 86
33. Ibid pp 88
34. Ibid pp 129
35. Ibid pp 119

Chapter 4

1. Grimwood, pp 132
2. Morse, pp 126
3. Ghose, Manipur, pp 115
4. Singh, Documents, pp 16

5. Majumdar, pp 2
6. P.P. 6353
7. Grimwood, pp 141
8. Ibid pp 142
9. IOL – LPS/18/B56
10. Ghose, pp 115
11. Grimwood, pp 144
12. GOV – Misc Papers, Foreign Dept Secret 1891
13. P.P. 6353
14. Majumdar, pp 5
15. GOV – Final Report on the Manipur Rebellion FDSE/Oct 1891/300
16. P.P. 6353
17. IOL – LMIL/17/19/33
18. Parratt, Court Chronicle, pp 262
19. Grimwood, pp 150
20. Ibid pp 155
21. Ibid pp 160
22. Ibid pp 163

Chapter 5

1. Bence-Jones, *Palaces of the Raj*, pp 45
2. Newton, *Lord Lansdowne*, pp 58–59
3. Bence-Jones, *Viceroys*, pp 153
4. Newton, pp 33
5. Ibid pp 57–58
6. Morris, *Pax Britannica*, pp 179–180
7. Bence-Jones quoting Curzon, *Palaces*, pp 64–65
8. Singh, Documents, pp 21
9. Johnstone, pp 278
10. Majumdar, pp 6
11. IOL – LPS/18/B56
12. P.P. 6353
13. Keen, pp 39
14. P.P. 6353
15. Ibid
16. Keen, pp 42
17. PP 6353
18. IOL – LMIL/7/15107

Chapter 6

1. Grimwood, pp 164–165
2. IOL – LMIL/7/15114
3. *The Times* newspaper 16 May 1891
4. IOL –LMIL/17/18/22
5. Ibid
6. IOL – Roberts Papers A164

7. P.P. 6353
8. Creagh & Humphris quoting citation
9. Couchman, pp 10
10. Heathcote, pp 136
11. P.P. 6353
12. Ibid
13. Grimwood, pp 174
14. Shakespear, *History of the Assam Rifles*, pp 176
15. Parratt, *Court Chronicles of Kings of Manipur*, pp 264
16. Grimwood, pp 178
17. Ibid
18. Ibid pp 182
19. Pioneer, pp 7
20. Singh, Documents, pp 20
21. Ghose, pp 117
22. IOL – LMIL/17/18/22
23. Grimwood, pp 185–186
24. Pioneer, pp 8
25. Majumdar, pp 11
26. PP 6535
27. Grimwood, pp 187
28. Morse, pp 29
29. IOL – LMIL/7/15114
30. Ibid – LMIL/17/18/22
31. Grimwood, pp 193
32. Ibid pp 196

Chapter 7

1. Wilson, pp 190–191
2. Willcocks, *From Kabul To Kumassi*, pp 91
3. Heath, *Armies*, pp 114
4. Keen, pp 62
5. Parratt & Parratt, pp 44
6. Keen, pp 64
7. IOL – LMIL/17/18/22
8. Ibid
9. Ibid
10. Pioneer, pp 15
11. Ibid pp 16–17
12. IOL – LMIL/7/15114
13. Ibid
14. Grimwood, pp 210
15. Pioneer, pp 18
16. IOL – LMIL/7/15107
17. IOL – LMIL/17/1822
18. Ibid – LMIL/7/15107
19. Ibid – Gimson Papers E3259

Chapter 8

1. *The Times*, 29th April, 1891
2. IOL – LMIL/17/18/22
3. Parratt & Parratt pp 52
4. Grimwood pp 217
5. *The Times*, 4th June, 1891
6. Parratt & Parratt pp 53
7. IOL – LMIL/17/18/22
8. Parratt & Parratt pp 54
9. Ibid pp 59
10. Ibid
11. Ibid pp 60
12. Grimwood pp 224–226
13. IOL – LMIL/17/18/22
14. Ibid
15. Parratt & Parratt pp 63
16. IOL – LMIL/17/18/22
17. Ibid
18. Ibid
19. Grimwood pp 229
20. Ibid pp 231
21. Ibid pp 236
22. Keen pp 78
23. Grimwood pp 240–241
24. Parratt & Parratt pp 66
25. IOL – LMIL/17/18/22
26. Ibid
27. Grimwood pp 248
28. IOL – LMIL/17/18/22
29. Ibid
30. Ibid
31. Ibid
32. Grimwood pp 266
33. *The Times*, 29 April, 1891
34. IOL – Wright Papers F174/2287

Chapter 9

1. IOL – LMIL/17/18/22
2. Ibid
3. Parratt & Parratt pp 76
4. IOL – LMIL/7/15114
5. Younghusband pp 94
6. Grimwood pp 292
7. Ibid pp 293
8. Keen pp 89
9. Pioneer pp 36
10. Grimwood pp 295

11. Ibid pp 296
12. Pioneer pp 36–37
13. Grimwood pp 299
14. IOL – LMIL/17/18/22
15. Grimwood pp 302–303
16. Pioneer pp 45
17. Grimwood pp 305
18. Ibid pp 306
19. Parsons pp 59
20. Ibid pp 308
21. *The Times*, 15 August, 1891
22. Younghusband pp 98–99
23. Grimwood pp 315
24. *The Times*, 11 May, 1891

Chapter 10
1. P.P. 6353
2. Ibid
3. Ibid
4. IOL – LMIL/7/15107
5. Grimwood pp 287
6. IOL – Roberts Papers Indian Series Vol IX
7. Pioneer pp 63
8. IOL – LMIL/7/15107
9. Ibid – LMIL/17/18/22
10. Ibid
11. Pioneer pp 69–70
12. Parratt & Parratt pp 93
13. Grimwood pp 311
14. Pioneer pp 55
15. Couchman pp 47
16. Grimwood pp 311–312
17. Couchman pp 47–48
18. Pioneer pp 57
19. Couchman pp 48
20. Buckle Vol II pp 24
21. IOL – Cross Papers E24/30
22. Ibid
23. Ibid
24. *The Times*, 29 April, 1891
25. Willcocks, From Kabul To Kumassi, pp 126
26. Morse pp 60
27. Pioneer pp 78

Chapter 11
1. Morris pp 261
2. Ibid

3. Newton pp 63–64
4. IOL – Cross Papers E24/30
5. Buckle Vol II pp 22
6. IOL – LPS/18/E56
7. *The Times*, 6 April, 1891
8. Ibid 10 April, 1891
9. Ibid 11 April, 1891
10. IOL – LPS/18/E56
11. *The Times*, 29 April, 1891
12. IOL – Cross Papers E24/30
13. *The Times*, 29 April, 1891
14. Ibid 5 May, 1891
15. Ibid 16 May, 1891
16. IOL – Cross Papers E24/30
17. Newton pp 83
18. Ibid pp 85
19. Pioneer pp 80
20. Ibid pp 81
21. NA – PRO/30/40/12/3
22. *The Statesman*, 3 June, 1891
23. Keen pp 124
24. IOL- LMIL/5/15107
25. Ibid
26. IOL – LMIL/17/18/22
27. IOL – Gimson Papers E325/9
28. Ibid
29. Ibid
30. Ibid
31. IOL – LMIL/17/18/22
32. Shakespear pp 178
33. Keen pp 132

Chapter 12
1. IOL – LPS/18/E56
2. Prakash pp 1,372
3. Parratt & Parratt pp 121
4. Gleichen pp 176
5. Malmesbury pp 236–237
6. N.A. – PRO/30/40/12/3
7. Ibid
8. Pearsall pp 231
9. Morse pp 98
10. Lyttelton Papers, Queen Mary Archives, UL Mss GB370 PP5
11. Grimwood pp 272–273
12. Ballhatchet pp 8
13. Gordon pp 119
14. HPL

15. Kipling vol II pp 19
16. Ballhatchet pp 147
17. Gilmour pp 117
18. Willcocks pp 96
19. Wilson pp 126

Chapter 13

1. Lutyens pp 76
2. Ibid pp 75
3. Balfour pp 128
4. Basu pp 101
5. IOL – Cross Papers E24/30
6. Buckle Vol II pp 24
7. Ibid pp 26
8. Ibid pp 28
9. Ibid pp 30
10. Ibid pp 31
11. Ibid pp 34
12. Ibid pp 35
13. IOL – Cross Papers E24/30
14. PP – 6353
15. Parratt & Parratt pp 125
16. Ibid pp 132
17. IOL – Roberts Papers A164
18. IOL – Temple Papers F86/289
19. Keen pp 140
20. Ibid pp 141
21. *The Times*, 23 June, 1891
22. Parratt & Parratt pp 147
23. Ibid pp 151
24. Ibid pp 159
25. Wilson pp 40
26. Buckle pp 44
27. Ibid pp 45
28. Ibid pp 46–47
29. Morse pp 81
30. Ibid pp 85
31. Parratt & Parratt pp 159
32. Wilson pp 39
33. Parratt & Parratt pp 160
34. Ghose pp 5
35. GOV – Misc Papers Foreign Dept Secret E Proceedings, July 1891
36. Morse pp 85
37. Buckle pp 55
38. Ibid pp 56–57
39. Ibid pp 57
40. Majumdar pp 19

41. James pp 332
42. Willcocks, Romance of Soldiering, pp 35
43. Wilson pp 40–41.

Chapter 14:
1. Parratt & Parratt pp 175
2. IOL – LMIL/17/18/22
3. IOL – Curzon Papers F111, Vol 160
4. Creagh & Humphris pp 104
5. *Daily Telegraph*, 6 January, 2015
6. Perham Vol I pp 285
7. Keen pp 130
8. IOL – Reid Papers E278/20
9. Parratt & Parratt pp 120
10. IOL – LMIL/17/18/22
11. Johnstone pp 281
12. Morse pp 112
13. Grimwood pp 102–103

Select Bibliography

Original documents
National Archives Of India, New Delhi (GOV)
Final Report On Manipur Rebellion (For., Dept., Secret External, Oct 1891 -100/186/91)
Statement Submitted By Tikendrajit To Court of Special Commission, Manipur (For., Dept., Sec E Sept 1891 –76)
Misc., Papers (For., Dept., Sec E, April 1891 – 3–55/91)
Law Member's Comments On The Trials (For., Dept., Sec E, July 1891 –3–53/91)
External A Proceedings Dec 1888 Nos 61–79 – Misconduct of the Senapati

India Office Library Collection, British Library, London (IOL)
Cross Papers – Eur/E243
Curzon Papers – Eur/F111
Gimson Papers – Eur/E325
Lansdowne Papers – Eur/D558
Reid Papers – Eur/E278
Roberts Papers – Eur/A164
Senior Papers – Eur/D507
Temple Papers – Eur/F86
Wright Papers – Eur/F174/2287
Military Department Papers – LMIL/17/5/1 – 17/5/2420
   LMIL/17/6 – 17/20
   LMIL/7/9717 – 7/13089
   LMIL/7/13206 – 7/16623

Political & Secret Department Papers – L/PS/7 – L/PS/10
L/PS/16–L/PS/19

National Archives, Kew (NA)
Ardagh Papers – PRO 30/40/12/3

Royal Archives, Windsor (RAW)
Letters of Her Majesty Queen Victoria, 1891

Wolseley Collection, Hove Public Library (HOV)
Letter of Garnet Wolseley to his brother, Richard Wolseley, 29th
November 1857

Printed works
Official Publications
Anon. *The Official Army List For The Quarter Ending 31st
December 1896*. Her Majesty's Stationery Office. London 1897.
_____ *Frontier And Overseas Expeditions From India, Vol IV,
North & North-Eastern Frontier Tribes*. Government Monotype
Press. Simla 1907.
Callwell (Maj. C.E.). *Small Wars: Their Principles And Practice*.
Her Majesty's Stationery Office. London 1899.
Cardew (Lt. F.G.). *A Sketch Of The Services Of The Bengal Native
Army: To The Year 1895*. Office Of The Superintendent Of
Government Printing. Calcutta 1903.
Couchman (Capt. G.H.H). *The Manipur Expedition, 1891*.
Intelligence Branch, QMG Dept., India. Simla 1892.
Parsons (Capt. J.H.). *History Of The Third Burmese War Period
VI The Winter Campaign Of 1890–91*. Government Central
Printing Office. Simla 1893.
Parliamentary Papers – *Correspondence Relating To Manipur*:
c.6353, c.6356, c.6410, hc.392

Other Publications
Allen (B.C.). *Assam District Gazeteers Vol IX: Naga Hills And
Manipur*. Government Press. Calcutta 1905.
Anon. *Manipur: Compiled From The Columns Of The Pioneer*.
Pioneer Press. Allahabad 1891.

Atteridge (A.H.). *The Wars Of The Nineties: A History Of The Warfare Of The Last Ten Years Of The Nineteenth Century.* Cassell. London 1899.

Balfour (Lady B.). *The History Of Lord Lytton's Indian Administration 1876 To 1880.* Longmans Green. London 1899.

Ballhatchet (K.). *Race, Sex And Class Under The Raj: Imperial Attitudes And Policies And Their Critics 1793–1905.* Weidenfeld & Nicolson. London 1980.

Battiscombe (G.). *Queen Alexandra.* Constable. London 1969.

Basu (S.). *Victoria And Abdul: The True Story Of The Queen's Closest Confidante.* The History Press. Brimscombe Port 2011.

Beaumont (P. & R.). *Imperial Divas: The Vicereines Of India.* Haus. London 2010.

———— (R.). *The Sword Of The Raj: The British Army In India 1747–1947.* Bobbs-Merrill. New York 1977.

Beaver (W.). *Under Every Leaf: How Britain Played The Greater Game From Afghanistan To Africa.* Biteback. London 2012.

Bence-Jones (M.). *Palaces Of The Raj: Magnificence And Misery Of The Lord Sahibs.* George Allen & Unwin. London 1973.

———— *The Viceroys Of India.* Constable. London 1982.

Boisragon (Capt. A.). *The Benin Massacre.* Methuen. London 1898.

Brown (C.). *Whitehall: The Street That Shaped A Nation.* Simon & Schuster. London 2010.

————(R.). *Statistical Account Of The Native State Of Manipur And The Hill Territory Under Its Rule.* Government Press. Calcutta 1874.

Bruce (G.). *The Burma Wars 1824–1886.* Hart-Davis, MacGibbon. London 1973.

Buckle (G.E.) ed. *The Letters Of Queen Victoria: Third Series – A Selection From Her Majesty's Correspondence And Journals Between The Years 1886 And 1901.* 3 vols. John Murray. London 1929.

Buckland (C.E.). *Dictionary Of Indian Biography.* Swan Sonnenschein. London 1906.

Coen (T.C.). *The Indian Political Service: A Study In Indirect Rule.* Chatto & Windus. London 1971.

Cotton (Sir H.). *Home And Indian Memories.* T. Fisher Unwin. London 1910.

Creagh (O.M.) & Humphris (E.M.). *The V.C. And D.S.O.* 3 vols. Standard Art Book Co. nd (c.1923). London.

Devereux (Capt. C.). *Venus In India: Or Love And Adventures In Hindustan.* 2 vols. Brussels 1889.

Edwardes (M.). *Bound To Exile: The Victorians In India.* Praeger. New York 1970.

Farwell (B.). *Queen Victoria's Little Wars.* Harper & Row. New York 1985.

_____ *Armies Of The Raj: From The Great Indian Mutiny To Independence.* W.W. Norton. New York 1989.

Ghose (M.M.). *Manipur: Did The Manipur Princes Obtain A Fair Trial?* William Hutchinson. London 1891.

Gilmour (D.). *The Ruling Caste: Imperial Lives In The Victorian Raj.* John Murray. London 2005.

Gleichen (Maj-Gen. Lord E.). *A Guardsman's Memories: A Book Of Recollections.* William Blackwood. Edinburgh 1932.

Gordon (I.). *Soldier Of The Raj: The Life Of Richard John Purvis 1789–1868.* Pen & Sword. Barnsley 2010.

Grimwood (E.). *My Three Years In Manipur And Escape From The Recent Mutiny.* Richard Bentley. London 1891.

Hare (Maj-Gen. Sir S.). *The Annals Of The King's Royal Rifle Corps Vol IV.* John Murray. London 1929.

Harfield (A.). *The Indian Army Of The Empress 1861–1903.* Spellmount 1990.

Heath (F.). *Armies Of The Nineteenth Century: Asia 3 – India's North-East Frontier.* Foundry Books. St Peter's Port 1996.

_____ *The North-East Frontier 1837–1901.* Osprey. Oxford 1999.

Heathcote (T.A.). *The Indian Army: The Garrison Of British Imperial India, 1822–1922.* David & Charles. Newton Abbot 1974.

Home (R.). *City Of Blood Revisited: A New Look At The Benin Massacre Of 1897.* Rex Collings. London 1982.

James (L.). *Raj: The Making And Unmaking Of British India.* Little, Brown. London 1997.

Johnstone (Maj-Gen. Sir J.). *My Experiences Of Manipur And The Naga Hills.* Sampson Low, Marston. London 1896.

Kanwar (P.). *Imperial Simla: The Political Culture Of The Raj.* University Press. Oxford 2003.

Keen (C.). *An Imperial Crisis In British India: The Manipur Uprising Of 1891*. I.B. Taurus 2015.

Khan (O.). *From Kashmir To Kabul : The Photographs Of John Burke And William Baker 1860–1900*. Mapin. Ahmedabad 2002.

Kipling (R.). *From Sea To Sea: And Other Sketches*. Macmillan. London 1914.

Lewinski (J.). *The Naked And The Nude: A History Of Nude Photography*. Weidenfeld & Nicolson. London 1987.

Llewellyn-Jones (R.). *The Great Uprising In India 1857–58: Untold Stories, Indian & British*. Boydell Press. Woodbridge 2007.

Lutyens (M.). *The Lyttons In India: An Account Of Lord Lytton's Viceroyalty 1876–1880*. John Murray. London 1979.

MacMunn (Lt-Gen. Sir G.). *The Martial Races Of India*. Sampson, Low & Marston. London nd (c.1920).

Malmesbury (Countess of.). *The Life Of Major-General Sir John Ardagh*. John Murray. London 1909.

Manning (S.). *The Martini-Henry Rifle*. Osprey. Botley 2013.

Mason (P.). *A Matter Of Honour: An Account Of The Indian Army, Its Officers & Men*. Jonathan Cape. London 1974.

_____ *The Men Who Ruled India:* Abridged Edition. Jonathan Cape. London 1985.

Massie (R.K.). *Dreadnought: Britain, Germany & The Coming Of The Great War*. Jonathan Cape. London 1992.

Morse (B.). *Calamity And Courage: A Heroine Of The Raj*. Book Guild. Brighton 2008.

Newton (Lord.). *Lord Lansdowne: A Biography*. Macmillan. London 1929.

Pakenham (T.). *The Boer War*. Random House. New York 1979

Parratt (J. & S.). *Queen Empress Vs. Tikendrajit, Prince Of Manipur: The Anglo-Manipuri Conflict Of 1891*. Vikas. New Delhi 1992.

Parratt (S.). ed. *The Court Chronicle Of The Kings Of Manipur: The Cheitarom Kumpapa Vol III, 1843–1892*. Foundation Books. New Delhi 2012

Pearsall (R.). *The Worm In The Bud: The World Of Victorian Sexuality*. Weidenfeld & Nicolson. London 1969.

Perham (M.). *Lugard*. 2 vols. Collins. London 1956–60.

Prakash (Col. V.). *Encyclopaedia Of North-East India*. Atlantic Publishers. New Delhi 2007.

Reid (Surg-Col. A.S.). *Chin-Lushai Land: Including A Description Of The Various Expeditions Into The Chin Hills And The Final Annexation Of Their Country*. Thacker, Spink. Calcutta 1893.

Riddick (J.). *The History Of British India: A Chronology*. Praeger. Westport 2006.

Roy (J.). *History Of Manipur: 2nd Revised & Enlarged Edition*. Firma KLM. Calcutta 1999.

Roy (K.). *The Army In British India: From Colonial Warfare To Total War 1857–1947*. Bloomsbury. London 2013.

Shakespear (Col. L.W.). *History Of The 2nd King Edward's Own Goorkha Rifles, The Sirmoor Rifles, Vol I*. Gale & Polden. Aldershot 1912.

_____ *History Of The Assam Rifles*. Macmillan. London 1929.

Singh (N.K.). *Documents Of Anglo-Manipur War*. N. Debendra Singh. Imphal 1984.

Various. *The British Empire: The Story Of A Nation's Heritage*. 6 vols. Orbis. London 1979.

Willcocks (Brig-Gen. Sir J.). *From Kabul To Kumassi: Twenty-Four Years Of Soldiering And Sport*. John Murray. London 1904.

_____ (Gen. Sir J.). *The Romance Of Soldiering And Sport*. Cassell. London 1925.

Wilson (Lt-Col. A.). *Sport And Service In Assam*. Hutchinson. London 1924.

Wright (M.J.). *Three Years In Cachar: With A Short Account Of The Manipur Massacre*. S.W. Partridge. London 1895.

Wright (W.J.). *Warriors Of The Queen: Fighting Generals Of The Victorian Age*. Spellmount. Brimscombe Port 2014.

Younghusband (Maj. G.J.). *Indian Frontier Warfare*. Kegan Paul, Trench, Trubner. London 1898.

Yule (H.) & Burnell (A.C.). *Hobson-Jobson: The Anglo-Indian Dictionary*. Concise Wordsworth Edition. London 2008.

Articles

Brett-James (A.). *Disaster In Manipur*. History Today, 1962.

Majumdar (R.). *The Manipur Rebellion Of 1891*. Bengal Past & Present, 1959.

Stearn (R.). *General Sir George Chesney*. Journal Of The Society For Army Historical Research, 1997.

Journals & Newspapers
The Daily Telegraph
The Pioneer
Illustrated London News
The Times
The Graphic
The Times Of India

Index